D0542125

UNIVERSITY OF GLASGOW SOCIAL
AND ECONOMIC STUDIES
General Editor: Professor D. J. Robertson

15

REGIONAL POLICY IN BRITAIN

By the same Author
(*in this series*)

REGIONAL POLICY
IN BRITAIN

BY

GAVIN McCRONE
Fellow of Brasenose College
Oxford

'We will build it here,' said Pooh, 'just by this wood, out of the wind, because this is where I thought of it.'

A. A. Milne

London
GEORGE ALLEN & UNWIN LTD
RUSKIN HOUSE · MUSEUM STREET

FIRST PUBLISHED IN 1969

SECOND IMPRESSION 1970

THIRD IMPRESSION 1971

FOURTH IMPRESSION 1973

*This book is copyright under the Berne Convention. All rights
reserved. Apart from any fair dealing for the purpose of
private study, research, criticism or review, as permitted
under the Copyright Act, 1956, no part of this publication
may be reproduced, stored in retrieval system, or transmitted,
in any form or by any means, electronic, electrical, chemical,
mechanical, optical, photocopying, recording or otherwise,
without the prior permission of the copyright owner.
Enquiries should be addressed to the Publishers.*

© *George Allen & Unwin Ltd* 1969

ISBN 0 04 330145 2

PRINTED IN GREAT BRITAIN
in 10 on 11pt Times
BY REDWOOD PRESS LIMITED
TROWBRIDGE & LONDON

To Alix

PREFACE

Throughout the time that I was working on this book I have benefited from frequent contact and discussion with Malcolm MacLennan and Kevin Allen, former colleagues at the University of Glasgow, whose book on the regional problem in Europe will shortly be published in this series. Their approach has many similarities to mine and indeed the two books are in many respects complementary to each other. While this book, though limited to the United Kingdom, makes several references to European problems, theirs, in studying the European situation, frequently draws comparisons with Britain. My book is much improved as a result of the comments made by them and by Professor D. J. Robertson on the original draft. I am also indebted to Jim Taylor and Donald Hay, both of whom read my Chapter II and suggested a number of improvements, and to Mrs B. Ashby who gave me much assistance in the preparation of statistical material. But, of course, no one other than myself is responsible for any errors of fact or judgment which remain.

I would like to thank Brasenose College, Oxford, for giving me a term's leave of absence and the Warden and Fellows of Nuffield for electing me to Associate Membership and putting all the facilities of the College at my disposal to enable me to get this book completed. My work on this subject began while I was at the University of Glasgow and was there associated with a study of European regional problems assisted by a grant from the Nuffield Foundation. The final version has been typed by Mrs J. Johnson and Mrs M. Cross and to them too I am most grateful.

GAVIN McCRONE

Brasenose College
Oxford

March 10, 1968

CONTENTS

TIMETABLE OF PRINCIPAL MEASURES USED IN BRITISH POLICY

Legislation	Area Scheduled	Special Assistance	Standard Grants		Tax Incentives	Controls	Other
			Buildings	Plant/Machinery			
1934 Special Areas Act	Special areas	Commissioner's Fund purposes limited			None	None	Trading estates started
1936		SARA loans		None			
1937 Special Areas (Amendment) Act		SALAC loans	None		Contributions to rent, rates, tax. National Defence Tax exemption		
1945 Distribution of Industry Act	Development areas	DATAC loans and grants			None	Building licences	Industrial estates. Advance factories built till 1948
1947 Town and Country Planning Act			None	None		IDC started	
1958 Distribution of Industry (Industrial Finance) Act	Development areas and additional places	DATAC aid extended to all trades					Advance factories restarted 1959
1960 Local Employment Act	Development districts	BOTAC loans and grants	Cost/value grant	None	None	IDC	Industrial estates reorganized
1963 Local Employment Act, Finance Act			25% cost grant	10% cost grant	Accelerated depreciation		Advance factories programme stepped up
1965 Control of Office and Industrial Development Act						IDC limit lowered. ODP started	
1966 Industrial Development Act	New development areas		Raised to 35% in certain cases	40% investment grants	Discontinued		
1967	Special development areas added			Raised to 45% 1967/8	REP started. SET rebate		

INTRODUCTION

The regional problem is a natural accompaniment to economic development. A rising standard of living necessitates changing industrial structures and patterns of trade all of which tend to favour some regions and disfavour others. These changes have always been taking place, but have been particularly marked since the industrial revolution fundamentally altered the economic structure of the more advanced countries. However, the idea that these forces could or should be controlled by Government policy is very recent. The origins of British policy may be traced to the 1930s, but for most European countries regional policy is a post-war creation. Nearly all Western European nations now apply measures which may properly be described as a regional policy, but, in many, such measures are still in the early stages of development and in no country of Europe can it yet be claimed that the measures have completely solved the problem for which they were brought into being. Regional policy has still a long way to go before it becomes a really effective part of Government policy.

In view of the long-standing nature of the problem, it is perhaps surprising that regional policy is such a recent creation. But it must be remembered that it was only with the last war that the Government's responsibility and power to control the level of economic activity came to be properly accepted. Acceptance of full employment as an objective, and of the goals of a welfare state, necessitated regional action. Discrimination against members of society can no more be accepted on a regional basis than it can on a social, racial or religious basis. Many therefore saw regional policy as justified primarily on political or social grounds.

But if the Governments of the 1940s and 1950s were largely preoccupied with achieving the Keynesian objectives of full employment and avoiding inflation, their successors in the 1960s have been increasingly concerned with the means of achieving faster economic growth. This has led to a new interest in the economic aspects of the regional problem in many European countries. Thus the potential contribution of the problem regions to national growth has been assessed, and major changes in regional policy have been made. As this book will show, the development of economic planning played an important part in enabling the economic, as distinct from the social or political, issues of regional policy to be understood.

The regional problem may take many forms, but three major types may be distinguished. First there are agricultural regions, untouched by industrialization, which, as national income rises, cannot provide their population with living standards comparable to the rest of the country. Sometimes the agricultural resources of these regions are themselves poor and offer little prospect of development. The result is either that increased labour productivity is achieved only by emigration, or that incomes lag well below the levels prevailing in the rest of the country. The second type of problem region is one which is industrialized, but whose industry is either stagnant or in decline, so that the region's economic growth is insufficient to maintain full employment. Unemployment rates rise, emigration takes place and the growth of incomes fails to keep pace with the national rate.

Both these types of problem region are alike in that they suffer from insufficient development to employ their labour resources. A third type is the congested region, whose further development entails high social costs and disproportionate public investment in various types of infrastructure. This is the opposite situation from the other two types of problem region, but the problems are linked and cannot be divorced from each other.

The concept of a region has provoked some controversy in the literature and attempts have sometimes been made to provide meaningful definitions. Some authors have tried to distinguish between administrative regions, economic regions based on a particular central urban area, and homogeneous regions defined according to the nature of the economy and its problems. This matter is further discussed in Chapter X when the nature of regions for planning purposes is considered. There is, however, no easy solution to this problem and much intellectual effort can be wasted in trying to find one. The type of regional definition which it is most appropriate to follow depends largely on the purpose for which it is required. Physical planners, for example, may find it necessary to use a different regional concept from economists. The latter have to be able to analyse the characteristics of a particular area yet see it within the perspective of the national economy. It is the nature of the regional problem that economic conditions vary throughout an economy, but to consider the economic conditions of each place separately would pose hopeless problems of economic management. It is the purpose of regional divisions to enable the more important of these differences to be analysed. It follows, therefore, that a regional division is largely arbitrary and many alternative schemes might have been put forward with as much or as little to be said for them. On the one hand, the regions must not be so aggregated as to conceal the differences which it is their purpose to illustrate, but, on the other hand, their number must be small enough to enable comparisons to be made and the priorities of policy between them properly co-ordinated.

THE NATURE OF THE REGIONAL PROBLEM IN BRITAIN

The development of British regional policy began in the 1930s with the Special Areas Acts of 1934 and 1937. The problem which this policy was designed to tackle was that of depressed industrial areas. Britain provides some of the best examples of this type of region to be found in Europe; and at least for the last thirty years, this has been regarded as the predominant type of problem region in Britain. The problem is therefore different in character from that which is typical in France and Italy, though similar in some respects to Belgium.

The reason for this is partly a matter of geography and partly economic history. The United Kingdom is a very densely populated country: with a population of around fifty-four million it has a land area only half that of France and a consequent population density of 222 persons per square kilometre. Moreover, part of the land area, especially in Scotland and Wales, is mountainous and therefore sparsely populated so that the population density on the remainder is greater than the average for the country as a whole would suggest. Some indication of this may be obtained if the United Kingdom is split up into its constituent countries. It then appears that, while Scotland and Wales are relatively sparsely populated, England with 344 persons per square kilometre has a higher population density than any country in Western Europe except the Netherlands, the comparable figures being France 88, Italy 170, West Germany 226, Belgium 307 and the Netherlands 361.[1]

Such a density implies, of course, a highly urbanized population. Indeed, over four-fifths of the population live in towns and 35 per cent are in seven conurbations of which six have more than a million people. It also entails a small proportion of total popula-

[1] UN *Demographic Yearbook* 1965, New York. Figures relate to 1964.

tion in agriculture; and indeed Britain with only 3.6 per cent of its labour force in this industry has by far the lowest figure in the world, the comparable figures for Italy being 25 per cent, 19 per cent for France, 12 per cent for West Germany and 8 per cent for Belgium. Here historical factors play a part, for, being the first nation to industrialize, it paid Britain to buy her primary products overseas, especially in Commonwealth countries, and to specialize in the production of industrial exports in which, initially at least, she had no competition. This was the policy throughout the long era of free trade from the middle of the nineteenth century until 1930. British prosperity was thus built on exports of textiles, iron and steel, ships and coal and her agricultural population had fallen to a very low percentage of the total labour force even by 1930.

It is really to the collapse of this policy that the regional problem, at any rate in the industrial areas, owes its origin. The over-valuation of the pound in the 1920s, the emergence of economic blocs in the 'thirties, changes in technology and competition from lower wage countries, all combined to produce a secular decline in the traditional export industries. When the cyclical effects of the great depression were added to these long-run trends, the result was acute economic distress and unemployment in the areas where these industries were concentrated.

The war brought full employment to the economy as a whole and boom conditions to the traditional industries. For a time, therefore, this aspect of the regional problem disappeared. After the war the continuation of these conditions coupled with a vigorous regional policy prevented the pre-war situation from recurring. The heavy dependence of these areas on the traditional industries continued, however, and although regional disparities in unemployment and income levels were greatly reduced compared with pre-war, they were not eliminated. In time shipbuilding caught up with the backlog of demand and coal and traditional textiles began to lose out to competition from other fuels and fibres; the secular decline returned and, towards the end of the 1950s, the regional problem became more acute.

The industrial areas most severely affected by this situation were the North-East coast of England, West Cumberland, Central Scotland, South Wales and Northern Ireland. In each case these are the main industrial areas in their respective regions: Northern England, Scotland, Wales and Northern Ireland. These are the four regions which are commonly termed the 'less prosperous' regions. Similar difficulties, however, have also affected Merseyside and

16

parts of Lancashire in the North-West region. This area has generally come within the terms of the regional development legislation though the region as a whole has not.

But although the regional problem in Britain is predominantly one of depressed industrial areas, it is far from being exclusively so. Areas of rural depopulation and underdevelopment exist, the best known examples being the Scottish Highlands and Mid-Wales, but the Scottish border counties may also be placed in this category, part of the West Country in the South-West region and part of Northern Ireland. These areas, like the industrial areas, are now included in the regional development legislation, though it was not originally designed for them. Various special measures have been in operation for some time for the Scottish Highlands and part of it was classified as a Development Area in 1948. Parts of the South-West were included after 1960, while Mid-Wales and the Scottish borders were scheduled in the new Development Areas introduced in 1966.

The problems of the rural areas, however, have never assumed quite the same urgency in the public mind, and this is at least partly because the population involved is small. The Scottish Highlands, although comprising approximately a half of Scotland's land area and one-sixth of Great Britain, have a population of only 280,000. All the areas together would not have a population much in excess of a million, while the depressed industrial areas, depending on how they are defined, account for six to eight million or around 15 per cent of the total population.

It would be a mistake, however, to imagine that the regional problem in Britain is purely an affair of the last thirty-five years, the time span of the legislation for depressed industrial areas. The problems of the rural areas go back much further than that and prior to 1922 the whole of Ireland was, of course, an integral part of the United Kingdom. This was a problem of the rural underdeveloped region *par excellence*, and indeed the economic position of Ireland within the United Kingdom offered as close a parallel to the problems of the Italian Mezzogiorno as may be found in Western Europe. Though joined in political and economic union to Great Britain in 1800, Ireland largely failed to industrialize in the nineteenth century. The *laissez-faire* free trade policies which Britain pursued were by no means appropriate to an agricultural Ireland. Thus the Irish population, which had been around eight million at the time of the famine or about 45 per cent of the figure for Great Britain, fell to just under three million at the present

17

Map 1

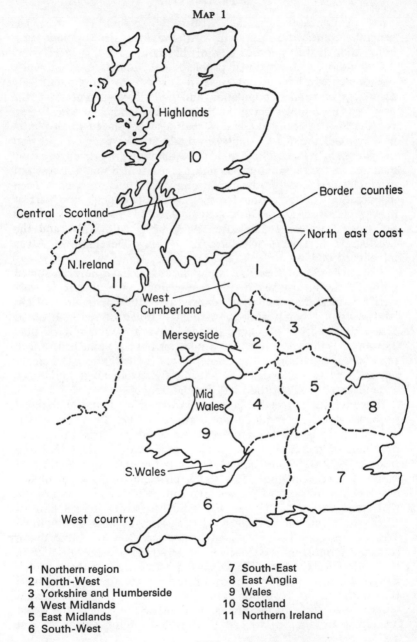

Highlands

10

Central Scotland

Border counties

North east coast

N.Ireland

11

West
Cumberland

Merseyside

1

3

2

Mid
Wales

4

5

8

9

S.Wales

7

6

West country

1 Northern region
2 North-West
3 Yorkshire and Humberside
4 West Midlands
5 East Midlands
6 South-West

7 South-East
8 East Anglia
9 Wales
10 Scotland
11 Northern Ireland

18

time, a mere 5½ per cent. The problem still remains and even with independence there are no barriers to labour or capital movements between the countries. For over a hundred years Irish emigration has exceeded the natural increase of the population and income per head is still only some 55 per cent of the British average. This disastrous economic performance no doubt played a part in bringing about political separation. But there is little doubt that if Ireland were still part of the United Kingdom, this would now be the dominant problem of British regional policy.

Another aspect of the regional problem is the congestion produced in densely populated areas, and undoubtedly these constitute a third type of problem region in Britain. The Royal Commission on the Distribution of Industrial Population drew attention to the social and economic costs of congestion before the war, but by 1960 this problem had assumed greatly increased significance.[1] The underlying purpose of *The South-East Study* was largely to see how the congestion in the South-East of England could best be coped with.[2] The London conurbation has a population of eight million, and if the whole 'metropolitan region' is considered, this rises to over twelve million, making it certainly the largest urban concentration in Western Europe.[3] Increasing attention is being paid to the costs of congestion as will be seen in the next section. But the gradual realization that this type of region, too, is a problem has meant that regional policy, which was previously inclined to be regarded by some as a fad of the Celtic fringe or the 'peripheral areas', is now increasingly seen in a national context.

These regional differences can be illustrated by means of the usual indicators: income levels, unemployment, activity rates and migration. These figures are presented in detailed form in a later chapter where they are fully discussed and the trends in regional disparity analysed.[4] Some of the more important statistics are, however, given in summary form in Table I to illustrate the nature of the regional problem. Because the main problem is that of depressed industrial areas, the indicator most commonly referred to is unemployment. At its worst during the pre-war depression, unemployment in the depressed areas rose to about 40 per cent of the employed labour force in 1933. Rates continued high up to

[1] Report of the Royal Commission on the Distribution of Industrial Population (Barlow Report), Cmd. 6153, HMSO, 1940.
[2] *The South-East Study*, Ministry of Housing and Local Government, 1964.
[3] *Ibid.* p. 5–6.
[4] See Chapter VI, pp. 151–64.

the war. Since then they have been relatively low, very low by some countries' standards, but still well above the national rate.

TABLE I

SELECTED INDICATORS OF REGIONAL DISPARITY

	Unemployment Average Annual % 1960–6	Activity Rates 1966 (Male & Female)	Migration 1951–66		Personal Income per head 1964–5
				as % of natural	as % of
			000s	increase	UK
United Kingdom	1.8	57.4	—	—	100
Northern	3.6	53.3	−113	38	82
North-West	2.0	58.3	−131	31	95
South-West	1.6	48.5	+212	112	91
Wales	2.9	48.5	− 41	28	84
Scotland	3.5	57.0	−476	89	88
N. Ireland	6.9	48.8	−131	53	64

Sources: Abstract of Regional Statistics.
Digest of Scottish Statistics.
Digest of Northern Ireland Statistics.
Reports of the Commissioners of Inland Revenue.

The rates for Scotland, Wales and Northern England have been almost twice the national rate while in Northern Ireland it has been three times as high. At the same time activity rates in these regions with the exception of Scotland and the North-West have been low, reflecting the lack of job opportunities. Productivity has also been well below average, especially in sectors such as distribution, construction and agriculture. This once again is probably due to overmanning in the absence of alternative employment. Migration has been another aspect of the problem. In part this may have acted as a safety valve preventing unemployment from rising; but migration tends to be largest among the skilled and enterprising section of the labour force, thus making the employment of the remainder and the ultimate redevelopment of the economy more difficult. Here Scotland has suffered most heavily. Her annual rate of population loss has risen from about 25,000 per annum in the 1950s to 47,000 in 1965, a figure exceeding the natural population increase. The South-West, on the other hand, has had a huge population inflow, exceeding the natural increase, but only a small part of this region is classified as a problem area. Income figures show that there is not nearly such a large dis-

20

parity in income per head as in Italy or even France. By far the worst off region is Northern Ireland with an income per head around 64 per cent of the United Kingdom level. The corresponding figures for Wales are 84 and for Scotland 88 per cent. Within Scotland, the figure for the Highlands is around 66 per cent of the British average. Gross domestic product figures for the only three regions for which they can be obtained are analysed in Chapter VI and these give similar results.

The problem is therefore clearly a matter of raising the rates of growth in the less prosperous regions, so that their labour reserves can be more fully utilized, migration reduced, and the income gap between them and other regions closed. In the congested regions, the primary problem is to plan the expansion in such a way as to make the best use of space, minimize the social and economic costs of congestion and preserve the amenity of the environment. This means that some urban concentrations, such as Greater London, for example, must be prevented from further population growth and expansion must be diverted to other centres.

It will be clear that the use of resources in the depressed regions and the effective use of space in the congested regions are important economic questions. Their importance was recognized, as will be seen, by the pre-war Barlow Commission which laid emphasis on the links between regional policy, urban redevelopment policy and transport planning.[1] It is surprising, therefore, that the regional problem was regarded by so many in the 1950s and early 1960s as primarily a social or political question. In 1955, for example, the Estimates Committee heard a witness from the Board of Trade say: 'The Board do not regard their Development Areas operations as trading, but rather as a social service.'[2] It must be considered one of the achievements of Britain's new-found interest in planning that the regional question has been brought back into economic focus.

It is not possible to tackle all the aspects of this important question in a book of this type. The economic theory relating to the regional problem, the problems of urban redevelopment and new towns, and regional planning could all provide more than enough material for separate books on their own, and it has been impossible to do any of these subjects the justice it deserves in the limited space available here. The emphasis of the present study is

[1] *Op. cit.* Cmd. 6153.
[2] Second Report of the Select Committee on Estimates: Session 1955–6, The Development Areas, HMSO, p. viii.

on the development of policy to influence the location of economic activity. A great wealth of specialist material on different aspects of this subject has appeared in recent years, but at the time of writing no book offering a general economic study of this question has been published since Professor S. R. Dennison's *Location of Industry and Depressed Areas* in 1939.[1]

The book is divided into three parts. The first outlines the case for a regional policy and attempts, in Chapter II, a general survey of those parts of economic theory which relate to the regional question. This chapter may be omitted by the non-specialist reader. Part II traces the development of regional policy in Britain from the early 1930s until 1967, and the final chapter shows how regional disparities have changed over the last twenty years. Part III attempts to evaluate the different policy measures and discusses how they might be developed in the future.

[1] S. R. Dennison, *Location of Industry and Depressed Areas*, Oxford.

PART I

THE BACKGROUND

CHAPTER I

THE CASE FOR A POLICY OF REGIONAL DEVELOPMENT

'The essential concept of the free market is trial and
error. . . . But can you say that this is a valid method of
control in matters where you may have to wait two cen-
turies before all the consequences of a decision are
apparent?'

Colin Clark

In most countries regional development policies have come about
in response to a mixture of political, social and economic pressures,
and it is not always possible to say which has played the dominant
role. The existence of regional unemployment on a serious scale
seems to be the factor which exerts the greatest influence in inducing Governments to take action. But this action is probably
prompted as much by the political consequences of unemployment
and the social need to give everyone an opportunity for work as
by considerations of making the best use of the nation's economic
resources. It is incomplete, therefore, to consider the case for a
regional development policy as if it were purely an economic
question. Indeed, in many cases Governments would adopt regional
policies even if the economic case was shown to be unconvincing.
In such cases the economists' role would still be important, because
whatever the factors which gave rise to a policy being adopted, it
is the economic development of the country which is being influenced to achieve the desired result. The way in which this can
best be done is therefore an economic question.

But, of course, it is seldom that a regional policy can fly in the
face of economic possibility and be based *purely* on political or
social considerations. Regional policy may be expensive; and it
may, if a misguided policy is persisted in, seriously affect a nation's
wealth and competitive power. For example, if attempts had been
made in the nineteenth century to preserve the geographical distribution of population exactly as it had been in the eighteenth, there
could scarcely have been an industrial revolution. Moreover, there
is no right entitling all regions of a country to equal rates of

economic growth. Mont Blanc, though a sizeable part of France, has no economic growth and it would be absurd to suppose it was entitled to any.

In many cases the economic issues are far from clear-cut and lack of data prevents them from being expressed in quantitative terms. A strong body of opinion thus remains unconvinced by the arguments. Thus much effort, which might usefully be devoted to designing an effective policy, is spent in debating the economic merits and demerits of having a policy at all. This is rather a pointless exercise, since the lack of data which makes it hard to prove the case for regional policy on economic grounds also makes it hard to disprove it; moreover, no Government in Western Europe is going to give up its regional policy in the light of such academic arguments. Yet the result in some cases is that policy is pursued in a half-hearted manner. The purpose of this chapter, therefore, is to set out the issues.

I. THE POLITICAL ISSUES

The political implications of the regional problem have been clearly illustrated in Britain by the electoral results of recent years. At the general election of 1959 there was a pronounced anti-Government swing in Scotland and Northern England, two of the areas whose economies were suffering; but the country as a whole was enjoying a boom and the Government's overall majority increased. In 1964 there was a national swing against the Conservatives, but again this swing was more marked in Scotland and the North than in the prosperous Midlands. Although much has been done to improve regional policy in recent years, the disparities in economic performance still remain; dissatisfaction is still widespread in the regions, particularly after the deflationary policies pursued by Labour. The election of Welsh and Scottish Nationalist Members of Parliament at recent by-elections is without doubt in part a consequence of this; and the regional swing which helped to put Labour in power in 1964 could just as easily put it out again next time. Of course, this type of situation does not hold everywhere. The province of Northern Ireland, whose economy is the most problematic of all the British regions, is dominated in its electoral behaviour by its history and its religion rather than its current economic circumstances. Nevertheless, it is clear that whatever Government is in power in the United Kingdom ignores the regional problem at its own peril.

These issues, however, are purely matters of Government self-interest. Of much greater potential importance are the effects of serious regional disparities on the cohesion of the State. This problem is most clearly illustrated by Belgium where the rivalry and antagonism between the Flemish and Walloon linguistic areas is undoubtedly aggravated by a sense of economic grievance. The situation is particularly complicated in that both areas claim such a grievance. Flanders because it has traditionally had lower incomes and higher unemployment than the rest of the country, the Walloon area because the run-down of the coal industry and disruption in steel has caused the economy to suffer from stagnation. A strong regional policy in the past might have done much to lessen these disparities and so reduce the disruptive forces.

Of course, Belgium, with its linguistic and cultural division, is particularly prone to separatist tendencies; but they exist also in other countries and may assume importance whenever a regional consciousness based primarily on cultural, linguistic or historical factors coincides with a serious economic grievance. The case of Ireland's separation from the United Kingdom may be seen in these terms and recent events have shown that separatist tendencies could also arise in Scotland and Wales. As is explained in a later chapter these factors are of the greatest importance for the cohesion of the Common Market and form an important reason for it adopting a strong regional policy.

II. THE SOCIAL FACTORS

Since the war, Governments in most Western European countries have attempted to redistribute income from rich to poor by means of the tax system, and they have also endeavoured to run their economies at full employment. These aims accord with most people's conception of social justice. To be properly effective, however, both of these objectives require some regional action. A progressive tax system will result in some transfer of real income from rich regions to poor, especially if it is accompanied by strongly developed welfare policies, while the aim of full employment will in many countries necessitate some type of regional policy if it is to be achieved. This has been clearly recognized in the British legislation. Since the White Paper on employment policy of 1944, British Governments have been pledged to full employment.[1] But it was recognized that regional imbalance made it

[1] *Employment Policy*, Cmd. 6527, HMSO, 1944.

impossible to achieve this goal merely by the operation of monetary and fiscal measures at national level; a regional policy was also required. Theoretically such action might either take the form of influencing the distribution of economic activity or of promoting the mobility of the labour force, or of both types of action combined. To deny that either type of action is necessary would seem an untenable position if full employment is accepted as a national goal.

Which type of action is preferred, will depend on two sets of considerations: first, relative effectiveness and cost; secondly, the preference of individuals concerned and the effect of the policy on their welfare. The effectiveness of different methods of tackling regional unemployment is a purely economic question. The issues here are by no means clear-cut, as will be shown later, since the movement of labour may set up cumulative forces of depression and raise the costs of public investment in congested areas. Nevertheless, even if economic analysis could prove that full employment could be achieved more efficiently or at lower cost by moving labour than by encouraging industry to move, it still does not necessarily follow that it is the right thing to do. For a variety of reasons the population is likely to prefer to be employed in its own region, and this preference may be particularly strong if there is some feeling of regional consciousness based on cultural or linguistic differences. The aim of the state should certainly not be the promotion of economic efficiency for its own sake, but rather the greater welfare of its citizens. It may be that the interests of economic efficiency were served by the forced migration of millions of Irish in the nineteenth century, but the loss of welfare on the part of those whom famine forced to leave was without doubt considerable. These factors may be hard to evaluate; but some attempt to consider them is necessary if a sensible policy is to be reached.

Even more intangible are the benefits which many believe our society obtains from the diversity of its cultural and regional background, differences of custom, of way of life and in some cases of language. Precisely because such factors cannot be scientifically assessed, it is easy to dismiss them in the words of one writer as 'springing from the less adventurous elements of society. Their resort to regionalism, in other words, is simply an expression of their fear of change.'[1] Yet, the people who express such scorn are

[1] E. G. West, 'Regional Planning: Fact or Fallacy', *Lloyds Bank Review*, April 1966, p. 37.

so often the representatives of the prosperous regions and the major cultural groups that one is tempted to ask if their attitude is not simply that of the conforming majority impatient with others for wishing to preserve their individuality. One may wonder, perhaps, if they would show the same impatience with regionalism if Britain became part of the European Community and were subjected to pressures which encouraged heavy migration from Britain to Europe or the submergence of British cultural differences in a wider European identity. The fact is that these are intangible matters. Different people will accord varying importance to them and those that are most dogmatic are likely to be the most prejudiced. It is hard to draw any conclusions for policy from this. Nonetheless, considerations of this type should not be overlooked just because they are intangible; it is for the politicians as representatives of the population to give them the importance that accords with their own value judgments.

There is likely to be rather more agreement on the social need to preserve the quality of the environment in which the population have to live and work. Economic growth is seldom achieved without costs of this nature.[1] The unrestricted growth of cities and built-up areas imposes heavy costs in congestion, air pollution, loss of recreation space, etc. The siting of public investment projects such as airports raises similar problems, as the Stansted affair has clearly demonstrated. At the other extreme, economic growth and rising productivity imply a declining population in many rural areas and the collapse of some rural communities with resulting hardship to those that have to remain. Of course, in such instances, the costs of economic growth may be much less than the benefits, but it does not follow that they should be ignored. Ideally it is the benefit, net of social and economic costs, which should be considered as a basis for action. If it had been possible to do this in the past, much of the country's economic growth might have taken place rather differently. In many instances there may be ways of obtaining the same economic growth at less social cost; in others, even if the apparent economic gain seems less, the benefit to the community may be greater if the smaller economic gain implies an even greater reduction in social cost.

This is of considerable importance to the regional pattern of economic activity. The lessons of nineteenth-century economic growth and urbanization, at least as exemplified by the British and Continental industrial towns, are that, left to themselves, free mar-

[1] E. J. Mishan, *The Costs of Economic Growth*, Staples, 1967.

29

ket forces will cause amenity to be lost and a most squalid living environment to be created. There is no reason to believe that unrestricted free market forces would achieve any better results in the twentieth century. Physical planners are therefore concerned with the immense task of urban renewal and of trying to create a new environment with some amenity. It is obviously of great importance that the mistakes of the past are not repeated with the development which takes place in the future. This may mean preserving green space for recreation, preventing the population from becoming too concentrated and avoiding excessive conglomerations of economic activity. Some of these issues can be considered by means of cost/benefit analysis and verge on economic factors which will be dealt with later. The importance of others is extremely hard to evaluate on any agreed basis. It is clear, however, that if unnecessary and undesirable social costs are to be avoided the distribution of economic activity and population over space cannot be left entirely to free market forces.

III. THE ECONOMIC ISSUES

The economic aspects of the case both for and against regional policy were first set out in detail as they applied to Britain by the Royal Commission on the Distribution of Industrial Population.[1] Recently, however, a number of articles have been devoted to this subject and the main lines of the argument are now clear.[2] The case rests on three main points:

(1) that free market forces cannot be relied on to operate satisfactorily in location decisions,
(2) that economic growth requires a policy to ensure that the economy's spare resources are as far as possible utilized,

---

[1] Report of the Royal Commission on the Distribution of Industrial Population (Barlow Report), Cmd. 6153, 1940.
[2] L. Needleman and B. Scott, 'Regional Problems and the Location of Industry Policy in Britain', *Urban Studies*, November 1964; L. Needleman, 'What are we to do about the Regional Problem?', *Lloyds Bank Review*, January 1965; Gavin McCrone, 'The Case for Regional Policy in Britain', *Cahiers Economiques de Bruxelles*, 1er Trimestre 1966; A. E. Holmans, 'Restriction of Industrial Expansion in South-East England: A Reappraisal', *Oxford Economic Papers*, July 1964, pp. 235–62, see also rejoinder by A. Thirlwall, *Oxford Economic Papers*, July 1965, p. 337; E. T. Nevin, 'The Case for Regional Policy', *Three Banks Review*, December 1966; H. W. Richardson and E. G. West, 'Must we Always Take Work to the Workers?', *Lloyds Bank Review*, January 1964, and E. G. West, 'Regional Planning: Fact and Fallacy', *Lloyds Bank Review*, April 1966.

(3) that the avoidance of inflation and achievement of steady growth are only compatible if wide differences in regional unemployment rates are avoided.

In addition, the need to utilize existing social capital has been put forward as an argument but this, as will be seen, is not a very strong one. A particularly important application of (i) is the excessive cost arising from congestion in urban agglomerations which have exceeded the optimum size. This case will be discussed separately.

(i) *Free Market Forces and the Location of Economic Activity*

One of the principal arguments against any attempt to interfere with business location decisions rests on the view that free market forces in this sphere, as in others, will bring about the best use of economic resources. Business, it is held, will naturally choose the locations where it will operate most effectively and, if this is upset, efficiency will be lost. This view ignores the interdependent nature of business decisions and the existence of externalities. A particular location is chosen often not because it has some particular natural advantage, but because a certain range of economic activity is, rightly or wrongly, already there. Even a bad location may, once developed, be superior in the mind of the individual firm to others which are potentially better but undeveloped, since they lack external economies and economies of scale.

Moreover, the free market view presupposes that businessmen are the best judges of a location appropriate for carrying out their activities, and that they do a critical evaluation of cost factors which lead them to a clearly defined optimum. It thus assumes that the costs which came into the businessmen's calculation are the only important ones; in other words, that there are no costs either of a social or economic nature that the community is obliged to bear as a result of the decision. It must also be assumed that industrial costs are very sensitive to location, so that if a firm is obliged to go to sites other than the one it first chose its costs will be affected.

The information on these questions is still far from adequate, but, to say the least, the evidence in support is far from compelling. In the first place, businessmen seem seldom to carry out a scientific analysis of all possible hypothetical locations. In many cases their inclination in setting up a new plant is simply to stay where they are already; and indeed one investigator found that some firms actually derived some benefit from being directed to another loca-

31

tion as a result of planning controls.[1] Where a firm is searching for a new location, though occasionally it may have certain specific requirements which are satisfied in only one or two places, quite often there are a number of possible locations which are equally satisfactory. Consequently the firm is simply concerned with finding a satisfactory location; and, once it has found one, it is not worth its while to consider the possible advantages and disadvantages of numerous alternatives. Furthermore, even if lengthy investigation revealed that one location had a small cost advantage over the others, this might appear insignificant when compared with the variations in costs which could result from the firm's own level of efficiency and technical advance. Indeed, so far from costs having a decisive effect on industrial location, it is not unknown for social and psychological factors to assume more importance. The quality of the environment, the facilities for education and recreation may all influence businessmen's decisions if the economic factors are not decisive.

It would equally be a mistake to go to the other extreme and suppose that the location of economic activity is almost entirely random or that Governments could oblige firms to locate anywhere without economic loss. Yet it is clear that there is substantial room for compromise between public requirements and those of the firm and that the Government should exercise considerable influence on the distribution of economic activity. Indeed, with a proper awareness of the costs involved, both public and private, economic and social, the Government ought to be able to achieve a distribution of economic activity which is much nearer to the optimum for the community than business could itself achieve purely on the basis of private commercial costs. But unfortunately information on costs is normally grossly inadequate which means that the Government, far from being aware of all the cost implications, usually has less useful data than the firm.

A second objection to the free market mechanism as a regulator in location decisions is that it depends on a process of trial and error. Businessmen cannot always evaluate market forces correctly and it is normally assumed that, where incorrect judgments are made, the forces of competition eliminate them. In location decisions, however, it may take a very long time for such processes to work themselves out. As Colin Clark has shown, the present European pattern of population settlement depends to a consider-

[1] B. J. Loasby, 'Making Location Policy Work', *Lloyds Bank Review*, January 1967, pp. 38–9.

able extent on what was determined by agricultural settlement in the eighteenth century. Moreover, he quotes an American investigator who found, in an area adjacent to Chicago, that no more than twenty location decisions made by major retailers would control the location of some 20,000 other retailers for the ensuing twenty-five years.[1] What if one of these original decisions was not optimal, or what if the pattern of land settlement appropriate for an agricultural age is by no means the best for an industrial era? Some adjustment may take place, but it will take ages to work its way through the system. More probably an area in which a particular economic activity is started, even if it is not optimal, will retain it, simply because, once begun, the external economies which are generated from its operation give it a lead over other areas as yet unstarted and exceed any advantages they might derive from being better locations. Bad location decisions, far from being corrected, may thus tend to be preserved unless they are so bad as to outweigh any advantage which derives from being first in the field. As Myrdal has aptly stated:

'Within broad limits the power of attraction today of a centre has its origin mainly in the historical accident that something was once started there, and not in a number of other places where it could equally well or better have been started and that the start met with success. Thereafter the ever-increasing internal and external economies—interpreted in the widest sense of the word to include, for instance, a working population trained in various crafts, easy communications, the feeling of growth and elbow-room and the spirit of new enterprise—fortified and sustained their continuous growth at the expense of other localities and regions.'[2]

(ii) *Regional Policy and Economic Growth*
The effects of regional policy on economic growth could be harmful in two ways. First, if, despite what has been said above, an unsatisfactory regional policy did result in locating industry in suboptimal locations where costs were high, this would harm its competitive position in international markets. Lack of export demand would thus discourage industrial expansion. Such a situation is indeed a possibility; but it ought not to arise if regional policy is well conceived.

[1] Colin Clark, *Population Growth and Land Use*, Macmillan, 1967, pp. 281–2.
[2] Gunnar Myrdal, *Economic Theory and Underdeveloped Regions*, Methuen University Paperback, 1963, pp. 26–7.

The other adverse effect on economic growth may come if the attempts to control industrial expansion in the prosperous areas result not in its diversion to problem regions but to the cancelling of expansion programmes or their diversion abroad. This is indeed a danger with all measures of control and it shows that there is a limit to their application. To prove that growth has been lost, however, it is necessary to show that capacity for growth exists which has not been utilized. If physical controls are used to check expansion in areas of the country which already suffer from over-employment and to divert it to problem areas, it is clear that, if inflation is to be avoided, the alternative is not unrestrained expansion but the checking of that expansion by greater dependence on fiscal or monetary means. In such a situation, even if the physical controls do not succeed in diverting growth to underdeveloped regions, it still cannot be claimed that they have affected growth adversely.

Many of those who have written on the regional problem appear to regard the movement of work to the workers and the movement of workers to the work as two alternative methods of reaching the same goal—the achievement of full employment and a higher level of economic activity.[1] They then commonly go on to argue that mobility of labour involves less obvious distortions to free market forces and is therefore preferable.

This is, however, rather too simplified a view of the problem. Of course, some mobility of labour is desirable and will take place. No doubt more could be done to assist this process with advantage. But there are several reasons why it is difficult to achieve full utilization of the nation's labour resources by this process. This becomes clear as soon as one examines what these resources consist of.

First, there are those registered as unemployed; and typically problem regions have higher unemployment rates than the nation as a whole. But not all those who might be working, if they lived in an area of labour shortage, register as unemployed; there are, for instance, the married women and those who have passed retiral age, who might well be glad to take employment if the opportunity were offered. Some idea of this effect may be gauged from activity rates, which in problem regions are normally below the national average. Thus NEDC found that all Britain's problem regions showed this characteristic, the female activity rate in Wales being particularly low owing to absence of employment opportunities in

[1] H. W. Richardson and E. G. West, *op. cit.*

an area which depended heavily on coal mining.[1]

Thirdly, there is under-employment. Where there is a labour surplus there is less incentive to maximize labour productivity. Labour is therefore retained in activities which in more prosperous areas it would have quitted for better paid work. Agriculture is commonly affected in this way, since it is a sector which, as productivity rises, must gradually shed labour. In depressed regions, where there is no alternative employment, this excess labour stays in agriculture longer than would be the case elsewhere. This phenomenon is common in all European countries and is perhaps most marked in the South of Italy. In Britain it is apparent especially in Northern Ireland, where it has been shown that the only way to raise labour productivity in agriculture to a satisfactory level is by expanding employment opportunities in other sectors.[2]

But this under-employment typifies other sectors too in depressed regions. In Scotland it appeared that the very low output per head in both distribution and construction might be explained in this way, while for Northern Ireland it was interesting to note that in 1958 labour productivity was below the United Kingdom level in every industrial sector of the Standard Industrial Classification.[3] Perhaps the existence of a labour surplus and slightly lower labour costs gave less incentive to businessmen to maximize labour productivity and employ capital intensive techniques.

If these labour reserves are to be fully utilized, dependence on increased labour mobility alone has its limitations. First, it is extremely hard to solve low activity rates in this way. Families like to keep together; the women would certainly not migrate to another region if their husbands were employed at home and both juveniles and the elderly would be reluctant to do so. It would also be much harder to persuade those in low productivity occupations to transfer to other employment if this involved leaving the region. Those actually registered as unemployed might more readily move, but normally these constitute a relatively small proportion of the under-utilized labour resources in a problem area. In the United Kingdom, for instance, the labour reserve of the problem regions has been put at approximately 500,000, though registered unemployment only accounts for about 20 per cent of this.[4]

[1] NEDC, *Conditions Favourable to Faster Growth*, HMSO, 1963.
[2] H. J. Shemilt, 'Adjustments in Family Farming in the Northern Ireland Economy', *Journal of Agricultural Economics*, Vol. XVI, No. 1, June 1964.
[3] Gavin McCrone, *Scotland's Economic Progress 1951–60*, George Allen & Unwin, 1965, p.56.   [4] NEDC, *op. cit.*

But even migration of the unemployed poses problems. The factors which cause migration need further study, but it would seem reasonable to suppose that it takes place in response to unemployment in some regions and job opportunities in others. It therefore depends on the existence of a pool of unemployment in the problem region. One may postulate that migration probably starts becoming important only when the regional rate of unemployment is already at some critical level well above the national rate and that it then rises rapidly the more the disparity grows. It may thus assume considerable importance when the regional and national rates differ very widely, but as the gap narrows so its importance falls fast. Thus it cannot be relied on to bring the regional unemployment rate down to the national level. A policy which relied on migration, therefore, even if it succeeded in removing many barriers and enabling the flow to take place more easily, would still be likely to involve some pool of unemployment in the problem regions, because without that there would be no migration flow.

There are other disadvantages associated with migration. Those that migrate first tend to be the most enterprising, the most skilled and the most employable. Their departure only makes it more difficult to employ the remainder. Regional enterprise is lacking and the skilled personnel are not available to man incoming industry. Moreover, if the migration takes place on a large scale, the local market becomes depressed, the tertiary sector suffers a loss of income and its employees become under-employed. This has occurred in many of the coal-mining areas of Walloon Belgium, where a large number of miners were of foreign nationality and immediately left when the mines were closed. Moreover, such depression has serious social and psychological effects and discourages new industry from coming to the area. These features all characterized the British Special Areas before the War and explained why the Special Areas Commissioners, who at first favoured a labour transference policy, ultimately came to the conclusion that its ability to help with the problem was limited.[1] The same difficulties have been encountered by the European Coal and Steel Community in operating a labour re-adaptation policy and account for the High Authority's decision to devote a much higher proportion of its expenditures to setting up new industries.[2] The

[1] See Chapter III.
[2] ECSC High Authority, 14e *Rapport Général sur l'activité de la Communauté*, Luxembourg, March 1966.

trouble is that migration may start off cumulative forces of decline, and if so it offers no solution. Thus a century of migration has never eliminated unemployment in Ireland, and ironically one of the main barriers to establishing new industry there now is that the market is too small to provide a base for many types of activity.

It follows, therefore, that a policy to influence the distribution of economic activity may be necessary if the labour resources of the economy are to be fully utilized and their contribution to national economic growth obtained. In the British case, NEDC estimated that by thus tapping the regional labour reserves so that the differences between regional unemployment and activity rates and the national average were reduced by one half, some 300,000 could be added to the labour force. This would represent a gain of 1.3 per cent.[1] In the National Plan a similar calculation was made: a reduction of the unemployment rate in the four problem regions by half its excess over the national rate was expected to increase employment by 50,000 and a corresponding increase in activity rates to add a further 100,000 to 200,000.[2]

Utilization of these labour reserves would, of course, require expenditure on regional incentives to attract industry to the areas where the labour was available. But this may be regarded as a good investment with a high rate of return not only in the form of growth but of increased Government revenue. This is well illustrated by some interesting calculations made by Needleman.[3] As later chapters show, Government expenditure on regional incentives in the United Kingdom during the 1960s was of the order of £900 per job created, but the greater part of this consisted of loans or of building factories on industrial estates which were subsequently let. The non-returnable cost per job may therefore be put at not more than £340. Against this, however, must be set the saving in unemployment benefit, which the Government would otherwise have to pay, and the loss of National Insurance contributions and taxes. Needleman estimates these at £175 per man for unemployment benefit and £115 for National Insurance contributions and taxes [i.e. approximately £290]. Employment once created, however, lasts for many years; the gain to the Exchequer is therefore the present value of £290 discounted for the time that

[1] NEDC, Conditions Favourable to Faster Growth, HMSO 1963, p. 16.
[2] The National Plan, Cmnd. 1764, HMSO, 1965, p. 38.
[3] Lionel Needleman, 'What are we to do about the Regional Problem?', Lloyds Bank Review, January 1965, pp. 54–5.

the employment lasts. If one assumes the employment lasts five years with a 6 per cent rate of interest, the value of the gain appropriately discounted comes to £1,200. Setting against this the cost of job creation to the Exchequer at £340 in non-returnable costs, Needleman shows that there is still a huge gain of around £900 per workless man employed. Yet this gain to the Exchequer is only a fraction of the gain to the country in higher output. These figures are, of course, very approximate, but they do demonstrate that the cost of utilizing spare labour resources is more than amply covered by the benefits.

(iii) *Regional Balance and the Avoidance of Inflation*
Disparities in regional economic conditions may affect the nation's ability to control inflation in two ways. First it may be impossible to apply general fiscal measures which avoid both excessive inflationary pressure and an unacceptable rate of unemployment; and secondly, large migration flows from one region to another may themselves have inflationary tendencies.

The importance to the control of inflation of a regional balance in the level of economic activity is fairly obvious. If full employment is an objective of the Government and regarded as socially necessary by the population, it may become extremely difficult to control the economy simply by general fiscal policies. If some region suffers a higher rate of unemployment than others, an attempt to eliminate this by boosting demand will generate inflationary pressure elsewhere. In the same way the reduction of inflationary pressure by cutting demand will raise unemployment in the problem regions to unacceptable levels. This has indeed been a characteristic of the British economy in the last decade and has contributed considerably to the problems of its management. In the 1967 economic crisis it was frequently reported that the Government's objective was to gain an acceptable level of employment by reducing unemployment in the problem regions, but without creating an inflationary labour shortage in the rest of the country. Regional policy measures may thus be regarded in large part as an attempt to manage the level of aggregate demand on a more selective basis than would be possible by the normal fiscal and monetary weapons. The difference is that whereas regional measures may be applied selectively to any area, fiscal and monetary policy, in the absence of differential regional tax rates, tends to be indiscriminate.

The effect of migration on inflation is much more complex. It is clear that migration into prosperous areas is not always inflationary. This is shown by the inflow of refugees from East Germany and the Polish territories to Western Germany or of Southern Italians up to the North. In both of these cases the additional labour prevented their respective economies from running into full employment bottlenecks sooner than they did and so made it possible for uninterrupted expansion to continue longer. The extent of the British labour reserve which is potentially mobile is, of course, tiny by comparison. Would it have a similar effect? Needleman claims on the contrary that labour movement in the British economy has aggravated the inflationary pressures.[1] The essential question is whether the inflow of labour to the prosperous areas adds more to demand than it does to supply. This in turn will depend on how much investment has to be undertaken to accommodate the additional population and whether this is offset by increased saving. It is clear that social capital is already more or less fully utilized in the Midlands and the South-East of England, that further population inflow would therefore be likely to require heavy investment expenditure and that this might well, at least for a time, outweigh any increase in output which the inflowing labour could contribute. If this is so the effect would be inflationary. But in any event it seems clear that, if investment in social capital has to be undertaken, this could be done with much less fear of inflationary consequences in the depressed regions where spare labour resources are available than in the prosperous regions where they are not. Moreover, as a later section suggests, there is evidence that, at least in the more congested parts of the prosperous regions, the cost of providing the necessary social capital is much higher than elsewhere.

(iv) *The Use of Social Capital*
It was argued, especially in the period before and after the War when a declining population still seemed a possibility, that the need to make the best use of existing social capital constituted a strong argument for regional development. Particularly at a time when there was an acute shortage of resources, the prospect of widespread labour movement, requiring heavy public investment in the areas of inflow, while infrastructure in other areas was under-utilized, seemed to impose a heavy burden.

In retrospect, however, this is shown to be a weak argument. With expanding populations in all the European countries, public

[1] L. Needleman, *op. cit.*, *Lloyds Bank Review*, January 1965, p. 47.

investment is required to cater for the increase in numbers; and even if the population of some regions has grown much more rapidly than others, it is a comparatively rare event for the population of a region to decline. In Britain none of the main planning regions has suffered a decline in population since the war.[1] All have had an increase, though this has been larger in some cases than others. All have therefore required increased public investment to cater for larger numbers, to meet the needs of higher living standards and to replace outworn infrastructure. Though new requirements have risen more rapidly in the regions with heavy population inflow, there is little evidence of under-utilization elsewhere. Indeed it is common knowledge that the nineteenth-century industrial towns of the North of England, Scotland and South Wales are the ones with the worst housing conditions and most in need of a large share of public investment for urban renewal. Thus, even if their populations were declining, this would not so much waste social capital as enable that capital which is already outworn to be discarded.

At the same time, it is hardly ever possible to write off an area, once it has been developed, and allow it to decline. Whatever economists may think of it as a location for new economic activity, social capital will be renewed in response to political and social considerations. It is understandable that it should be so. Yet if social capital is to be renewed at heavy cost in any case, it may enable much better use to be made of public investment if it can be combined with other measures to encourage new industrial growth. In this way the overheads of the investment will be spread and it will provide an economic as well as a social return.

Generally speaking, the only places where an actual decline in population has taken place have been rural areas. Such areas may be extensive, as in the case of the Scottish Highlands, the Border Counties or Mid-Wales; but it happens, according to the way in which Britain is divided into planning regions, that none of these constitutes a region of its own and that the decline of such areas is matched by the expansion of urban areas elsewhere in the region. This decline is the result mainly of increasing productivity in agriculture, a consequent reduction in the number of people required to run the industry and a drop in the proportion of the total population engaged in it. Clearly this may lead to under-utilization of social capital, but it is hard to see how an infrastructure designed

---

[1] A map showing the planning regions of the United Kingdom appears on page 18.

for a primarily agricultural community could be made to serve the needs of other activities.

Nevertheless, this may pose problems in some countries. In Ireland or in parts of France, for example, where vast areas are primarily agricultural and where the population in consequence is now very sparse, public investment such as railways, roads and schools which were originally laid out in days of greater population density have become under-utilized; the costs of maintaining them per head of the population rise and they become increasingly uneconomic. The burden of supporting such regions may be partly avoided if centres of new economic activity or poles of development can be created within them; and, though these cannot use the infrastructure exactly as it existed, they may make an important contribution to the viability of the region as a whole.

(v) *The Costs of Economic Concentration*
A much more important argument connected with social capital, and one most commonly used to support a regional development policy, is associated with the costs of congestion. Basically this is no more than a special case of the arguments against unrestricted use of the free market mechanism already outlined in section (i) above. It is, however, a particularly important case and therefore deserves to be considered separately.

In Britain no official estimates are available of the costs of providing social capital in different parts of the country, but the view is commonly held that such costs are excessively high in the London Metropolitan Region. Even in the 1930s the London County Council in submitting evidence to the Barlow Commission had expressed the view that: 'the urban development of Greater London already exceeds the aggregate which would have been desirable on general principles of town planning and in the interests of the well-being of the population of London'.[1] The Commission gave this view considerable emphasis in their report and saw the 'problem presented by the excessive growth and future excessive industrialization of London and the Home Counties' as linked to the solution of unemployment in the Depressed Areas. Nothing that has happened in the intervening thirty years has in any way reduced the problem of congestion. Indeed the rapid development of motor traffic must have made the costs of development in congested areas even more excessive. Though not expressed

[1] Report of the Royal Commission on the Distribution of the Industrial Population, Cmd. 6153, p. 84.

41

in quantitative terms, this was the premise on which the South-East Study was based and which underlies much Government thinking on regional policy.[1]

This problem arises because those who have to decide on the location of economic activity do so in the light only of those private costs which fall on them as entrepreneurs; it is not their business to consider all the costs which may fall on the community as a result of their decisions. These comprise not simply the social costs, such as lack of amenity and air pollution which were referred to earlier; they also include the public investment required in housing, schools and transport facilities for an increased population.

Such costs may vary substantially depending on where they have to be carried out. One might expect them to be high in sparsely populated areas where the population is insufficient to support them and also in congested areas where not only will the cost of land be higher, but physical difficulties will occasion higher costs. Moreover, as far as transport is concerned, since in large urban areas the population tends to travel further to work and spends longer in so doing, the amount of public transport facilities required per head are likely to be greater than in other areas. Such public services in large urban areas almost always operate at a commercial loss and thus require subvention from public funds; the excessive costs incurred therefore do not fall directly either on those responsible for location decisions or on the public which makes use of the services. If they did, there might be a significant effect on the location of economic activity.

Other costs associated with congestion will also arise, though their importance will be harder to assess and may even depend on individual value judgments. Commuting, for example, tends to increase, the larger congested areas become. The opportunity cost of the time thus spent, either in potential production or in leisure, may well be high. Traffic congestion and lack of amenity are also likely to be important considerations.

These questions have been formally illustrated by Klaasen in a model designed to give the theoretical basis for Dutch regional policy.[2] The optimum size of an agglomeration is illustrated in the

[1] *The South-East Study 1961–1981*, Ministry of Housing and Local Government, HMSO, 1964.
[2] L. H. Klaasen, 'Regional Policy in the Benelux Countries', published in F. Meyers (ed) *Area Redevelopment Policies in Britain and the Countries of the Common Market*, US Dept. of Commerce and Area Redevelopment Administration, US Government Printing Office, Washington, 1965, pp. 21–85.

diagram below which measures cost and revenue on the Y axis and population size on the X axis. The curve AB measures gross income *per caput* and since there are assumed to be economies of agglomeration this curve rises with population. It is assumed, however, that these economies are not such as to occur at a constant rate. Beyond a certain point the slope of the curve therefore declines. The curve CD illustrates operating cost of the agglomeration *per caput*. Here it is assumed that after a certain point increasing costs *per caput* prevail and that the increase in costs accelerates. The optimum size of agglomeration is therefore where the difference between the two curves is widest, illustrated in the diagram by point P.

Diagram I.

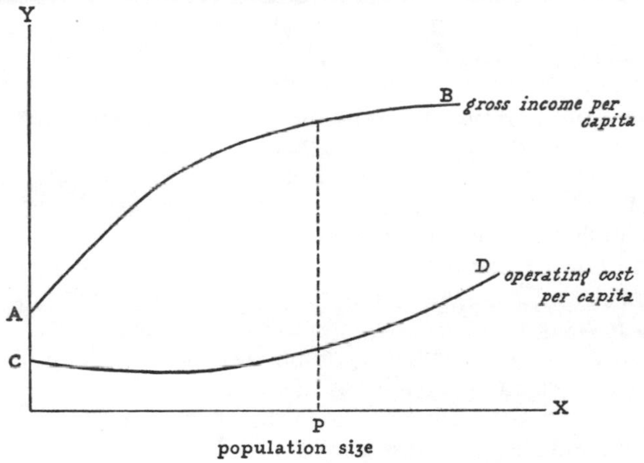

population size

There will be no tendency, according to this model, for an agglomeration to come to rest at the size indicated by P. Entrepreneurs, who play the largest part in location decisions, are influenced only by the curve AB and so long as this yields further economies, even at a diminishing rate, they will carry expansion past P. The costs represented by CD fall on public authorities and therefore will not influence the growth of the agglomeration unless these authorities attempt to influence the entrepreneurs.

A by-product of this drive towards agglomeration is that uneconomic units will also appear at the opposite end of the scale. The drain from peripheral or rural areas will leave communities

43

there which become increasingly uneconomic because they are too small. The cost of essential public services rises per head of population and costly subventions are required from the State. The process of agglomeration, if left uncontrolled, may therefore give rise to uneconomic units at both ends of the scale.

It therefore appears quite probable, both that there is some optimum size of urban agglomeration and that there is no mechanism to prevent this size being exceeded in practice. In the United Kingdom, which expects a population increase of some twenty million by the end of the century, it may thus make an immense difference to the costs of providing for the expansion whether it is allowed to be absorbed into the existing large conurbations or is distributed in new urban centres. This is undoubtedly one of the main economic arguments for a regional policy.

Unfortunately, the curves illustrated in the diagram are extremely hard to estimate in practice, though a number of attempts have been made. It is therefore difficult to establish what the optimum size of agglomeration actually is. This optimum may depend considerably on how the agglomeration is constructed; and it may vary according to time and technical advance. Increasing use of private motor transport, for example, may well lower the optimum size of unit. It would be possible for the curves to be of very different shapes and still give an optimum. For example, even if gross income continuously rose at an accelerating rate, an optimum would still be reached if operating costs after a certain point accelerated *faster*. Only if the curves showed increasing divergence could it be argued that unlimited agglomeration was economically desirable. This seems improbable, but since adequate data is not available, it is impossible statistically to disprove such a hypothesis.

But attempts have been made to estimate some of these variables and they do tend to support the argument. Clark, for example, working with American, British and Australian data, attempted to estimate what size a city had to be to provide the inhabitants of its region with a full range of service and manufacturing activity.[1] He came to the conclusion that a region can give its inhabitants a full range of commercial services when the population of the principal city is somewhere in the range of 100,000 to 200,000. On the other hand, he found that a size of 200,000 to 500,000 was necessary for the full development of manufacturing activity. Lomax, working on the cost of municipal services per head of population

[1]Colin Clark, 'Economic Functions of a City in Relation to its Size', *Econometrica*, April 1945, p. 97 ff.

in England and Wales, found from this point of view 100,000 to 200,000 was the optimum size.[1] Over 300,000 the cost of municipal services per head rose sharply. More recently, Neutze, working with Australian data, attempted to discover the optimum size of cities by considering the advantages to manufacturers, the costs to local government and the cost of traffic congestion.[2] Much of his evidence is extremely tentative, but he too came to the conclusion that medium-sized centres in the range of 200,000 to one million offered the most advantages:

'Our contention is that the medium-sized centre can support most of these industries and services and that it provides a large enough market for most of them to produce at near minimum costs. . . . In addition large cities suffer from important diseconomies. Traffic congestion is the most obvious. That, and growth of journey to work, are probably the most important examples of the increasing cost of communication within the city.'[3]

But even if it is accepted that there is a need to plan the use of space so as to avoid very large agglomerations or to control those that already exist, there are various ways in which this might be done. These do not necessarily correspond to the way in which regional policy is at present operated in many countries. Indeed, as Holmans has argued, it does not follow that the whole of the South-East of England and the Midlands are congested in this way or that development should only be directed to the less prosperous regions.[4] The problem might be tackled by checking the growth of London and building up new towns, satellite towns or expanding existing towns within the South-East. This policy was indeed that proposed in the *South-East Study* and subsequently implemented.[5] In favour of this it may be said that it is easier to check the growth of a large city and overspill its population into

---

[1] K. S. Lomax, 'The Relationship between Expenditure per head and Size of Population of County Boroughs in England and Wales', *Journal of the Royal Statistical Society*, Pt. I, 1943, p. 51 ff.
[2] G. M. Neutze, *Economic Policy and the Size of Cities*, Australian National University Press, 1965.
[3] *Ibid.*, p. 110.
[4] A. E. Holmans, *Restriction of Industrial Expansion in South-East England: A Reappraisal*, Oxford Economic Papers.
[5] *The South-East Study, 1961–81*, HMSO, 1964. The South-East Economic Planning Council have carried this approach further in their report *A Strategy for the South-East*, HMSO, 1967.

other centres within the region than to divert such growth to the other end of the country. On the other hand, the promotion of new centres of growth or growth poles within the South-East will absorb some of the mobile industrial development which might have gone to the problem regions. At any one time the amount of new development which can be moved to a new location is not very large.

But the effect of this policy in checking the growth of large agglomerations may not be as great as appears at first sight. Development taking place anywhere has a multiplier effect. It is true this is not likely to be very large at the regional level, but it nonetheless exists. The development effects of building up new centres in the South-East will thus not be limited to the new centres themselves, but will be spread throughout the region, particularly in London. London being much larger than any other centre in the region will continue to be the market for many of the specialized goods and services in the region. Smaller centres which in a more remote region might be large enough to support all sorts of specialist activities, do not do so when in proximity to a very large city. And the larger the city the wider the area it seems to dominate in this way. Thus, even if some economic activity can be diverted from a major agglomeration to new centres within the region, the effect of such development is likely to stimulate, at least in some degree, the agglomeration which it is the object of policy to control. If, on the other hand, the new development took place in a depressed region, these spread effects would be wholly beneficial.

The congestion argument, however, applies not only to the prosperous regions. Many problem regions, particularly those that have been industrialized, have large urban agglomerations which may be beyond the optimum size. Thus it may make little economic sense to control development in the more remote parts of the South of England only for it to take place in Glasgow or Liverpool. Indeed, so far as the congestion case is concerned, the most appropriate policy might entail the building up of centres which are at present somewhat below the optimum size and the development where necessary of new ones. The British new towns, as originally conceived, were mostly too small for this purpose; but in recent years schemes for much larger ones have been started. Against this background the various proposals for new cities at Humberside, Solway, Tayside and the Moray Firth offer the prospect of being able to play a valuable role in accommodating the increase in Britain's population during the next half-century and deserve very serious consideration.

IV. CONCLUSION

The first conclusion which may be drawn from the foregoing discussion is that it would be wrong to regard regional policy as if it were purely an economic issue, a mistake economists are rather inclined to make. The case cannot properly be considered without reference to political and social factors as well. The relative strength of these factors will vary, depending on the particular situation in any country, but all three need to be considered. The economist has, however, a particularly important role insofar as any regional policy, even if justified solely on political or social grounds, must influence the pattern of the country's economic development if it is to have any hope of success. Alternative strategies for achieving this must be thought out and their economic implications assessed. It is claimed in later chapters of this book that policies have sometimes been adopted primarily in response to political and social factors and have failed to achieve the desired results because they have been insufficiently based on economic realities.

As for the economic issues, the full force of many of the arguments remains untested owing to lack of data on many of the key questions. The economic growth argument shows that a distribution of industry policy to tap regional reserves of labour can substantially raise the level of economic activity in the short run. Over the long run, however, the advantages are less clear-cut. If it were true that such a policy led to industries being sited in locations from which they suffered a *permanent* handicap in operating efficiency, and if it also resulted in less migration, then over the long run the effects would be harmful to the country's rate of growth. But such a clash between short-term and long-term interests seems unlikely, because there is little evidence so far that operating efficiency is adversely affected in this way.

The congestion argument depends on the hypothesis that, as an urban area grows, the increasing social and economic costs after a certain point exceed the increasing gain in operating efficiency which is obtained by activity. This seems a plausible argument and such evidence as there is is fairly consistent in suggesting in what range the optimum size of agglomeration lies. But more data are badly needed. The results undoubtedly depend not only on the size of the urban area, but also on its type, particularly its density and the way it was planned.

It is important to resolve these gaps in our information not only so that the case for adopting a regional policy can be proven to the satisfaction of economists. What is much more vital is that such data should form the basis for regional planning. Regional plans are concerned with the distribution of economic activity over space and, in setting the objectives here, it is of fundamental importance to know the effects of concentration and regional dispersion on efficiency and economic development.

But despite the gaps in information a decision has to be taken on whether there should be a regional policy, and if so, what kind. The one argument that seems open to little dispute is that a better regional balance of economic activity enables inflationary pressure to be controlled more easily without creating excessive pools of unemployment. For the rest a judgment simply has to be taken on such evidence as is available. This suggests that there is a wide range of industry which can operate without permanent disadvantage in most of the major industrial areas of Britain. Against this, regional policy may secure higher economic growth by utilizing spare labour resources and avoid the high costs of excessive concentration. The case therefore seems strong.

The type of policy to which this discussion leads is one which minimizes any adverse effects of locational disadvantage while securing the benefits of growth and avoidance of congestion. This might best be done by giving a particular boost to those areas within the problem regions which have the best growth potential, by regrouping population through a new towns policy and by giving them priority in public investment. This is the essence of a growth area or development pole policy. It will be argued in later chapters that any disadvantage, which a firm experiences in operating in a particular place, is at least as often due to lack of facilities or external economies as to the enduring features of the location itself. Such deficiencies can be remedied and this is one of the prime functions of regional policy.

CHAPTER II

ECONOMIC THEORY AND THE REGIONAL PROBLEM

'Spatial problems have been so neglected in economic theory that the field is of interest for its own sake.'
Paul Samuelson

In the last chapter the view was expressed that the lack of data necessary for a proper cost-benefit analysis of the principal issues of regional policy was an important source of weakness in regional economics. Another is the comparative neglect of this subject in economic theory; in consequence, the factors which govern the dispersion of economic activity over space are very poorly understood, as are the causes of regional depression and growth.

The purpose of this chapter is to examine those parts of economic theory which relate to the regional question. The subject deserves a book on its own, and it cannot be claimed that the following pages take it very far or open much new ground. In the space available here it is impossible to do more than attempt a general survey of some of the more important ideas and discuss their relevance to the regional question. It will be plain that many of the theories are extremely crude and have little application to reality in the form they were originally presented. And obviously much work remains to be done before economic theory can play the role in regional economics which it plays in other spheres. Nevertheless, a discussion of the existing body of theory does raise some important issues and may shed insight into various aspects of regional economics.

Despite the major advances in economic theory that have been made in the present century, most economists have completely ignored the use of space. Even the theory of international trade was built up without the factor of distance being properly analysed. Its consideration would involve no less than the addition of a new dimension to a large body of current economic theory. Attempts have, of course, been made to tackle this question: location theory

49

started in Germany where the works of von Thünen, Weber, Christaller and Lösch were among the most important contributions; in recent times Hoover and Isard have developed the subject in the United States; while in France Perroux has developed the pole of growth idea, which has been further elaborated by Davin and others.[1]

It is, perhaps, useful to start by considering what aspects of the regional question economic theory may be expected to elucidate. It would seem that the subject falls into three main parts:

(1) The microeconomic aspects. If the spatial pattern of economic activity is given, how does the individual firm determine its location?

(2) The macroeconomic aspects. The factors which determine how economic activity comes to be spread over the available geographical space.

(3) The dynamic factors. The factors which cause some regions of an economy to grow while others stagnate or contract.

Rather surprisingly it is the first of these aspects which has received the greatest attention in the written work, though from the point of view of regional policy the second and third are probably of greater importance.

I. LOCATION OF THE FIRM

(a) *Agricultural Location—von Thünen*

The first important work on the economics of location is that of von Thünen in 1826.[2] von Thünen was concerned to show how location affected agricultural production. Taking the sites of towns as given, he demonstrated that distance from the markets would

---

[1] J. H. von Thünen, *Der Isolierte Staat in Beziehung auf Landwirtschaft und Nationalöknomie*, Hamburg 1826 (translated into English by C. M. Wartenberg and edited by Peter Hall as *von Thünen's Isolated State*, Pergamon Press, 1966); Alfred Weber, *Uber den Standort der Industrien*, Tübingen 1909 (translated into English with notes by C. J. Friedrich as *Alfred Weber's Theory of the Location of Industries*, Chicago, 1929); Walter Christaller, *Die Zentralen Orte in Suddeutschland*, Jena 1933 (translated by C. W. Baskin as *Central Places in Southern Germany*, Prentice-Hall, 1966); August Lösch, *Die Raumliche Ordnung der Wirtschaft*, Jena 1940, 2nd ed. 1944 (translated into English as *Economics of Location*, Yale University Press, 1954); E. M. Hoover, *The Location of Economic Activity*, McGraw-Hill, 1948; Walter Isard, *Location and Space Economy*, MIT Press, 1956; Francois Perroux, *L'Economie du XXe Siecle*, PUF, 1964, pp. 123–276; Louis E. Davin, *Economie Regionale et Croissance*, Genin, 1964.

[2] J. H. von Thünen, *op. cit.* von Thünen's theory has been recently re-examined by M. Chisholm in *Rural Settlement and Land Use*, Hutchinson, 1962.

determine what agricultural products were produced and that these would vary even if the quality of the resources and technical possibilities of agriculture were everywhere the same. This would arise because the relationship of transport costs to the total value of the product differ from product to product. Thus those products where transport costs were relatively heavy in relation to total value would be produced near the market and those where transport costs were less important could be brought from further afield. von Thünen then developed his notion of rings surrounding each market showing how each type of agricultural product would be located.

The theory is clearly of great importance in explaining the phenomenon of economic rent.[1] As originally developed economic rent was most commonly thought of as relating to the quality of the factors of production; but it may be just as easily applied, and indeed is perhaps more commonly found, associated with their locations. In the form stated the theory is valuable in explaining the factors determining agricultural location; and it may indeed have some interesting applications to the present-day world in helping to analyse the effects of a new town or a newly established *pôle de croissance* on the surrounding agricultural area. But it is of little help in explaining the location of activities other than agriculture and it offers no guidance to the factors which determine the general distribution of economic activity over space. Its main relevance to the present survey was that it was the first theory to emphasize transport costs as the chief factor in determining location.

(b) *Weber's Theory of Industrial Location*

The first systematic attempt to tackle the problems of industrial location was made by Alfred Weber.[2] Though called a theory of industrial location, it was really a theory of location for the firm or plant. The firm was seen as deciding its location in response to: (*a*) transport costs, (*b*) labour costs and (*c*) the economies of agglomeration or deglomeration. The emphasis of the theory was, however, on transport orientation and this may be seen from the

[1] See, for instance, Bertil Ohlin, 'Some Aspects of the Theory of Rent: von Thünen vs. Ricardo' in *Economics, Sociology in the Modern World: Essays in Honor of J. N. Carver*, Camb., Mass., 1935.

[2] Alfred Weber, *op. cit.* Weber's theory together with the criticisms made of it is admirably summarized in S. R. Dennison, *Location of Industry and Depressed Areas*, Oxford, 1939, pp. 1–27. Although written over twenty-five years ago this book still provides a most useful discussion of the theory of location.

fact that Weber expresses labour costs in 'ton miles' in order to include them in his model.

The mechanism of the model was most simply explained with the aid of the following simple device. A stiff map is taken and perforations made at the supply points for raw materials and at the market. Lengths of string knotted together at one end are then passed through the perforations. Weights are then attached to the ends of the pieces of string proportional to the amount of goods which have to be transported from each point. Where the knotted end of string comes to rest on the map is then the optimum location. Such a simple device can, of course, only be made to work with a very limited number of points on the map: a market and two sources of raw material, for instance. Moreover, it assumed transport costs to be proportional to distance. If these assumptions are relaxed it breaks down.

Weber was aware that there might not be one single optimum location and for this reason he developed the concept of the isodapane. Conceivably there might exist an area on the map where a movement of location towards the market or towards one source of supply might result in a reduction of transport costs from that point which was exactly counterbalanced by the increase in transport costs from the other supply points. Transport inputs, in other words, could be substituted for each other without affecting total costs, and within such an area, the isodapane, location would be a matter of indifference.

This situation, in Weber's view, was even more likely to arise if labour costs were considered. If labour costs vary significantly over space, there might well be an isodapane within which labour and transport costs could be substituted for each other to give the same average costs of production.

Weber was clearly aware of a third factor, the 'economies of agglomeration or deglomeration' which might affect the optimum location. But he did not carry the analysis of this very far, and did not, for example, distinguish between internal and external economies of scale.

Weber's theory of location was entirely cost orientated in that it was concerned simply with finding the lowest combination of production and transport costs. But as Lösch has pointed out, the theory of location is not complete without consideration of the effect of the location chosen for production on the demand for the product.[1] Only if demand is completely inelastic, with respect

[1] August Lösch, *op. cit.* English Edition, pp. 25–35.

to location of the firm, may one be justified in deriving an optimum location entirely from the cost factors as Weber does. In fact, the effect of location on demand may vary considerably from one form of economic activity to another. At one extreme the location of many types of activity in the services sector of the economy may be primarily determined by demand factors, while at the other the demand for some manufacturing products may be very little affected by the location of their production and a theory which is based entirely on minimizing cost factors may give adequate results. In contrast to Weber, the works of Hotelling and Chamberlin, both of whom approach location theory from imperfect competition, emphasize demand factors almost exclusively.[1] The well-known example is cited of ice-cream sellers each trying to position themselves on a beach in such a way as to maximize their share of the trade.

To be complete, Lösch emphasizes, the theory of location of the firm must be based on profit maximization in which both cost and revenue factors would be considered. The optimum location may be neither where costs are at a minimum nor where gross revenue is at a maximum, but where the difference between these two, net revenue, is maximized. But in Lösch's view, while such a theory offers a complete consideration of the relevant factors, it is a most complex matter to work them out. Firms are unlikely, therefore, to be able to identify their optimum location readily, and will proceed on a basis of trial and error. Those firms which are badly located being driven to close down or to move to a better location. By such a means firms will tend towards their optimum location rather as the theory of the firm postulates that industries will tend towards long-run equilibrium.

Such a theory suffers from some of the disabilities of the profit maximization theory of pricing behaviour. In a dynamic economy optimum locations may change, and in consequence there may be, at any point in time, a large number of firms in suboptimal locations. Moreover, considerations of long-run growth may be much more in businessmen's minds than immediate profit maximization and this might conceivably lead to a different choice of location.

Despite these criticisms, Weber's theory, particularly as amended by Lösch, does present many of the most important factors in determining the location of the firm. Moreover, it shows that the

[1] H. Hotelling, 'Stability in Competition', *Economic Journal* 1929, pp. 52 ff; E. H. Chamberlin, *The Theory of Monopolistic Competion*, Harvard, 1933, Appendix C, *Pure Spatial Competition*, pp. 260–65.

greater the transport costs of the final product the more production will be dispersed over space, whilst the greater the economies of agglomeration the more it will be concentrated. This may well explain why different types of economic activity are spread over space with differing degrees of intensity; and it is a proposition which will be examined further in the second section.

(c) *Transport and Distance Costs*

The theory, even as modified by Lösch, however, is primarily based on transport costs and this is a matter which needs further examination. In the first place, plant location is more frequently concentrated either at the market or at one of the sources of raw material than the simple Weberian theory with transport costs proportional to distance would lead one to expect. Secondly, for a wide range of economic activity it is held that transport costs are not an important element of total cost, and therefore in such cases seldom an important element in determining location. A variety of studies have attempted to investigate the importance of transport costs both in Britain and in other European countries.[1]

The reason for production units tending to concentrate themselves either at the market or at one of the sources of material supplies arises for a number of reasons as Hoover has clearly shown.[2] In the first place, there are many types of economic activity where the transport cost of the finished product or of one of the raw material inputs simply predominates to such a degree that it outweighs all other transport costs. Thus the fluid content added to beer in the process of manufacture makes the final product expensive to transport and in consequence it tends to be located near the market.[3]

More commonly, however, the important factor is that transport costs are not proportional to distance as the simple Weber model assumes. Frequently transport rates per ton mile fall as distance increases, since the costs of loading and unloading are a fixed element of cost which has to be covered whatever the length of journey. The longer the journey, therefore, the smaller the average fixed cost per mile covered and the more nearly total costs may

[1] W. F. Luttrell, *Factory Location and Industrial Movement*, NIESR, 2 vols., 1962; Report of the Committee of Inquiry into the Scottish Economy (Toothill Report), Scottish Council Development and Industry, 1961, pp. 72–75.

[2] E. M. Hoover, *op. cit*, pp. 27–46.

[3] This is one of the examples most commonly cited of a market-oriented product, but the advent of bulk carrying is reducing its validity. Other examples are bricks and cement.

approach variable costs. This means that it will normally be cheaper to transport 100 tons of one raw material 200 miles than to move 100 tons of two separate raw materials 100 miles each. Thus, an industry using two raw materials, A and B, in equal quantities would be more economically located at A or at B than at any point in between.

This also explains the tendency for economic activity to be located at transport interchange points such as ports. Here goods have to be loaded and unloaded as they change from one type of transport to another. It is often cheaper, therefore, to site manufacturing processes at such a point than to transport the goods and unload them yet again elsewhere. The position of ports is further strengthened by the widely differing costs per mile of transport by sea and transport by land. This means that bulky raw materials, such as iron ore, raw materials for fertilizers or crude oil may be economically transported by sea, but the cost of a relatively short distance overland is prohibitive. The process of manufacture, on the other hand, greatly increases the value in relation to volume and so diminishes the burden of transport costs.

These factors are well illustrated by the changes which have taken place in the European steel industry in the last ten years. This industry used to be based on local resources and tended most commonly to be sited on coalfields such as South Wales, Central Scotland or the Walloon area of Belgium, since the cost of transporting coal outweighed the other transport factors. Now that the industry is relying mainly on imported ore, that other fuels may be used instead of coal and American imported coal is often cheaper than European, the industry is tending to relocate on the coast. The modern European steel mills are therefore at places like Europort, Ghent and Dunkirk and the older sites such as Charleroi and Liège are encountering severe economic difficulties.

The other question is whether transport costs are a relevant factor at all for a wide range of activities. Isard states: 'If there is any sense at all to location economics, it is because there are certain regularities in the variations of costs and prices over space. The regularities arise primarily because transport cost is some function of distance.'[1] Yet it is clear that many industries pay little regard to transport costs in choosing a location, at any rate in Europe. Luttrell found that the majority of manufacturing activity in Britain was footloose in the sense that it could operate satisfac-

[1] Walter Isard, *op. cit.*, p. 35.

torily in any of the major industrial centres in Britain.[1] The Toothill Committee studied the effect of transport costs on firms which had chosen a location in Scotland and found them to amount to less than 2 per cent of total costs, a figure which they did not consider to be significant.[2] Similar conclusions were found in France.[3] For many activities, therefore, it may be assumed that transport costs are no longer the key factor in determining whether a particular area can or cannot be developed; what matters more is the extent to which a firm can benefit from external economies in a particular location.

Clearly the importance of transport costs in determining location has altered substantially over time. In the early days of the industrial revolution the situation was quite different from what it is now. Even the typical nineteenth-century industries were based on coal as a source of energy and used raw materials, such as iron ore, which were expensive to transport. The products were likewise heavy and bulky in relation to their value. The railways must clearly have made an immense impact in enabling firms to serve a wider area; but the continuing revolution in transport, especially the introduction of motor transport and air travel, has constantly reduced the importance of transport in the total cost of a firm and thereby diminished its importance as a factor determining location. At the same time the new twentieth-century industries are typified by products where the value in relation to bulk, or cost of transport, is high. Industries such as wireless and electronics, for example, are far less influenced by transport considerations than the typical industries of a hundred years ago, both because of the developments in transport and the nature of their products.

At the same time one cannot completely reject transport costs as a relevant factor in determining location. It is clear that in heavy industry they still have a vital role, as the relocation of the European steel industry, already alluded to, exemplified. A limited number of other industries are also very largely transport orientated. Transport considerations apply to the service sector of the economy, though here convenience and accessibility to the main points of consumer demand are more important than a strict evaluation of transport costs.

[1] *Op. cit.*
[2] *Op. cit.*
[3] *Les Régions Sous-Developpées en France*, Report for a Conference on Backward Regions in Industrial Countries, Rome 1966.

Even for those manufacturing industries, however, where it has been shown that transport costs on finished goods or material inputs are not a significant item, it would be a mistake to assume that location is therefore a matter of indifference and that distance has no meaning economically. Despite the findings of Luttrell and Toothill, two recent studies by Cameron and Clark and Cameron and Reid have shown that businessmen are nonetheless influenced to a significant extent by the factor of distance in choosing a new location.[1] The advantages of being in daily contact with raw material and component suppliers, with customers and distributors, do not fit very easily into the traditional Weberian conception of transport costs; they are more easily defined as external economies of agglomeration, but they are associated with distance all the same. Similar considerations apply with branch factories. Branches which are far from the parent unit have to be run to a greater extent as separate entities than those located, say, within reasonable driving distance. Such distances, therefore, give rise to diseconomies in management. Costs of this nature are much harder to quantify than the traditional transport costs associated with materials or finished product. They are nonetheless important, and it may well be that, thus defined, distance costs can provide location theory with the degree of rational motivation which is required if it is to be called a theory at all.

It is an idea of this kind which underlies Colin Clark's conception of economic potential.[2] While rejecting a simple transport cost theory as too crude, Clark noted that there was a tendency for economic activity to concentrate in the areas of greatest population density and that the most densely populated agricultural areas in a pre-industrial age often turned out later to have the greatest industrial growth. This appeared to give evidence that economies of scale and external economies were associated with proximity of location either to the market or to other suppliers and to labour and that distance from these implied diseconomies. Population itself, however, seems unlikely to be the attractive force so much as income, and it is the concentration of incomes in a particular spot which Clark suggests attract industrial development.

[1] G. C. Cameron and B. D. Clark, *Industrial Movement and the Regional Problem*, and G. C. Cameron and G. L. Reid, *Scottish Economic Planning and the Attraction of Industry*, University of Glasgow Social and Economic Studies, Occasional Papers Nos. 5 and 6, Oliver and Boyd 1966.
[2] Colin Clark, 'Industrial Location and Economic Potential', *Lloyds Bank Review*, October 1966, and *Population Growth and Land Use*, Macmillan, 1967, Chapter VIII.

This is the concept of economic potential which Clark defines as the sum of incomes in areas adjacent to a particular geographical point divided by their distances from that point. This gives varying levels of economic potential for different parts of the country, and the higher the economic potential of an area, the greater its power, Clark suggests, to attract economic activity.

This hypothesis appears to give plausible results. Maps may be drawn to show the areas of high and low economic potential in a country; and in Britain's case these appear to correspond to the regional pattern of economic growth. The hypothesis does, however, require further testing and elaboration to include other factors. The underlying theory is not yet fully worked out. Nevertheless, compared with a simple transport cost model the concepts of distance costs and economic potential appear to offer a more satisfactory basis for a theory of location of the firm or plant.

Distance costs, thus defined, are really the same thing in reverse as economies of agglomeration. Whereas the economies of agglomeration are concerned with the cost advantages of geographical association either with suppliers, selling outlets or kindred firms, distance costs express the cost disadvantage of not associating with them. It would seem that as a location factor such forces are widespread over a much larger section of economic activity than transport costs narrowly defined. Their effect will, however, vary from one form of activity to another. In some cases a basic industry, such as steel, may be located in a particular area by simple transport cost factors on its materials or product, while distance costs will encourage other related industries, for example steel-using industries, to form a complex in the area.

But while the theory is no doubt much more applicable to a firm's behaviour if modified in this way, it is still essentially a theory of location of the firm. It cannot properly explain regional economic structure nor the spread of economic activity over space. Even less can it explain differences in economic performance between regions.

II. THE PATTERN OF REGIONAL DEVELOPMENT

(a) *An Historical View*

The way in which economic activity has come to be spread over space is to a great extent due to historical factors; and it may therefore be useful to analyse these factors before developing any purely theoretical conceptions. Associated with the process of the industrial revolution and rising living standards have been immense changes in the relative importance of the primary, manufacturing and tertiary sectors of the economy which have had profound implications for the spatial distribution of economic activity.

In a pre-industrial era agriculture employs the greater part of a country's population and most of the industrial and service activities which exist are closely associated with it. In such circumstances regional development in a given state of technology is widely dependent on the distribution of agricultural resources. Generally speaking, where such resources are rich, populations are of higher density, and living standards better, than where resources are poor. Such factors seem to have been largely responsible for the distribution of population and wealth in pre-industrial Europe. The assumption of a given level of technology is, however, unrealistic; in fact, there will be an interaction between the level of wealth and the state of technology. In wealthy areas a greater surplus available for investment, better education and greater possibilities of specialization may lead to more rapid technical progress than in poorer areas. To the extent that it does so, the development that the richer areas can support will in turn be increased and the disparity between rich and poor areas further emphasized.

The need for specialization in such a pre-industrial society will lead to the development of towns. This will be essential if trade between areas is to take place and if service activities are to be developed. Such centres will also be important for military and administrative reasons. The sites chosen will either be at important transport intersections, at ports or at the central focal point of an agricultural area. In some cases military considerations may dictate that they should be on sites that are easily defended. Such were probably the original functions of the English county towns and the main reasons for their siting. Once established, however, as it were to serve the needs of the agricultural hinterland, the town itself interacts on the pattern of agricultural production. Because of transport costs, as von Thünen's theory shows, the areas closest to the town will command higher rents, be farmed with a greater degree of intensity and specialize in different products than those further away.

This pattern of economic activity was completely disturbed by industrialization. Many of the first industries to develop were heavy industries depending for their location on supplies of water-power, coal or iron ore. Often, therefore, they established themselves in areas which had not hitherto been able to support high population densities. The rapid development of trade with the American altered traditional transport patterns and caused new ports to develop. At the same time rapid increases in agricultural productivity reduced the population that was necessary to work the land; the revolution in transport altered the size of market areas and made it possible for agricultural products to be available to consumers far outside the immediate region of their production. These changes, therefore, broke the connection between the population density of an area and the wealth of its immediate agricultural resources.

As the process of development continues, so the developments in different means of transport go on. Light industries are developed for which materials are drawn from innumerable sources and the value of the product in relation to its bulk or weight is very high. Market areas are thus continually widened, the importance of transport costs as a factor in determining location are reduced and the spatial pattern of economic activity is increasingly decided by economies of agglomeration. In some instances this may result in firms locating beside heavy industries on whose products they depend; but the majority of firms seem to be influenced rather by the market, whether one sees this as the external economies gained by being close to the market or the distance costs of being away from it. Such firms, of course, have a very wide market area and the issue is really a matter of siting within the area. The tendency will probably be for gravitation to take place towards the centre of this area where demand is greatest. Where market areas cover the whole country, as is increasingly the case in Europe, the economy will tend to get more and more centralized; and the more it does so, the stronger the centralizing forces, at any rate from the point of view of the individual firm, will become. These forces will be greatly strengthened in countries which are politically and administratively centralized and where this centre also coincides with the economic centre.

From the economic point of view this process of agglomeration may easily go further than is economically justified. This may arise (as Chapter I showed) because the private costs of an entrepreneur which influence him in choosing his location may differ substantially from the social costs which the community as a whole must bear. Indeed, it is possible that there may be an increasing divergence between the two as the process of agglomeration continues. This divergence may arise in either of two ways.

First, as Giersch has pointed out, a firm in deciding to move from the edge of a market area to the centre will be attracted by the external economies of agglomeration which can be obtained at the centre.[1] His departure from the periphery, however, especially if it leads to a reduction in economic activity there, will lead to a loss of external economies to those who remain in operation. Since this is not borne by the entrepreneur who moves, it will not enter his calculations.

Secondly, and of greater importance than the above, are the increasing social costs at the centre which the move may incur. This question was analysed in the last chapter. Continued economic growth requires public authorities to provide infrastructure, roads, public transport systems, schools, housing, etc. These things are necessary in some degree whatever the location; but the costs incurred per head may be particularly high in very congested areas. There is, therefore, good reason to suppose that the natural process of development will reduce the connection between the spatial pattern of economic activity and its raw material resources, and will result in a growing tendency towards concentration which may exceed what would be desirable on economic grounds.

(b) *Theories of the Spatial Distribution of Economic Activity*

The two principal pioneering works on the spatial distribution of economic activity are those of Walter Christaller and August Lösch.[2] Both authors are German, as have been many of the contributors to this field, and their two theories have some important points of similarity. Both develop a structure of hexagonal market areas, both offer an explanation for different sizes of urban settlement, and both theories depend heavily on transport costs to give the market structure which they indicate.

Christaller is obviously concerned primarily with the services sector of the economy, since the examples he uses for illustration are drawn almost entirely from it. His towns and villages (central places) are sited in such a way that those offering an equivalent range of goods and services are equidistant from each other, since only in this way can the population be served with the minimum of transport costs. This condition is best satisfied if the central places are each at the points of an equilateral triangle. Such a system continued all round any one central place will form a regular hexagon. Different goods and services, however, will have

[1] H. Giersch, 'Economic Union between Nations and the Location of Industries', *Review of Economic Studies*, 1949/50.
[2] Walter Christaller, *op. cit.*; August Lösch, *op. cit.*

market ranges of differing sizes. Central places will therefore be of varying importance, depending on whether they form the market centres simply for the immediate neighbourhood in its most pressing needs or whether they supply a wide range of goods and services to a large area. According to Christaller's system the central places will form a hierarchy, each town fulfilling the same functions as other towns of similar size and including all the functions of towns smaller than itself.

The size of the hexagonal network will, of course, depend on the functions of the central place. Villages, for instance, would form a network of small hexagons, county towns a much larger one and cities a larger one still. Christaller distinguishes a great variety of types.[1]

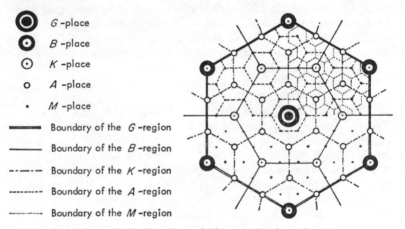

G -place
B -place
K -place
A -place
M -place
———— Boundary of the G -region
———— Boundary of the B -region
—··—··— Boundary of the K -region
-------- Boundary of the A -region
············· Boundary of the M -region

Reproduced from Christaller, *Central Places in Southern Germany.*

A problem with this type of system is that whereas a hexagonal system may represent the best layout of market areas, the scattered nature of the central places which it entails poses problems for a communications system. Christaller recognizes a direct conflict here. He suggests that on occasions the requirements of the communications system may distort the hexagonal framework so that central places are formed in lines giving access to communications. This he suggests is most likely to occur in difficult terrain.

Christaller applies his system to the towns of South Germany, taking Munich as his principal central place. Allowing for frontiers,

[1] For a fuller description of this system and the definitions of the different regions, see Christaller, *op. cit.*, p. 58–80.

for difficult terrain, etc., he finds that the spacing of towns of different rank accords quite well with his theoretical framework. There is no doubt that this theory is an important contribution. Perhaps its greatest shortcoming is that it passes over the difference between market areas and the location of industrial activity. In a region which is primarily made up of towns which are market centres and provide services for the surrounding area, it might be expected to give good results. But it is much less likely to be satisfactory where there are heavy concentrations of manufacturing or extractive industry whose products are sold all over the country and exported. Under the Christaller system these would be concentrated in the largest central places, but they do not fit in with his hierarchical framework, since it is the characteristic of these goods to be concentrated in particular areas in such a way that the economic structure of towns of equal size may be very far from being alike.

Lösch's theory is worked out with much greater precision in its economic aspects. The theory starts by assuming that there is a plain on which agricultural population and natural resources are evenly dispersed. If industrial activity is to be introduced, it therefore follows that this would also be dispersed if economies of scale were completely lacking and if the costs of transport were high. On the other hand, such activity would be completely centralized if the economies of scale, either internal or external, were infinite or if the costs of transport were insignificant. On these two factors, therefore, the settlement of industrial activity depends.

Lösch illustrates this theory with the example of the brewing industry. Because economies of scale exist, each man will not brew his own beer, but breweries will be set up surrounded by circular market areas, the limits of these areas being determined where distance from the brewery gives rise to transport costs which equal or exceed the economies to be gained from scale production. At such a point an individual could brew beer for his own personal consumption; and although he would enjoy no economies of scale, he could nonetheless produce beer as cheaply as he could obtain it from the brewery.

It makes a difference to the system whether transport costs are assumed to fall on the producer or the consumer. Lösch assumed that they were borne by the consumer, and this situation can be shown to give a market area which is clearly defined by the limits of demand. The further the consumer is from the point of production, the higher the transport costs he will have to meet in relation to the production cost of the product. This will have the effect of raising the price he has to pay for the product the further he is from its point of manufacture. The increasing cost will cause less of the product to be demanded the further the distance over which it has to be transported. Finally, a point will be reached when the consumer will either prefer to do without the product than pay so much for it, or where he could produce it for his own personal consumption, even without economies of scale, at a price no greater than he was paying for the factory-produced product including its transport.

<u>Diagram II.</u>

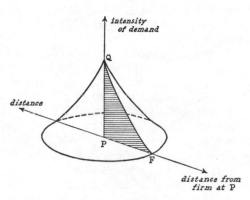

Lösch is thus able to construct a 'demand cone' giving a clearly defined market area as shown in Diagram II. The base of the cone represents geographical space and the height the quantity of the product sold at any point. At the centre of the cone, the point of manufacture P, transport cost will be minimal and the cost of the product to the consumer at its lowest; demand for the product will here be at its greatest and output PQ will be sold. The further one is from P, so the output sold will diminish, until beyond F sales cease altogether. A circular market area is therefore described by the radius PF from the production point P. In practice the limit of the market area will not be set by the costs of individuals producing the product for their own personal consumption, but by competition from other firms. Spaced at intervals, these will eat into each other's market areas until excess profits are eliminated and the average costs of production are only just covered.

This will cause the market areas to lose their circular shape and assume that of hexagons, as will shortly be shown.

If transport costs are borne by the firm the situation will be rather different. This assumption is not examined by Lösch and it is therefore worth considering in detail what it involves. Price to consumers will now be uniform regardless of where they are and the intensity of demand will be everywhere the same; but the cost to the firm of supplying the product will vary. Reverting to Lösch's example of the brewing industry; suppose in Diagram III that an individual at O could produce beer to meet his own requirements at cost ON per pint. A brewery, since it could obtain economies of scale, would, if sited at O, sell beer across space in the direction of P. As output expanded, costs of production per unit would fall, while costs of transport per unit would rise. Thus, at point O there are no transport costs and total costs are equal to production costs. If output is expanded to supply the area OE, average production costs per unit fall from ON to OD, but the firm's total costs including transport are equal to EI. Similarly, when the area OH is supplied, average production costs fall to OA, but total costs including transport are equal to HL. When area OK is supplied maximum economies of scale are being obtained; production costs do not fall below OB with any further increases in output, but since the average transport costs are still rising with distance, any increase in output and area over which it is sold beyond OK must entail a rise in average total costs per unit. But so long as the increment in costs per unit is less than that unit's contribution to profits, marginal cost, though rising, will still be less than marginal revenue. The brewery will, therefore, expand output beyond what is necessary to cover the area OK. Indeed, in the absence of competition from other firms, it would sell over a wider area until it reached point P. At this point its average production and transport costs per unit are again equal to ON, the cost at which an individual could produce his own beer for his private consumption in the absence of economies of scale. The market area for each brewery is thus clearly defined.

If transport costs are borne by the firm, the validity of the theory depends on the assumption of a U-shaped curve indicating costs of production and transport. If transport costs are borne by the individual consumer, the firm's cost curve need not be U-shaped for the theory to apply; but it is still essential for the increase in transport costs per unit of output as distance increases sooner or later to exceed the fall in production costs obtained

65

Diagram III.

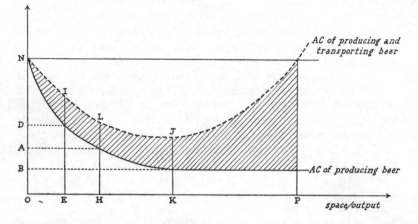

from increasing economies of scale. Basically, therefore, the same conditions apply. It is perhaps easier to see the implications of this if we assume that the firm bears the transport costs. The actual shape of the average total cost curve will then depend on both transport and production costs and on the technical conditions which affect each.

Provided that the transport and production costs, when added together, give a U-shaped cost curve as shown in Diagram III, there will be a clearly defined market area with a limit. If, on the other hand, transport costs are never sufficiently significant, or the economies of scale from extending the market so vast, that they counteract the effect of transport costs and the total average cost curve is not U-shaped, then there will be no limit to the market area. This does not mean that location is random, since some locations may have cost advantages. And these may even be due to transport, because although transport costs may be small in relation to economies of scale, the firm which minimizes transport costs, other things being equal, will still be the most profitable. In such conditions, however, from whatever point production is started, there is no limit to the market area and the Löschian system does not operate, since the average cost curve, including production and transport costs, will either fall with increasing output or remain constant.

It is possible, of course, that the curve for average production costs is itself U-shaped, as is commonly assumed in much of the literature on the theory of the firm. This merely indicates that the economies of scale are not limitless; that there is a definite optimum combination of factors of production and that further expansion involves diseconomies of scale. In these conditions the production costs will themselves set a limit to the size of the market even if transport costs are zero. Without transport costs, however, the firms could all be concentrated in one place, even though this meant they were far removed from the market areas they served. If transport costs are significant, the firms will once again be scattered over space; but, if average transport costs rise per unit of output, their potential size and the size of their market areas will be less than if it had been determined by production costs alone.

In any of the cases where transport costs are significant and where the rise in transport costs over space sooner or later exceeds the fall in production costs with increasing output, the firm will have a clear market area with a finite limit. The production unit will normally be situated in the centre of the market area, this being the way in which transport costs are minimized. Lösch devotes considerable thought to this. Provided that transport costs are identical in every direction from the firm's location the market area would tend to be circular with the firm's location as the centre. A series of circular areas if drawn on the map, however, will either leave some awkward spaces uncovered by any market area, or, if the whole map is to be covered the circles will overlap considerably. Such areas of overlap will signify areas of competition between two production units. However, as shown in Diagram IV, firm A will be in a stronger competitive position on the left of the line MN and firm B on the right. Lösch, therefore, shows that from this situation will evolve a system of hexagonal market areas which prove to be the ideal shape in a competitive situation.

Each industry, therefore, according to the Löschian system, will develop a hexagonal system of market areas. The technical conditions, however, especially the relationship of production and transport costs, will differ considerably from one industry to another. The size of the hexagonal market areas which is ideal for one type of industry will therefore be quite unsuitable for another. Thus, though each industry will evolve a hexagonal network, the size of the mesh, as it were, will differ from one form of activity to another. When the systems come to be imposed on a map the different hexagonal systems will not be set up in complete disregard of each other. Rather the hexagons will tend to be

Diagram IV.

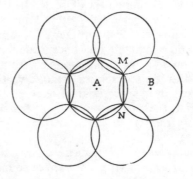

aligned in such a way as to enable the centres to coincide as far as possible. A system will, therefore, tend to evolve with economic focal points of different sizes. A number of small centres will exist which are the focal points of market areas only for the industry with the smallest mesh network of hexagons. Every now and then one of these centres will coincide with the centre of a larger mesh network and less frequently still several hexagonal systems will converge on one central point. Thus, at one extreme will be the largest focal point in the country which is the centre of all hexagonal systems and at the other extreme the small centre for only one type of economic activity.

At this point Lösch's system has great similarity to Christaller's. But there are some important points of difference. While Christaller's central places were arranged in a hierarchy, each fulfilling the same functions as towns of similar size and including all the functions of smaller places, the same is not necessarily true of Lösch's system. Lösch's system, too, gives towns of different sizes, but this arises through the chance of the central point of several hexagonal systems coinciding in one spot. If two towns are the same size in Lösch's system this does not necessarily imply an identical range of activity: one may happen to be the central point of hexagonal systems relating to activities A, B and C, while the other might be the focus of systems X, Y and Z. In the same way the system does not necessarily require that each town fulfils all the functions of towns smaller than itself. The Lösch system, therefore, while offering an explanation of different sizes of urban

68

unit, is not a hierarchical system in the strict sense. The communications problem which, as has been seen, gave Christaller considerable trouble, also arises under the Lösch system and it is therefore suggested that the larger centres will tend to be grouped so that there are, say, three sections of the hexagon with large centres as well as small where the main transport links are and three other sections with only small centres.

Lösch's theory is a work of great originality and it is highly ingenious, but it does not lack serious shortcomings. The first of these is that the whole system depends on the initial assumption whereby agricultural population and natural resources are evenly distributed across economic space. This population constitutes the initial demand in search of which industry is in turn obliged to disperse. Today this obviously makes little sense when the agricultural population in most industrialized countries is only a small proportion of total population. Indeed, in Britain the agricultural population is now no more than 3.5 per cent of the labour force; and since their incomes are usually below the national average, the proportion of total demand which they represent is lower still. It may be, nonetheless, as indicated in the earlier part of this section, that historically such an assumption is defensible. In pre-industrial days agriculture did largely determine the spread of population and the early industries and services would have to locate themselves in response to this. But later as the agricultural population declines in importance it is the centres themselves, which have by then evolved, that determine the spread of economic activity in space.

Another weakness of the Lösch system is the importance attached to transport costs. This has already been criticized in discussing Weber's theory of location. If a uniform distribution of population and proportional transport costs in every direction from the market centre cannot be assumed, the hexagonal system will become seriously warped and distorted. Thus physical barriers such as water or a mountain range will affect the cost of transport adversely, while if particularly highly developed transport facilities exist in other directions the cost will be lowered. Christaller fully recognized this problem and emphasized the need to think in terms of economic rather than physical distance, but Lösch devotes little attention to it. In reality, therefore, a much distorted system bearing little relation to hexagons might result.

More important than this, however, is the objection that, for a considerable range of economic activity, transport is not an important element of cost. Either a U-shaped average cost curve is not found to exist or, if it does, the U-shape derives from production characteristics alone. A firm could thus exhaust its economies of scale without at any time finding that the increase in transport costs exceeded the gains from scale production. Indeed it might be that the market is large enough to enable several production units to reap the advantage of scale without transport considerations being strong enough to make them disperse.

If this is so, there would be several producing units within one market area. This, though commonly the case in the real world, seemed an improbable circumstance from Lösch's theory in the way it was developed. Such producing units may site themselves largely at random within the market area; they may tend to cluster together, if external economies can be obtained from associating with each other; they may alternatively associate themselves either with their suppliers or with the market. Instances such as these would be fully compatible with the conception of distance costs as outlined in discussing the location of the firm. Lösch was fully aware of the tendency for firms to associate with each other, indeed he devotes considerable space to discussing it; but it does not fit in well with his theory.

Another weakness of Lösch's theory is that, as developed, it is entirely static and therefore does not explain changes in regional economic structure. Again, Christaller recognizes the importance of this and attempts to consider the changes brought about by dynamic factors. It is the forces governing these changes which have to be understood if policies for growing and declining regions are to be sensibly pursued. An attempt will be made to investigate some of these forces in the third section of this chapter.

The essence of both the Christaller and Lösch systems was to give a spatial distribution of economic activity which minimized the combination of production and transport costs. Since it was supposed that under free market conditions firms would be working to this objective, it appeared that a theoretical construction on these lines could explain the *actual* spatial pattern of economic activity. Obviously this is in part a substitution problem: the more dispersed an activity is, the lower its transport costs to the market, but the less economies of scale it can gain; the more concentrated, the lower its production costs may be, but the higher its transport costs.

Clearly, the recent development of input/output models and programming techniques may have much application to this problem, and this is the approach followed by Professor Bos.[1] With an evenly-spread agricultural population, he uses programming techniques to show what the spatial distribution of other forms of activity should be. However, this type of approach is most complex. Ordinary linear · programming uses constant input/output relationships; yet a theory which attempts to explain the spatial dispersion of production must take account of indivisibilities. These indivisibilities lead to economies of scale or agglomeration and they do not permit proportionality to be maintained at all levels of production between all inputs in the production process. External economies, where these exist, have the same effect, in that a given increase in inputs will produce a more than proportionate increase in output. For these reasons programming techniques in this field are hard to handle.

The type of approach followed by Bos and also by Tinbergen, however, strays some distance from simply offering an explanation of the spatial dispersion of economic activity and the forces governing it.[2] Rather what they are concerned with is discovering the *optimum* dispersion. But there are a great variety of reasons for supposing that in real life actual location decisions may be very wide of the optimum, as has been shown in the last chapter. Not least of these is the interdependent nature of business location decisions so that one firm in making a location decision accepts as datum the location of others whether they are optimal or not. Results obtained by the programming approach might, therefore, differ very widely from the actual situation; and the great value of those techniques would therefore seem rather to be in spatial planning for future development than in offering an explanation of the forces which determined the existing situation.

(c) *The Theory of Poles of Growth*
Another theory which may be used to explain spatial distribution of economic activity is based on the idea of the *pôle de croissance* or pole of growth. The idea of the growth point or growth pole has appeared in the writings of a number of economists from time to time but the theoretical conception as outlined here originates

[1] H. C. Bos, *Spatial Dispersion of Economic Activity*, Rotterdam University Press 1965.
[2] J. Tinbergen, 'Regional Planning some Principles', *Revista del Banco Central de Venezuela*, 176–8, 1959; 'The Spatial Dispersion of Production: A Hypothesis', *Schweizerische Zeitschrift für Volkswirtschaft und Statistik*, Vol. 97 No. 4, 1961; 'Sur un Modèle de la dispersion géographique de l'activité économique', *Revue d'Economie Politique*, Numéro Spécial 1964.

from Francois Perroux and has been developed by a number of other Continental economists such as Davin and Boudeville.[1]

The notion is basically a simple one: an industry tends to start up in a particular area either because of proximity to natural resources or possibly for some entirely fortuitous reason. In growing it will develop economies of scale which will give it competitive advantages over other firms in the same industry which are trying to start up either in the same area or elsewhere. More importantly, however, it will attract a variety of industries which either supply it with components or use its products. These industries will be attracted to the location by the external economies which may be obtained by being in close association with the key industry or *industrie motrice*. A pole of growth thus consists of a sort of industrial complex of related industries which derive considerable economic advantage from locational association. Perroux lays some stress on the fact that the competitive power or economic vitality of such a complex is intertwined in such a way that the complex needs to be considered as a whole. Since each industry's input is another's output a weak link in the chain will weaken the competitive power of the whole complex. This would be most likely to happen, of course, if there was some weakness in a key industry such as steel or energy. Higher cost sheet steel, for instance, would clearly injure the competitive position of all steel-using industries in the complex.

Often the reasons which induced the key industry to set up in the area, if these were other than mere chance, disappear with the passage of time. A natural resource which originally attracted an industry becomes inadequate for its needs and is exhausted. By such a stage the complex has often acquired such a momentum that imported supplies are substituted with no adverse effects on its growth. Italy's industrial growth, for example, is originally supposed to have started in the area bounded by Turin, Milan and Genoa because of the existence of mineral deposits. These have long since ceased to be of any importance, yet the area is industrially more dynamic than ever. What this illustrates is that an industrial complex, for whatever reason it started, tends to perpetuate itself in a position of strength because the combination of scale and external economies, or economies of agglomeration, give it a competitive edge on another area which is only just starting and is therefore unable to obtain such advantages.

In some cases, however, adjustment is more painful. Demand

[1] *Op. cit.* The literature on this subject in Britain is referred to in Chapter IX.

for the product of a key industry may decline, as was the case with shipbuilding and cotton; or changing technical conditions may make the area no longer ideal for the key industry. In these cases the closely-knit nature of the complex means that it is all affected by the decline; and the consequence may be widespread regional depression.

There is nothing particularly new in this notion of the pole of growth. Basically it is an elaboration of the concept of external economies which goes back a very long way. The form of its development by Perroux and others, however, is original and it focuses attention on aspects of the idea which might otherwise have been overlooked.

All theories described above offer some useful insights to the working of the economic system in space; but all have their limitations. The chief trouble with Lösch's system is that the basic assumptions are such an over-simplification of the real world as to destroy much of the theory's usefulness. The hexagonal framework depends on an evenly dispersed population, on a transport rate structure which is uniform in all directions, and on economic activity which is market oriented in accordance with transport costs. Lösch is clearly aware of the limitations of these assumptions and in elaborating his theory he considers their implications at some length. But since the structure of the theory depends on these assumptions, their removal and replacement by a series of *ad hoc* rationalizations, though necessary if it is to be applied to the real world, destroy its value as a theory. The position is not unlike that of the theory of perfect competition whose assumptions, while giving it the virtue of simplicity, render it of limited application.

The pole of growth theory is almost the opposite of the Lösch system in that transport costs have no part and the emphasis is placed on external economies or the economies of agglomeration. The theory is more limited than the Lösch system, however, in that it does not attempt to explain fully the economic use of space but merely shows how economic activity will tend to form in clusters.

But the two theories need not be mutually exclusive. In many respects the service sector and certain types of market-oriented manufacturing come close to the type of system expounded by Lösch and Christaller. If limited to these sectors these theories may be of considerable analytical value. A second category of activities, mainly basic industries, are limited to a small range of possible locations because of their need for raw material resources, labour facilities, cheap power supplies, etc. For a third category, and one which forms a very large and growing proportion of manufacturing activity, some form of distance costs form the main economic motivation for choosing a location. These may take the form of external economies which arise either from close proximity to the market or from association with suppliers. Thus, there are links between this third category of economic activity and the basic industries; and the sites on which the latter are established may become the location of large industrial complexes the greater part of whose economic activity has only been indirectly influenced in favour of the locations. It is this type of situation that the pole of growth theory explains.

What neither theory considers satisfactorily is the interaction between the distribution of population and the pattern of economic activity. Clearly it is not satisfactory to regard the distribution of population which provides both the market and the labour force as independently determined; yet this is what the Lösch system assumes. As Britain's economic history shows so clearly, the early industries whose sites were determined by water power, by mineral deposits or by access to ports, attracted to hitherto sparsely populated areas huge concentrations of population which provided the labour both for these industries and for the complex of related activities associated with them. At the other extreme there are those activities whose locations are mainly market oriented. These activities tend to settle in the larger urban concentrations; but their growth attracts further supplies of labour to the concentrations thus in turn increasing their market potential and making them even more attractive to market oriented activities. A cumulative process thus develops, which is of the greatest importance in explaining inter-regional differences in economic performance, the subject of the next section.

III. GROWTH AND REGIONAL EQUILIBRIUM

(a) *Market Areas and Poles of Growth in a Dynamic Setting*
It is perhaps surprising that very little of the theoretical work on the regional question has attempted to show why some regions grow and others decline. Yet it is precisely this varying performance among regions of a national economy which has made the regional problem an important issue for public policy. Most countries of Western Europe, for example, have adopted measures to influence the pattern of regional development; and some of

74

these might have been better conceived if the forces giving rise to the situation had been more fully understood.

Christaller gave considerable thought to the changes in his system which would result from dynamic factors. But most of the theories fail to tackle this question because they originate in a static framework. The Löschian system, for example, might be expected to undergo change over time in a number of important respects. First, as the economy develops the proportion of the labour force engaged in agriculture will steadily fall and that in industrial and service activities rise. Firms will, therefore, be less market oriented towards the countryside and more towards the towns. Economic activity will, therefore, tend to be sited in such a way as to serve the existing towns, rather than the agricultural population as Lösch postulated. In doing so it will attract labour to the towns thereby increasing still further their relative importance and their attractiveness to industry.

Secondly, changes in techniques of production over time tend to lead in many industries to increased economies of scale. This will have the effect of widening the market area for a given producing unit, putting it in strong competition with those of neighbouring market areas, and possibly driving less competitive units out of business. In other words, the size of the hexagons will alter over time. In the real world this process may well offer some explanation of the tendency for business in Scotland or Northern England which in the nineteenth and early twentieth century were predominantly independent to come increasingly under the ownership of larger enterprises in the South.

Thirdly, the revolutions in transport and in the nature of the products produced, which have already been referred to in discussing the location of the firm, are bound to critically alter the structure of market areas. As a result of these changes, firms which are some distance apart and previously had distinct market areas will find that they can readily sell in each other's market areas as indicated in Diagram V. In V (a) three firms at X, Y and Z, with average cost curves including transport ab, a' b', a" b", each had distinct market areas originally, limited by the intersection of each other's cost curves. With transport costs remaining the same, the introduction of economies of scale by the firm at X as shown by the new cost curve AB would enable it to outsell both Y and Z so that all production would come to be concentrated at X. In V (b) it is assumed that there is no change in production techniques or costs, but transport costs are greatly reduced.

The effect of this is to reduce the slope of the three firms' cost curves till it is almost a straight line. Thus, whereas each firm had a virtual monopoly in its own market area before, the three market areas are now fused into one and the firms are in competition. Over time it may be that the original sites cease to be ideal and that some new location would offer more ready access to the greater market potential in the new area.

Diagram V.

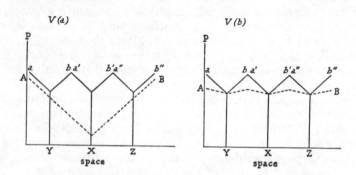

For all these reasons, therefore, changes in the regional balance of the economy may be expected. Economic activity will tend increasingly to be centred in the towns rather than being spread throughout rural regions; firms serving large urban areas will be in a position to develop to the point at which they gain economies of scale which enable them to buy up or drive out of business those serving smaller areas; and the tendency for market areas themselves to enlarge will lead increasingly to economic activity being concentrated in the densely populated zones of high market potential at the centre of these areas.

In Perroux's theory of poles of growth the effect of dynamic forces can very easily be seen. Changing patterns of demand, changing techniques of manufacture, the development of different sources of energy and raw materials, may cause some key industries to contract or stagnate while others develop. The areas in which the former predominate will tend to become industrial depressed zones. Regeneration requires the reorientation of the regional economy round new key industries and the building up of a new type of industrial complex. This, however, is seldom easy to accomplish since a depressed industrial zone loses its entrepreneurship and skilled labour to other areas and is seldom attractive to new capital once a buoyant and expanding market are lacking. State incentives, therefore, have to be provided if the obstacles are to be overcome and if self-generating growth is to be got under way.

Two types of problem area may thus be expected to develop: areas of comparatively slight development, often in peripheral locations, which lose out increasingly to the growing dominance of more developed urban concentrations; secondly, developed urban areas which have depended on a key industry that changing technical conditions or an altered pattern of demand have made obsolete.

(b) Regional Theory and International Trade Theory

Another useful way of looking at inter-regional development is by the application of the theory of international trade to regions. Regions are, after all, subject to the same sort of trade flows as nations; some of them were even in previous times nations in their own right. The main difference is that, being generally smaller than independent nations and unprotected by tariffs or import restrictions, they are all the more dependent on trade for their economic health. A theory which can therefore demonstrate how these flows operate, and to which region's advantage, could be of considerable value in explaining the relative prosperity and pace of economic advance of different regions.

The first approach along these lines was that of Ohlin.[1] He regarded inter-regional and international trade as essentially the same; the latter being only a special case of the former. According to his interpretation the main difference is that greater barriers to commodity movement, and more especially to factor mobility, exist in international trade. Furthermore, Ohlin shows that the more factor mobility is impeded, the more international commodity flows will tend to be stimulated. These conclusions are of the first importance for the operation of the theory and in due course it will be necessary to examine their implications more closely.

To start with, it may be supposed that regions, like nations, will specialize in the form of economic activity to which they are best suited according to the principle of comparative advantage. According to this principle two economies should still be able to gain from trade even in conditions in which one economy is technically

[1] Bertil Ohlin, Inter-regional and International Trade, Cambridge, Mass. 1933.

77

superior in the production of all commodities. All that is necessary is for prices when translated into each other's currencies to give each country the ability to sell the product in which it has a comparative advantage and for the earnings of the factors of production in each country to reflect the differing levels of productivity. Thus, countries such as the United Kingdom and the United States, despite the much lower levels of productivity in the former, can both gain from trading with each other; real incomes in both will be higher than in the absence of trade; and there is no reason why both economies should not enjoy a satisfactory rate of growth.

But those who have developed this theory have sometimes devoted too little attention to the conditions which must be fulfilled if it is to work. At the international level, balance of payments equilibrium between two nations trading according to the principles of comparative advantage will only be obtained if it is possible to set an exchange rate which brings imports and exports into balance. It is conceivable that no such equilibrium exchange rate can be found: either the demand for the exports of one of the countries may be perverse so that the cheaper they become the less is sold; or, more likely, the supply elasticity of exports in one country is so low that it is never possible to expand them sufficiently to meet demand. This is not unusual in underdeveloped countries where much of the population is at subsistence level: exports cannot then be increased at the expense of home consumption but only as a consequence of increased productivity. In other words, the cut in living standards which a reduction in the exchange rate would entail cannot be supported by a population already at subsistence level.

But if there are reasons why the principle of comparative advantage cannot always bring equilibrium to nations trading with each other, these problems are magnified in inter-regional trade. Indeed, the most serious problem for equilibrium in inter-regional trade is that the principle of *comparative* advantage is rarely able to apply. This arises for two reasons. In the first place, exchange rate adjustment is clearly impossible between the regions of an economy with a unified money system. Secondly, if the costs and prices which prevail do not properly reflect regional differences in productivity or if they give the result of over-pricing the products of some regions and under-pricing those of others in relation to demand, it will be impossible for regions to achieve balance of payments equilibrium by specializing in the products in which they have a comparative advantage.

Here the question of inter-regional factor mobility is of the greatest importance. As already stated, Ohlin assumed that there was much greater factor mobility between regions than between nations. As a starting point it will be convenient to postulate that there is complete inter-regional factor mobility. This would imply that there must also be inter-regional equality of factor earnings. For example, if the earnings of one factor, labour, were lower in one region than another, this would tend to be corrected both by an outflow of labour to other regions and by an inflow of capital and enterprise wishing to take advantage of cheap labour costs. Sooner or later a shortage of labour will develop as a result of which wage rates will rise to the levels prevailing elsewhere. There would thus be a tendency for the marginal product of each factor to be equalized in all regions and *per caput* income levels between different regions of an economy to converge, except where they were accounted for by differences in skills or types of labour.

If inter-regional equality in factor earnings is assumed, trade between regions can no longer take place on the basis of *comparative* advantage but only as a result of *absolute* advantage.[1] A region which is less efficient than the others at all forms of production, a consequence perhaps of inferior natural resources or inability to gain economies of scale, will be unable to establish prices at which it can sell its products to the other regions. In consequence its economy must contract, and factors of production must move to other regions; but since complete mobility of factors is assumed, this need not lead either to regional unemployment or to depressed factor earnings. Thus there is the contrast between international trade where differences in productivity can be matched by differences in factor earnings, where exchange rates can be adjusted to ensure trade can take place on the basis of comparative advantage, and where all participants in trade no matter what their level of efficiency or their endowments may enjoy economic growth. And, on the other hand, inter-regional trade with complete factor mobility which implies equality of factor earnings, trade only on the basis of absolute advantage, no regional unemployment, but a tendency for regions with below average efficiency to decline while others expand.

Of course, this picture differs substantially from the real world.

[1] That inter-regional trade is conducted on the basis of absolute advantage is argued in P. P. Streeten, *Economic Integration, Aspects and Problems*, European Aspects, Sythoff Leyden, 2nd edn. 1964, pp. 57–66; Bela Balassa, *The Theory of Economic Integration*, George Allen & Unwin 1962, esp. p. 191 ff.

Although capital approximates to complete mobility between regions, labour is far from being perfectly mobile. Consequently, it is possible for some regional unemployment to persist, though probably not on the same scale as if there was complete immobility of labour. At the same time, although some differences in regional earnings do exist, institutional factors such as national collective bargaining and social resistance to regional differences in earnings for comparable types of employment, prevent wide disparities in income levels from arising except in agriculture and self-employed activities. A situation approximating to equality of factor earnings therefore exists although labour is not perfectly mobile. This is borne out by the lack of evidence in any Western European country of a firm being attracted to a particular region by low labour costs.

As a result, regions neither have the advantage of factor immobility, which enables nations to trade on the basis of *comparative* advantage, nor do they enjoy complete factor mobility, which would make persistent unemployment impossible. It is therefore possible for a region to find that there is no product it can produce which other regions cannot produce more efficiently. Moreover, there is nothing to prevent a region from remaining in an adverse balance of payments relationship with the rest of the country for an indefinite period of time. Such a situation would pose no financial problem as it does internationally; indeed, it is rare that figures even exist at a regional level for this relationship. Yet an adverse balance of payments has a depressing effect on an economy in the same way as an excess of savings over investment, and will tend through the multiplier to produce regional depression and unemployment. Under these conditions the region finds that there is a poor demand for its own output both within the region and elsewhere, while a buoyant demand exists for the products of other regions.

Once a region gets into this position, the situation may well become self-perpetuating. Indeed, as Myrdal and Hirschman have both argued, far from any tendency for convergence to manifest itself, depression is liable to breed depression and success to produce further success.[1] A depressed region with stagnant income, unemployment and high rates of net emigration does not provide a buoyant market to encourage new enterprises. It is not, therefore, attractive to capital from other regions and, since there is no

[1] Gunnar Myrdal, *Economic Theory and Undeveloped Regions*, Duckworths 1957. A. O. Hirschman, *The Strategy of Economic Development*, Yale 1958.

barrier to movement of capital, it is likely that capital from this region invested elsewhere will exceed any inflow from other regions. Emigration tends to be heaviest among skilled manpower and those who are potential entrepreneurs. Moreover, the atmosphere of pessimism which this situation engenders is extremely discouraging to initiative and entrepreneurship within the region. Low incomes mean low tax revenue for local authorities, so that the public investment, which is so essential if the position of the region is to be changed, tends, unless corrective measures are taken by the State, to be on a lesser scale than in other regions.

As a result of these factors the region will tend to have less investment, less technical progress and benefit less from economies of scale than other regions. Yet these are precisely the things it needs if it is to have any hope of catching up and putting its economy on a firm competitive basis. So much economics tends to be built around the idea of static equilibrium that economists are rather too apt to assume that an uncompetitive industry or region will sooner or later get into balance if allowed to contract. As Myrdal emphasizes so strongly, however, ability to compete with rivals comes in many cases as much from the state of technical advance which has been reached and the economies of scale which are obtained as from any initial endowment of resources. Insofar as these factors can be influenced they are more likely to speed up with expansion and slow down with contraction. Success breeds success and failure leads to further failure.

Thus, the vicious circle will tend to persist and will only be ended by intervention from the State or by such pressure on resources being reached in the prosperous regions that firms are forced to look elsewhere if they are to find the labour, the space, the supplies of fresh water, the harbour facilities and other things that they need for development. These spread effects, as Myrdal calls them, will tend to manifest themselves as an economy approaches full employment. There is some evidence that these effects explain the post-war dynamism of the Southern and Western United States, of the Flemish region of Belgium which has witnessed a substantial inflow of German capital since the latter economy achieved full employment, and of South Wales which has increasingly developed since the war as a kind of offshoot from the English Midlands.

As a result of this vicious circle of cumulative causation, Myrdal takes a gloomy view of the prospects for regional development. He clearly thought it improbable that the spread effects would be strong enough to prevent disparities from widening. But the strength of these spread effects depends on a variety of factors. In the first place much depends on the Government's determination to intervene successfully. Equally important, however, is the extent to which the economy can be run with resources fully utilized without running into inflationary or balance of payment difficulties. It is not easy to pursue different economic policies in different regions of the same economy; and so expansion in underdeveloped or depressed regions is generally most successful in times when there is an impetus for expansion in the economy as a whole. It follows that an economy which can run for a considerable time without full employment leading to severe inflationary pressures, as Germany managed to do in the 'fifties and early 'sixties, has a greater chance of getting development to spread out to its problem regions than one which is chronically in the grip of 'stop-go'. The degree of centralization is also important: an economy which is heavily concentrated on one or two massive conurbations may be expected to have more difficulty in getting development to spread to its regions than one which already has major industrial centres throughout most of the country. Here again Germany's relative absence of concentration both politically and economically is an advantage when compared with France.

The contrast, therefore, of the effects of trade on a region and on a nation therefore illuminates a number of interesting points. The fact that comparative advantage cannot apply regionally makes it more likely than would otherwise be the case that development will tend to concentrate in some regions and others will be liable to stagnation and unemployment. The existence of the vicious circle accentuates any disparity which appears and may produce the result that those regions which get an initial lead continue in it long after the reasons for their original advantage have disappeared.

But having drawn attention to the differences between inter-regional and international trade, it is perhaps worth taking the analysis a little further. Some of the disadvantages of inter-regional trade have now been shown; but does it follow that some of the problem regions might do better as sovereign States? What, for instance, might have been the consequences for Scandinavia if it had been a region of the European economy instead of several independent States? In its present form, despite its peripheral location to the main European economy, it has been prosperous and the *per caput* income levels of Sweden, Norway and Denmark are amongst the highest in the world. If these countries had been part of a united European economy, might they not have suffered a drain of capital, enterprise and labour to the industrial centres of Britain and Germany? Moreover, if these countries have done well from independence, does it follow that a similar status would benefit Scotland or Wales? These are important questions. To answer them properly would require a lot of detailed analysis which is beyond the scope of this book and cannot be attempted here. Some of the factors may, however, be outlined and their implications considered.

A State has the advantage over a region that it is more likely to be able to pursue an independent economic policy. If it is a small State, however, it will be very heavily dependent on foreign trade and its control over its own economy will thereby be seriously curtailed. Decisions of foreign governments which lead to a rise or a fall of its exports may be every bit as important as any action it can initiate on its own. Nevertheless, compared with a region of similar size and importance, it will have a greater array of weapons at its command. It can alter its exchange rate, raise or lower tariffs and pursue its own fiscal policy. National barriers to factor movements make it more likely that it can establish trade on the basis of comparative advantage and that it will be able to achieve balance of payments equilibrium with full employment and growth.

On the other hand, compared with a region, it will also suffer some serious disadvantages. If the economy is small, it may be unable to offer the economies of scale necessary for the efficient operation of a large proportion of industry. Its exports will have to sell at world market prices instead of having a subsidized or guaranteed market; this is an important factor particularly with agricultural products, coal and ships. Advantages of specialization may be lost with factors of production being applied to inferior natural resources. Public expenditure on investment and social services which a region may obtain at the expense of the rest of the country may be beyond the resources of an independent State. Thus, while it is theoretically possible that there may be full employment and economic growth, it is also likely that the area's standard of living would be lower as an independent State than as a region.

But although a lower standard of living is likely, it is not an inevitable conclusion. The standard of living of a country depends not only on its resources but the effectiveness with which they are used, on technical progress, on the amount of national product devoted to investment, education and so on. Efficient management might make up for physical handicap, and separate States may be able to follow policies more appropriate to their individual needs than if they were all regions of one economy. Nor is this quite so fanciful as might appear. The fastest rate of growth which a country can achieve is determined by the need to avoid inflation and consequent balance of payments difficulties; but this pace is commonly set by the regions where labour is scarce and where over-full employment may very easily cause inflationary pressure. The depressed regions might have sustained a more rapid rate of growth as separate States, since they would not be held back by the slower ships in the convoy. This would also be subject to balance of payments constraints since their exports would feel the effect of restrictions imposed on other economies; but they would have a variety of weapons with which to manipulate the balance of payments and their wage levels would not necessarily move in line with the wage-price spirals of inflation-prone economies.

But, while this scope for independent action may exist for a State which has always been independent, it may be hard to establish if it has not always existed. Ireland, despite nearly fifty years of independence, has never achieved full employment. But neither has it broken all the links which typify a region of the British economy rather than an independent State. Free factor mobility still remains and devaluation against the British £ has never been attempted. These links would not be easily broken, since a common language makes labour movement easy. Any attempt to achieve lower production costs by devaluation would encounter severe inflationary pressures; the drop in living standards involved would be strenuously resisted, and if in any way successful, would merely stimulate emigration. Such a policy would therefore be unlikely to be accepted politically, and economically any long-term benefits which it might produce would probably be frustrated. Any problem region becoming independent is likely to encounter similar problems: either the free movement of factors of production cannot be stopped, or if it can the resulting unemployment and drop in living standards in the short term would be impossible to withstand politically and socially. In the end these factors might, by lowering production costs, lead to the establishment of new export-oriented growth industry which could undercut foreign competitors; but this is something of a gamble and long-term in its effects.

But there is no reason why some lessons should not be learnt from this for regional policy. If the processes of inter-regional trade produce some depressed regions whose redevelopment is considered an important objective of policy, this might be achieved by trying to emulate some of the policies which independent States would pursue in the same circumstances. Devaluation is, of course, out of the question, so is a drop in regional real wage levels, but the purpose of these measures is to reduce home production costs so that import demand is reduced and exports increased. These effects may also be achieved by fiscal and budgetary means. Differential regional taxes or subsidies may be used as a quasi-devaluation to stimulate regional production and at the same time restore something of the comparative advantage principle to inter-regional trade. As will be seen in Chapter VIII, these arguments played an important part in the case for the Regional Employment Premium.

A crucial question may be the part played by exports.[1] A balance of payments deficit is debilitating; and it is a feature of many problem regions that their traditional export industries can expand no further or are in decline. If policy can produce a regional balance of payments surplus, this might produce the advantages that are often claimed for export-led growth in the national economy. An export surplus would, through the multiplier, stimulate regional expansion which would in turn encourage investment and generate further expansion. From the point of view of the national economy this would be a wholly advantageous effect: an improvement in the competitive position of a depressed region so that the demand for its products was increased compared with other areas, would tend to reduce the pressure on overstretched fully-employed regions, damp down inflationary pressure and improve the country's overall balance of payments. Regional export-led growth may thus be the only way that a government may stimulate regional development without also adding to the strain imposed on the fully-employed regions. From the problem region's point of view it may also be essential, since regions in peripheral locations seldom offer an attractive site to market oriented industry but may have few disadvantages for exporting industry. Just as the industries of small countries cannot obtain economies of scale if based on the home market and must therefore be specialist and exporting, so it is with regions.

A properly developed regional policy should thus be able to

[1] See D. C. North, 'Exports and Regional Economic Growth', in J. Friedman and W. Alonso (editors), *Regional Development and Planning*, MIT Press 1964.

apply, where appropriate, the advantages of both systems. The policies which independent States might follow in similar circumstances may be simulated without entailing the disadvantages. And, while regions are perhaps more liable to suffer from unbalanced growth than if they were each separate economies, the State undoubtedly has far greater resources at its disposal to use for the development of problem regions than each region could hope to muster on its own, if it were a separate economy.

CONCLUSION

The application of economic theory to the regional problem, like any other piece of economic theory, can do no more than yield a set of hypotheses to explain the operation of forces which determine the spatial distribution of economic activity. But how much importance should be attached to different factors or whether the hypotheses offer a satisfactory explanation of the problems under analysis can only be established by reference to the facts. Inadequate knowledge of the factual situation, already referred to in the last chapter, makes it impossible to test the theories properly or to replace them with better hypotheses. But in many instances it is easy to see that the theories are far too crude.

The Weberian theory of location of the firm, for example, adopts a far too simple view of the importance of transport costs and gives insufficient weight to external economies and economies of scale. Colin Clark's concepts of distance costs and economic potential offer a much more fruitful approach to this question and will no doubt be further refined and tested. But account needs to be taken of availability of suitable labour, a factor frequently cited by firms as determining their location. This is distinct from the cost of labour which, despite Weberian theory, does not appear to play a very important role. There are also a host of incidental non-economic factors which are hard to fit into a theory but, nonetheless, influence the location of firms.

The theories of Christaller and Lösch are still a long way from explaining the spatial distribution of economic activity. This type of approach is inapplicable to much of manufacturing industry and the fierce national and international competition in manufactured goods is hardly compatible with it. It may, however, have some application to the services sector of the economy and undoubtedly may explain reasonably well the location of market towns in a primarily agricultural region such as Southern Germany, rural France or, possibly, Ireland. The location of manufacturing is probably better explained by Clark's economic potential or Perroux's poles of growth. The poles of growth theory, however, explains quite plausibly why many types of economic activity develop in clusters, but it cannot offer an explanation of the location of the clusters, other than natural resources or pure accident. It, therefore, is not really a theory of the spatial distribution of economic activity.

The forces causing regional growth and depression could be analysed by means of inter-regional and international trade theory. This seemed to throw up a number of interesting insights. Most important of these was the suggestion that the principle of comparative advantage did not apply to trade at the regional level owing to factor mobility and the tendency towards equality of factor earnings. This seemed more likely to make regions prone to depression and stagnation than independent nations; and the function of regional policy was, therefore, in some degree to fill the place that policies to make the balance of payments balance with full employment would play in an independent State.

The inter-regional trade theory seems one of the more fruitful approaches to the regional question. By itself, however, it is hardly sufficient, since factor movements remain insufficiently explained. This leads back to the spatial distribution of economic activity, market areas, economic potential and distance costs. New work here, both theoretical and empirical, is undoubtedly required.

PART II

THE DEVELOPMENT OF POLICY

CHAPTER III

PRE-WAR POLICY

The inter-war years were a period of high unemployment throughout Britain. The total number unemployed was normally in excess of one million during the 1920s and touched three million in the worst years of the 1930s. Expressed as a percentage of insured employees, the figures for those out of work ranged from around 10 per cent in the 1920s to 23 per cent in January 1933. As explained in the introduction to this book, this situation had a number of causes of which the loss of export markets through foreign competition and the uncontrolled operation of trade cycle were the most important. Added to this in the 1920s was the handicap which an overvalued rate of exchange imposed upon the export industries.

The effects of the depression, however, were not uniform everywhere. Whereas London and the South-East had unemployment rates of around 5 or 6 per cent in the 1920s which rose to 15 per cent in 1932-3, Scotland, Wales, Northern England and Northern Ireland had unemployment rates of 12 to 15 per cent in the 1920s and these rose to between 25 and 35 per cent in 1932. In individual towns some astronomical rates were recorded at the depth of the depression. In January 1933, to take a few examples, 91 per cent of the labour force were out of work in the Yorkshire town of Saltburn, 77 per cent at Jarrow and 64 per cent at Cleator Moor in Durham. In Scotland, 70 per cent were out of work at Stornoway, 60 per cent at Wishaw and 54 per cent at Clydebank. In Wales, 82 per cent were unemployed at Taff Wells, 72 per cent at Pontycymmer, 68 per cent at Merthyr and 66 per cent at Abertillery. The depression, therefore, carried with it a regional problem in the acutest form.

It was clear that the severity of the depression was associated with the industrial structure of the regions. Generally the worst hit areas were those which specialized in coal mining, ship-building, iron and steel and textiles.[1] All of these were traditional export industries, and they had been the foundation of Britain's prosperity in the nineteenth century. In these areas unemployment rates averaged about 40 per cent in the early 1930s. Decline was due to the emergence of competitors in other countries, to technological change, and to the generally unfavourable export situation. But what was perhaps less clear was the extent to which depression was cumulative. Depression in the basic industries of a region would, of course, affect all the suppliers of components in other industries, but it would also lower regional incomes so, through the multiplier, affecting the service sector and creating conditions very unfavourable to expansion in other industries. At a time of general labour surplus new industries had no incentive to go to such areas and indeed tended to avoid them.

Regional problems were not new to Britain, but previously they had been confined, in the main, to declining rural areas; the Highlands of Scotland and Ireland being the most obvious examples. On occasion special legislation had been passed to assist these areas, but this could hardly be described as a regional policy. In the middle of the nineteenth century, when the crisis in these areas was at its worst, governments had neither the economic understanding nor the means to promote regional development. But in the inter-war years the unemployment was on such a scale and the social distress so great that it eventually compelled the adoption of a policy. Indeed, seen from the standpoint of thirty years later, the only astonishing feature of this is that such high rates of regional unemployment had been allowed to continue for so long, right through the 1920s, without any measures being adopted to reduce them.

The first step towards a regional policy in Britain was the setting up of the Industrial Transference Board in 1928. The purpose of this policy was to retrain labour which had originally been trained in the skills of the declining industries and to provide grants and loans to enable it to move and find employment in the expanding industries elsewhere. The policy continued through the 1930s, the number of persons transferred reaching a peak in 1936 and thereafter declining. However, this was more of a labour policy than a regional policy; the start of the latter came in 1934 with the Special Areas Act.

[1] The national unemployment rate in shipbuilding was 61 per cent in March 1933, in metal manufacture it was 35 per cent, in coal mining 26 per cent and in textiles 24 per cent.

In the early 'thirties the Government had commissioned studies covering some of the worst hit areas where the average unemployment figure was around 40 per cent of the labour force.[1] Following on this the Special Areas (Development and Improvement) Act designated four Special Areas; South Wales, North-East England, West Cumberland and the Clydeside–North Lanarkshire industrial area of Scotland. Commissioners[2] were appointed, one for England and Wales and one for Scotland to promote the rehabilitation of the areas.

The particular areas designated were open to some criticism. As Professor Dennison points out, some very depressed parts of the country, such as parts of Lancashire and Teesside for example, were not included even though they were worse hit than some parts of the Special Areas.[3] Moreover, major towns were excluded from the Areas. Thus in South Wales, Newport, Cardiff, Swansea, Neath, Porthcawl and Barry were excluded from the surrounding Special Area and therefore not covered by the legislation. The same was true of Glasgow in the Scottish Special Area, and Newcastle, Darlington and Middlesbrough in the North-East. The reason was, undoubtedly, that unemployment in these towns was not quite so severe as in the surrounding areas. But it was to prove extremely difficult to tackle the problems of economic regeneration in an area when the towns which formed the focal points of development were excluded.[4]

It was envisaged that the legislation should be temporary to meet an unusual emergency, and it was the Government's belief that they were conferring exceptional powers on their Commissioners. The Prime Minister, Ramsay MacDonald, said in the House of Commons:[5]

'Who is going to say how much is going to be required? It would be sheer folly for us to have said £20 million, £50 million or £100 million. . . . The ground has been surveyed. The problem is now clear. You face it. You deal with it. You spend money on it and I will stand by you.'[5]

[1] Reports of the Investigators into Industrial Conditions in Certain Depressed Areas, Cmd. 4728, Ministry of Labour, HMSO 1934.
[2] They were originally known as Depressed Areas but were changed to Special Areas as a result of an amendment while the Bill was going through Parliament.
[3] S. R. Dennison, *Location of Industry and Depressed Areas*, Oxford University Press 1939, p. 126.
[4] The same mistake was made in the Belgian legislation of 1959.
[5] Hansard, November 20, 1934.

MAP 2
THE PRE-WAR SPECIAL AREAS

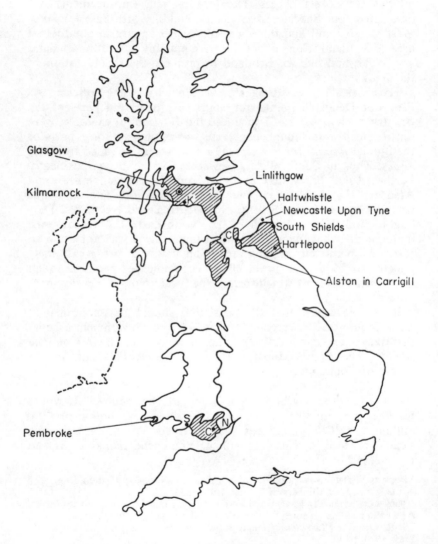

Glasgow

Kilmarnock

Linlithgow

Haltwhistle
Newcastle Upon Tyne
South Shields
Hartlepool

Alston in Carrigill

Pembroke

A sum of £2 million was paid over to the Commissioners, but this was supposed to be only a start. In fact, however, the power of the Commissioners turned out to be extremely limited. They were not allowed to finance projects for which a Government grant from other sources was received or was payable, neither were they allowed to provide funds for profit-making enterprise. This ruled out direct assistance to private industry and also made ineligible all the major public works projects. Accordingly, in the first year or so, the Commissioners' expenditure was almost entirely limited to sewerage schemes and settlement of labour on the land. Indeed, the Scottish Commissioner spent no less than 90 per cent of his money on sewerage. Despite the fine words in the House of Commons, this was indeed a feeble approach to the problem.

I. FINANCIAL ASSISTANCE

The inadequacy of these powers was commented on at length in the second and third reports of the English Commissioner, Sir Malcolm Stewart, who, despite his official position and unlike his Scottish colleague, was prepared to speak plainly about the inadequacies of the legislation.[1] In his second report, he draws attention to the need for additional finance beyond the very limited conditions under which the Commissioners themselves can authorize expenditure. Accordingly in April 1936, the Special Areas Reconstruction Association (SARA) was set up by the Bank of England with Government backing and a nominal capital of £1 million. Its function was to provide loan capital for small business in the Special Areas. Advances were generally to be limited to £10,000. The State was to pay the management expenses and guarantee SARA against loss.

Since the operations of SARA were limited to small firms, however, it was clearly insufficient to exert a major influence on the economic structure of the Special Areas. Therefore, following the

[1] Reports of the Commissioners for Special Areas (England and Wales), 1934–5 Cmd. 4957; 1935–6 Cmd. 5090; 1936–7 Cmd. 5303; 1937–8 Cmd. 5595; 1938–9 Cmd. 5896.

Reports of the Commissioners for Special Areas (Scotland) 1934–5 Cmd. 4958; 1935–6 Cmd. 5089; 1936–7 Cmd. 5245; 1937–8 Cmd. 5604; 1938–9 Cmd. 5905.

The five reports of the English Commissioners give a detailed account of policy in this period. The Scottish Commissioners particularly in the early years were very much less informative. An excellent survey of the pre-war situation is available in Professor S. R. Dennison's *Location of Industry and Depressed Areas*, OUP, 1939.

continued failure of policy to have any major effect and the outspoken review of the measures given by Sir Malcolm Stewart in his third and final report as English Commissioner, further steps were taken. In December 1936 Lord Nuffield, on his own initiative, set up a Trust of £2 million to be spent in helping undertakings to set up in the Special Areas; within a year the greater part of this money had been promised to some fifty undertakings. And under the Special Areas Amendment Act of 1937 the Treasury were empowered on the advice of a Special Areas Loans Advisory Committee (SALAC) to give loans to firms in the Special Areas. An initial sum of £2 million was provided and it was intended that this assistance should be available for larger undertakings than those covered by SARA.

II. TRADING ESTATES

A characteristic of British policy from the early years has been the provision of trading estates operated by non-profit-making companies. This was one of the few really important policy measures which the Commissioners were able to institute even with their inadequate powers under the 1934 Act. The idea was first mooted in the 1936 report. The first estate was set up at Team Valley in the North-East to be followed by a similar one at Treforest in South Wales. A similar estate was established at Hillingden in Scotland in 1937. From the first these estates proved a useful instrument of policy. The companies operating them laid on the necessary public services and would construct factories to meet a firm's requirements to be rented on a cover cost basis.[1]

In 1937, therefore, the Special Areas Amendment Act encouraged this development and gave the Commissioners wide powers to let factories to private enterprise in any part of the Special Areas for which the trading estate companies would act as agents. A new company was formed to start a trading estate in West Cumberland, the only Special Area which did not already have one, and a number of additional smaller estates were started in each of the other three Special Areas. The estates attracted quite a number of foreign firms which has been obliged to flee from the Continent, and the success of those who set up destroyed

[1] In practice rents of Government sponsored factories came to be set at 6 per cent of the cost of building them with the aim of producing 4 per cent on the Government's total outlay (Second Report of the Select Committee on Estimates on the Administration of Development Areas, 1955/6, p. xv, para. 55).

the idea that it was impossible to establish new industries in the Special Areas on an economic basis.

III. TAX INDUCEMENTS

Following the apparent failure of the policy measures to produce results during the first two years, the Special Areas Amendment Act of 1937 introduced a number of tax incentives along with the financial provisions already mentioned. The Special Area Commissioners were enabled to make contributions in respect of a firm's rent, rates or income tax for a period not exceeding five years. At the same time, firms in the Special Areas could be exempted from the new National Defence Tax which was started in 1937. This was the first time tax incentives had been given on a regional basis in the United Kingdom and they were not to be used again until Mr Maudling's 1963 budget.

IV. INDUSTRIAL TRANSFERENCE

Complementing these measures, all of which were intended to attract industry to the Areas, was the policy of industrial transference. As already mentioned, the measures to promote industrial transference were introduced following the report of the Industrial Transference Board in 1928, and they continued throughout the period.[1] The policy is of interest because it is the principal instance in the history of British regional policy of an attempt to promote the movement of workers to the work.

It cannot be said, however, that the Industrial Transference Board took a very imaginative view of the problem. It is clear from their report that they regarded the wholesale movement of the population out of the Depressed Areas as the *only* solution to the problem. While they commend the Depressed Areas to manufacturers as sites for new plants, they expect little success from this quarter and they have no notion of any kind of State intervention to encourage such development. They state their view as follows:

'It is a bad thing to tell numbers of men and even whole communities that unless they leave all their familiar surroundings they will not be able to earn a living, but we should be shirking every inference from the fact, if we did not emphasize this as the first and strongest of the lessons that our work has provided.'[2]

[1] Report of the Industrial Transference Board, Cmd. 3156, HMSO 1928.
[2] *Ibid.*, p. 54.

97

They also advocated large-scale emigration as a solution to the problem:

'As regards overseas settlement, it is a matter for regret, and indeed astonishment, to find out how disappointingly slow has been the rate of settlement of British people in Australia and Canada.'[1]

The principal measures introduced comprised the provision of grants and loans to help cover the cost of their removal to another area and the setting up of training centres to enable such labour to acquire new skills. A substantial number of persons were transferred during the years that the scheme was in operation as the following Table shows:

TABLE I

LABOUR TRANSFERENCE FROM DEPRESSED AREAS 1929-38*

	Adults	Juveniles	Families
1929	32,000	6,456	—
1930	30,000	3,021	2,100
1931	19,000	2,854	1,680
1932	12,000	3,130	990
1933	8,000	4,172	605
1934	12,000	5,173	1,308
1935	20,000	10,024	3,718
1936	28,000	15,407	10,025
1937	24,000	14,125	7,673
1938	18,000	9,627	3,500

* The transference scheme covered a wider range of depressed areas than those that were designated Special Areas.
Source: Annual Reports of the Ministry of Labour.

This movement of labour did not, however, provide a solution for the problem of the Depressed Areas. Little could be achieved by retraining and transferring labour when there was already a surplus of labour all over the country. If a retrained man was lucky enough to get a job in one of the more prosperous parts of the country it was merely at the expense of someone already there. In fact, many of those transferred, especially juveniles, returned to the Depressed Areas.[2] At the same time the exodus of the more enterprising and skilled section of the labour force from the Areas, far from relieving the problem, only aggravated it. This was pre-

[1] Ibid., p. 55.
[2] Third Report, p. 3.

98

cisely the section of the labour force needed to man new industry if it could be established in the Areas; and their departure both reduced local purchasing power and contributed strongly to the atmosphere of depression.

At the start, the Special Areas Commissioners, while not sharing the extreme views of the Industrial Transference Board, regarded the measures as an essential element in a solution to the problem. It was clear to them that at least certain parts of the Special Areas, notably some depressed mining villages, could not expect to attract sufficient new industry on any reasonable economic terms, and that therefore some transfer of population was both desirable and inevitable. As time went on, however, the failure of the policy became apparent and its harmful effects more obvious. Both the English and Scottish Commissioners became disillusioned with it and were glad to see the figures fall after 1936.

But it is perhaps unfortunate that the failure of this policy in the 1930s and its undoubted unpopularity led to post-war policy being concentrated so heavily on taking work to the workers no matter where they happened to be. Measures to promote labour movement have played little part in post-war policy. Yet while wholesale migration from the problem regions is probably both undesirable and unnecessary, there is little doubt that the regrouping of the labour force within them around locations which are suitable for growth may be an essential part of a successful policy.

The Results of the Policy

By 1939 the trifling powers which the Commissioners had been given in 1934 had been turned into a complete armoury of weapons consisting of provision of finance to private industry, tax incentives, trading estates and labour transference. There were no measures to control development in the more congested and prosperous areas and, no doubt, some of the measures might have been more generously applied; but otherwise they embraced a wider range than regional policy was to acquire again until the 1960s.

The position of the Special Areas did, of course, improve in the 1930s as the unemployment figures in Table II show. From 35–40 per cent of the labour force unemployed in 1932–4 the figure fell to 25 per cent in 1938. There is little doubt, however, that the main reason for this reduction was the gradual upturn of the trade cycle which enabled the old basic industries to take on more labour. The economic structure of the Areas was substantially the same in 1938 as it was in 1934. The policy was particularly ineffective up to 1937; as Sir Malcolm Stewart wrote of the legislation in November 1936: 'It has to be admitted that no appreciable reduction in the number of those unemployed has been effected.'[1] Later in the same report: 'Seeing that the Special Areas Act provides no means of directly reducing unemployment, the all-important question that arises . . . is whether the time is not now ripe for a second experiment.'[2]

Even if the 1937 Act made the measures much more effective, the results were still small. As Table III shows only a very small number of new factories were opened in the Special Areas in the years 1934–6 and these were often more than offset by closures.

TABLE II

UNEMPLOYMENT BY DISTRICTS IN SELECTED YEARS
1929–38

as a percentage of insured employees

	1929	1932	1934	1936	1938
London	5,6	13.5	9.2	7.2	7.8
South-Eastern	5.6	14.3	8.7	7.3	7.7
South-Western	8.1	17.1	13.1	9.4	8.1
Midlands	9.3	20.1	12.9	9.2	10.0
North-Eastern	13.7	28.5	22.1	16.8	12.9
North-Western	13.3	25.8	20.8	13.1	17.7
Scotland	12.1	27.7	23.1	18.7	16.8
Wales	19.3	36.5	32.3	29.4	25.9
Northern Ireland	14.8	27.2	23.4	22.7	24.4
United Kingdom	10.4	22.1	16.7	13.2	12.9

Source: 22nd Abstract of Labour Statistics of the United Kingdom, Cmd. 5556, 1939, Ministry of Labour Gazette.

Note: The Administrative divisions were as follows:

South-East: London, Bedford, Bucks, Cambridge, Essex, Herts, Kent, Middlesex, Norfolk, Suffolk, Surrey, Sussex.

South-West: Berks, Cornwall, Devon, Dorset, Gloucester, Hunts, Oxon, Somerset, Wilts.

Midlands: Derby, Hereford, Huntingdon, Leicester, Northants, Notts, Rutland, Salop, Stafford, Warwick, Worcester, Soke of Peterborough and Stamford.

North-East: Durham, Lincoln (less Stamford), Northumberland (less Berwick), Yorkshire.

North-West: Cheshire, Cumberland, Lancs, Westmorland and Glossop and New Mills from Derby.

[1] Third Report, p. 3.
[2] Ibid., p. 4.

The effect of the trading estates may be seen in 1937 and 1938 figures for factory openings, which show a marked increase compared with any other year. But even in 1937 the twenty-three factories opened in the Special Areas amounted to only some 4½ per cent of the factories opened in Great Britain, while the population of the Special Areas was around 10 per cent of the British figure. Certainly 1938 was much better with around 17 per cent of the new factories opening in the Special Areas. But by contrast, Greater London, during all these years, was attracting about 40 per cent of the new factory development in Britain.

TABLE III

INDUSTRIAL DEVELOPMENT IN SPECIAL AREAS
1932–8

	1932	1933	1934	1935	1936	1937	1938
No. of Factories opened:							
South Wales	1	1	—	—	—	5	19
West Cumberland	—	1	2	—	1	—	2
North-East	7	6	5	2	5	14	26
Scotland	7	3	6	2	6	4	14
Total Opened	15	11	13	4	12	23	61
Total Closed	12	10	22	5	10	6	13
Extensions	6	2	3	8	5	4	6
No. of Factories opened in Great Britain	636	463	478	514	942	522	414
Of which:							
% opened in Special Areas	2.3	2.4	2.7	0.8	2.2	4.4	17.1
% opened in Greater London	41.0	47.1	49.2	41.8	47.3	39.1	40.6

Source: Board of Trade, Survey of Industrial Development, 1938.

It may seem surprising, in view of the extensive range of measures available, that pre-war policy was not more effective. But it must be remembered that most of these measures only came into operation in 1937, some five years after the lowest point in the depression and less than two years before rearmament was to temporarily abolish the problem of the Special Areas. It is clear, too, that the absence of control on development elsewhere in the country made it very difficult to operate an effective policy. The number of firms setting up in the Special Areas during most of the pre-war years was trivial compared with the national figure. At a time when labour was in surplus supply all over the country, an industrialist had no need to go to the Special Areas to find manpower; and the fact that such areas were depressed meant that their purchasing power was low and therefore made them unattractive for new industry. The most important factor in the failure of the policy was surely the low level of aggregate demand in the economy as a whole. Not only did this mean that there was surplus labour all over the country, but in such conditions the possible extent of industrial movement was very small. Few firms were considering expansion, and when they did it was on a very limited basis. Thus even if the inducements which were offered in the Special Areas had been extremely generous, few firms would have been interested when the national demand for their products was depressed.

Royal Commission on the Distribution of the Industrial Population
In his third report as Special Areas Commissioner, Sir Malcolm Stewart put forward the view that further development of the congested areas, notably Greater London, must be controlled if the Special Areas' problems were to be satisfactorily solved. By that time it was clear to all that unemployment was persisting and that the problems of the Special Areas were proving much harder to tackle than had at first been expected. Moreover, the increased concentration of the population in areas where congestion already existed, and where overcrowding and slums were a pressing problem, clearly raised important social and economic issues. At the time in question it was also a matter of considerable strategic importance. The Government, therefore, appointed a Royal Commission under the chairmanship of Sir Montague Barlow to examine the whole question. The terms of reference required the Commission 'to inquire into the causes which have influenced the present distribution of industrial population . . . to consider what social, economic or strategical disadvantages arise from the concentration of industries . . . and to report what remedial measures, if any, should be taken in the national interest'. Alike on strategic, social and economic grounds, its report published in 1940 found that the trends in the geographical distribution of industry and population were undesirable.[1] There was agreement that steps must be taken to influence this geographical distribution in future, agreement too on the need to check the growth of London. The main proposals were as follows:

(i) That national action was required to influence the distri-

[1] Report of the Royal Commission on the Distribution of Industrial Population, Cmd. 6153, HMSO 1940.

102

bution of industry and population and that a Central Authority should be set up for this purpose.

(ii) The objectives were to redevelop the congested urban areas coupled with decentralization of industry and population, and to achieve a regional balance of diversified industry.

(iii) The use of garden cities, satellite towns, expansion of rural towns and trading estates was to be reviewed as a means of implementing this policy.

(iv) Assistance should be given to Local Authorities to tackle the problem regionally and the Central Authority was to have the right to inspect all planning schemes.

(v) The Authority was to be responsible for research on the location of industry and the use of natural resources. It was to be able to anticipate depression in particular areas and encourage development before depression occurs.

There was less agreement, however, on the detailed measures required to implement this policy. The majority of the Commission went on to recommend that the proposed Authority should take the form of a Board with research, advisory and regulating functions on the location of industry; that the Board should have power, in London and the Home Counties, to regulate the establishment of additional industrial undertakings, but not distributive trades, housing or storage; and that provision should be made for these powers to be extended to other areas.

A note of reservation by three of the Commissioners proposed, in addition, that regional or divisional bodies should be set up related to the National Board; that the Board should prepare at once a report on positive measures to promote regional development and diversification which would go hand in hand with the negative power of control; thirdly, that the power of control should cover the whole country, though applied in the first instance to London and the Home Counties; and fourthly, that the power of the Commissioners for Special Areas should be transferred to the Board.

Three other members of the Commission could not accept the majority recommendations and submitted a separate minority report. Their main difference from the majority was that they wanted a Government Department to be responsible for the distribution of industry and population, instead of the proposed Board. They envisaged that such a Department should prepare a national plan for the distribution of industry. They also proposed that it should take over the powers of the Special Area Commissioners and be able to apply them to any part of the country; it should be thus enabled to promote satellite towns, trading estates, public utility companies, etc., wherever the need arose. The Ministry was to have power to schedule (a) those areas in which industrial development would be unrestricted, save for the normal local planning regulations, and (b) areas in which further development would be prohibited subject only to certain exceptions. The Ministry was also to set up Regional Boards through whom the Department would act and to establish a permanent Research Commission.

When the Report of the Royal Commission appeared the War was in progress, attention was diverted to more urgent matters and the problem of the Special Areas had in any case, for the time being, disappeared. The Report did, however, form the background to the Distribution of Industry Act 1945 which incorporated some of its recommendations.

In many respects, the Barlow Report was a landmark in the development of thought on the regional problem in Britain. At the time of writing it still provides the most comprehensive review yet to be undertaken in Britain of the case for a regional policy. In several respects it was ahead of its time and many of the innovations which have been introduced into British regional policy in the 1960s were given clear expression in this report some twenty years earlier. Thus the report laid emphasis on the economic case for regional development. It regarded the congestion problems of some cities and the unemployment of the depressed areas as different aspects of the same problem; yet in the 1950s the Board of Trade regarded their regional development activities mainly as a social service for the peripheral areas. It was not until the 1960s, with the publication of the South-East Study, that the economic interconnection between congestion and the problems of the depressed regions was again brought into perspective.

Since the Barlow Commission were convinced of the economic case for regional development, they emphasized the need for research to promote sound economic development and to identify the problems of regions in advance of a critical situation arising so that appropriate redevelopment could be undertaken. Yet only in recent years has there been any major research activity by Government on the regional problem and much remains to be done.

Likewise, the Report emphasized the role of planning and the relationship of regional economic planning to physical planning. It stressed the importance of using new towns and public investment in infrastructure to spearhead regional economic development. The concept of growth areas is alluded to when it is suggested that some depressed areas may be incapable of development and the resources may have to be regrouped in those locations within the region which offer an environment suitable for development. These ideas were never properly developed in post-war legislation. Regional planning after the physical plans of the 1940s was abandoned until 1963; new towns were developed more as an instrument of urban and social policy than regional or economic; and, though some references were made to growth areas in post-war legislation, subsequent changes tied regional policy more closely to the criterion of unemployment with little regard for development potential. Yet in the 1960s these ideas were to reappear and form the basis of many of the changes in regional policy.

CHAPTER IV

POST-WAR POLICY TO 1960

During the War unemployment throughout Britain fell to an extremely low level. All the traditional industries in the Special Areas were working full out; the need for armaments and the shipping losses together restored the ship-building and steel industries to full capacity. The huge increase in public expenditure raised the level of aggregate demand to such a degree that only the strictest controls prevented an inflationary situation from getting out of hand. These factors together accounted for the drop in the number unemployed to the record low figure of 75,000 for the whole United Kingdom in 1944.

Fears of unemployment in the post-war period were, however, very much alive. There seemed every possibility that the pre-war situation could recur; but the War had converted all major political parties to Keynesian economics and they determined to prevent it. The result was the White Paper on Employment Policy published by the Coalition Government in 1944.[1] This was an epoch-making document in that for the first time a British Government pledged themselves to maintain full employment. The White Paper opens with the sentence: 'The Government accept as one of their primary aims and responsibilities the maintenance of a high and stable level of employment after the war.'

It was, of course, obvious that although the Government might succeed in controlling the level of aggregate demand in the nation as a whole, this could not be relied on to get rid of acute structural unemployment in certain areas. Some areas would be likely to have an excessive share of stagnant or declining industries so that a level of demand which was appropriate for national economic policy would result in inflationary pressure in some areas without eliminating unemployment in others.

Chapter III of the White Paper, therefore, outlined the measures which would be used to tackle the regional imbalance. These comprised:

[1] *Employment Policy*, Cmd. 6527, HMSO 1944.

(i) Increasing the efficiency of basic industries so that they could secure overseas markets. (As pointed out in Chapter III, many of these industries were originally strongly oriented towards exports.)

(ii) Influencing the location of new industries.

(iii) Reducing the obstacles to transfer of workers by such measures as resettlement allowances and providing an adequate supply of housing to rent.

(iv) Providing retraining facilities.

It was seen that the problem areas, however they might be scheduled, would be likely to require redesignation as the situation developed; and it was indicated that prime responsibility for implementing this policy would be given to the Board of Trade, though the Ministries of Transport, Labour, Town and Country Planning and the Scottish Office would also be involved.

With regard to the location of new industries and the prospects for particular areas, the White Paper expresses its thinking with clarity: 'There may be some small and isolated villages, especially in mining areas, which, owing to permanent changes in industrial conditions, offer no hope of sound economic revival.'[1]

This implies that policy was to be soundly based economically, that some labour movement within areas would be necessary and that not every depressed hamlet could be assisted. As will be seen, this makes better economic sense than some of the policies which were pursued later.

DISTRIBUTION OF INDUSTRY ACT 1945

The foundation of British regional policy from 1945 to 1960 was the Distribution of Industry Act of 1945. The Act was supplemented by the Distribution of Industry Act of 1950 and some important changes were introduced in the Distribution of Industry (Industrial Finance) Act of 1958, but the basic character of the 1945 Act remained unchanged during the period.

The Act replaced the pre-war legislation for the Special Areas. The Areas themselves were redefined and renamed Development Areas (see map). The boundaries of the Areas remained approximately the same except that the new Areas included the towns Glasgow, Cardiff, Swansea, Darlington, Newcastle, etc., which had been omitted from the Special Areas which surrounded them. In

[1] *Ibid.*, para. 29.

MAP 3
THE DEVELOPMENT AREAS 1945–60

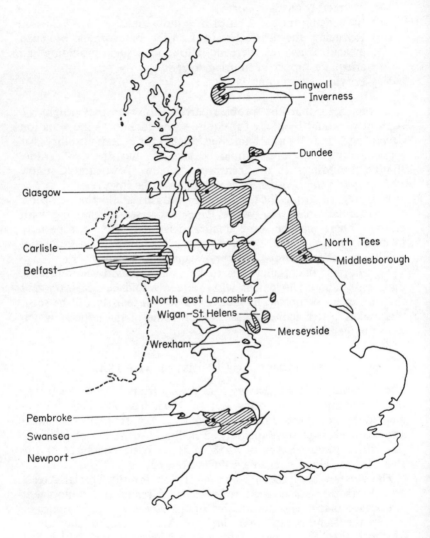

the words of the Act, the Areas were now 'in the main continuous and compact regions and are suitable economic and social units for development as a whole'.[1]

Some external changes in boundaries were also made. The most important of these was that Dundee and its immediate surrounding area, though geographically separate, became part of the Scottish Development Area. A substantial area to the west of the old Welsh Area taking in Swansea, Llanelly and Ammanford was included in the new Development Area, and in the North-East the Area was extended to include Teesside in the south and a small area in the north, while a part of the old Special Area in the west was excluded.[2] The West Cumberland Area remained unchanged. The effect of including the main towns was that whereas the 1939 population of the Special Areas was four million or 8½ per cent of the British total, the equivalent population of the four Development Areas was 6½ million or 13½ per cent.

These four Areas were added to in 1946 with the inclusion of Wrexham and the Wigan—St Helens district of Lancashire. The former Area was expected to suffer severe unemployment following the closure of Royal Ordnance factories. In 1948 three other Areas were added: North-East Lancashire, Merseyside and the Highlands of Scotland. In the case of the latter, however, the whole region of the Highlands was not scheduled, but only a nucleus area in which it was thought development could be most economically established and where its concentration would increase its chances of success. As the White Paper of 1948 said:

'There is a case for making Development Area powers available in a district chosen because of its suitability as a focal centre of industrial development for the Highlands as a whole and not merely because of its local unemployment.'[3]

This reflects the view of the White Paper on Employment Policy to which attention has already been directed and again stands out in contrast to later policy. After the addition of these five new Areas to the four original ones, the geographical definitions of the Development Areas were to remain unchanged until 1958.

But certainly the worst problem area, in terms both of un-

[1] *The Distribution of Industry*, Cmd. 7540, HMSO, London 1948, para. 31.
[2] Maps showing the details of these changes are given in *The Distribution of Industry, op. cit.* pp. 50–52.
[3] Cmd. 7540, para. 108.

employment percentages and the low level of income per head, was Northern Ireland, which, with its heavy dependence on linen textiles, ship-building and a low productivity agriculture, suffers all the symptoms of the other problem regions in more acute form. Since it is self-governing, however, it is not the concern of Westminster Departments, but passes its own legislation to attract industry to the province. It was, therefore, not scheduled as a Development Area, but inducements were offered under the Northern Ireland Capital Grants to Industry and Industries Development Acts and industrial estates organized and run by the Ministry of Commerce. On the other hand, the province has benefited substantially from the measures the United Kingdom has taken to restrict development in the more prosperous and congested parts of Britain.

The main responsibility for policy in Great Britain was given neither to a Board, as the majority of the Barlow Committee had recommended, nor to a new Department, but to the Board of Trade which was to take over the work of the Special Area Commissioners. Its powers were to be similar in many respects to those that the Commissioners had enjoyed after 1937. The Board of Trade was enabled:

(1) To build factories in Development Areas, buying land by compulsory purchase if necessary.
(2) To make loans with the consent of the Treasury to industrial estate companies (as the trading estate companies were now called).
(3) To make provision for basic public services.
(4) To reclaim derelict land.
(5) In addition, the Treasury could give grants or loans to assist specific industrial undertakings on the advice of the Development Areas Treasury Advisory Committee (DATAC) *provided* that the Committee were satisfied both that the project was commercially sound, and that finance could not be raised from another source.

The provision of payments to cover part of the cost of rates, rent and taxes, which the Special Area Commissioners had been empowered to make before the War, was not included in the new legislation. It therefore contained no form of tax incentive as a means of promoting regional development. Otherwise the powers were very similar to pre-war with the small difference that the loans to small companies which had pre-war been the concern of

SARA (Special Areas Reconstruction Association), and the loans to large companies made by SALAC (Special Areas Loans Advisory Committee) were amalgamated and extended to include grants under DATAC.

These powers were, however, reinforced by two important additions. The first was the control of new factory development which corresponded to the recommendation of the Barlow Commission. This was achieved by means of the building licence system originally introduced as a wartime control and now vigorously used to control the location of new development. This was, however, a temporary measure, and although it remained in use up till 1950, a substitute had to be found for the long term. Accordingly the system of Industrial Development Certificates was introduced by the Town and Country Planning Act of 1947. This made it compulsory for a new industrial development of more than 5,000 square feet to have a Board of Trade Certificate before planning permission could be granted.

The second important measure was the building of new towns. Slum clearance, the rehousing of the urban populations and repair of war damage together required a policy of urban development. The fact that when an area was rebuilt it was impossible, with acceptable population densities, to rehouse the whole of the population which the area had previously held, necessitated the development of new urban areas. At the same time awareness of the congestion problems of large cities, and the social desirability of cutting down travel to work, seemed to indicate that new towns would be the most satisfactory type of development. Although the new towns were, therefore, thought of first and foremost as a measure of urban redevelopment policy, they also had a potential role in regional economic policy. This was realized in the 1948 White Paper where the linking of the new towns of Aycliffe and Peterlee with industrial estates in the North-East was referred to[1]; but in the event most of the post-war new towns were sited purely to serve the needs of urban development policy and the greatest number were established round London. It was only in the 1960s, after more than a decade of experience, during which the new towns in Central Scotland and North-East England had demonstrated their success as centres for industrial growth, that their role as an important weapon of regional policy came to be properly recognized and their size and siting began to be considered with this end in view.

[1] Cmd. 7540.

111

The Policy in Practice 1945–60

The period from 1945 to 1960 demonstrates that the emphasis a government puts on its regional policy is at least as important to securing success as the measures themselves. Broadly speaking, the legislation remained unchanged, at least until 1958, but the priority given to regional policy did alter and so consequently did the results achieved.

During the immediate post-war years the Labour Government was very anxious to avoid the situation which had arisen in the Special Areas pre-war and accordingly gave high priority to regional policy. Circumstances could not have been more favourable. After the destruction of the War, the control of investment and the restriction of demand for all sorts of products, there was a tremendous impetus for industrial expansion and development. Moreover, the Government were determined to keep the level of aggregate demand high to secure full employment. With such a large amount of new development ready to take place, the potential industrial mobility was probably greater than at any other moment in Britain's recent economic history. Thus the situation was highly opportune for steering industry to new locations.

The Government entered into this situation with enthusiasm in 1945. The building licence system was used to keep a very strict measure of control in parts of the country which were not scheduled as Development Areas. In the Areas themselves the Government not only converted a large number of munitions factories for commercial use, but also built factories on its industrial estates both to order and in the form of ready-made advance factories

TABLE I

POST-WAR INDUSTRIAL BUILDING IN THE DEVELOPMENT AREAS

	No. of square ft. of Industrial Building approved in Development Areas	Development Areas as % of all Industrial Building in GB	Insured Population of Development Areas as % of GB
Annual Average			
1945–7	15.7	51.1	19.9
1948–50	7.5	17.2	18.3
1951–3	8.1	21.7	18.2
1954	12.8	18.1	18.1

Source: Second Report of the Select Committee on Estimates, Session 1955/6: The Development Area, HMSO, p. vii.

TABLE II

EMPLOYMENT IN BOARD OF TRADE FACTORIES, 1955/6

	BOT Factory Space 000 sq. ft.	Numbers Employed	Total Insured Employees May 1954 000s
North-East	11,617	49,000	1,020
South Wales	12,869	63,800	716
Scotland	14,358	62,300	1,194
West Cumberland	1,413	5,500	52
North-West (inc. Merseyside, S. Lancs and NE Lancs	1,271	5,300	857
	41,528	185,900	3,839

Source: Second Report of the Select Committee on Estimates, Session 1955/6: The Development Areas, HMSO.

built to several standard specifications. The consequence of this was that although the Development Areas had only 20 per cent of the nation's total population they received over 50 per cent of the new industrial building in the years 1945–7 (see Table I). Compared with the miserable percentages in the pre-war years, this was indeed a considerable achievement. In evidence submitted to the Estimates Committee in 1946–7 the Government expected the employment eventually resulting from these developments to be around 149,000 and including factories built by the Special Area Commissioners, pre-war Royal Ordnance factories and other Government factories, the total expansion of employment was expected to be 242,000.[1] Sizeable though this is, it may be seen in better perspective if compared with the unemployment which exceeded 800,000 in 1932 and 400,000 in 1937.

Moreover, it turned out to be a considerable overestimate. Reporting to the Estimates Committee in 1955–6, the Board of Trade showed that by that date it had 41 million square feet of factory space occupied by 1,085 tenant firms. The employment which had thus resulted was 185,900 compared with an insured population of 3.8 millions in the Development Areas in 1954 (see Table II). Board of Trade factories thus accounted for only 5 per cent of the insured population in the Development Areas, and as

[1] Second Report from Select Committee on Estimates 1946/7: The Administration of Development Areas, HMSO.

113

the Estimates Committee commented, the 'effect of the Board of Trade's powers were strictly limited'.[1]

Nor was the position altered much by 1960. According to a later report of the Estimates Committee, by that date the Board had 45 million square feet of factory space, for 1,095 tenant firms, and the total employment was 201,000. This shows an increase in five years of only 4 million square feet, ten tenant firms and 15,000 workers.[2]

TABLE III

EXPENDITURE ON REGIONAL POLICY UNDER THE
DISTRIBUTION OF INDUSTRY ACTS

£ million

	Board of Trade	Treasury	TOTAL
1946/47	5.7	0.2	5.9
1947/48	12.5	0.3	12.8
1948/49	11.0	0.5	11.5
1949/50	6.5	0.6	7.1
1950/51	5.0	0.8	5.8
1951/52	5.0	0.8	5.8
1952/53	3.7	0.3	4.0
1953/54	3.1	1.1	4.2
1954/55	4.5	1.7	6.2
1955/56	5.9	0.4	6.3
1956/57	4.9	0.3	5.2
1957/58	2.7	0.1	2.8
1958/59	1.5	2.1	3.6
1959/60	5.6	3.0	8.6

Source: Reports of the Estimates Committee, op. cit. A. J. Odber, op. cit.

Moreover, the provision of factories and industrial estates was the main form of government action in regional policy during these years. During the whole period of the Distribution of Industry Acts 1945–60, expenditure by the Treasury through the loans and grants authorized by DATAC totalled no more than £12 million, equal to about half the expenditure on lime and fertilizer subsidies to agriculture in one year. The Board of Trade's total expenditure on construction of factories and industrial estates, on the other hand, was £77.7 million. Even this sum is by no means large

[1] Second Report from the Select Committee on Estimates, Session 1955/6: The Development Areas, HMSO, 1956.
[2] Seventh Report from the Estimates Committee, Session 1962/3: Administration of the Local Employment Act 1960, p. 2.

when it is remembered that it is an investment in real assets on which a return in the form of rent on factories let will be paid.

Obviously, therefore, the basic industrial structure of the Areas was still not greatly changed by this new development. Moreover, the maintenance of unemployment at reasonable levels would require the economic expansion of the Areas to be at least as fast as the national average; but given that they were still dominated by the old industrial structure, this might eventually prove to be difficult.

The very success of policy in the immediate post-war years resulted in it being accorded a lower priority thereafter. Although unemployment rates continued above the national average in the Development Areas, the level was very low compared with pre-war and lower than many people had expected the national unemployment rate to be. Accordingly, when the country found itself in balance of payments difficulties and suffering from inflationary pressure, some retrenchment in government expenditure was necessary and Development Area policy was among the casualties. The building of advance factories was stopped altogether in 1947 and did not start again till 1959, and at the same time the pressure on businessmen to go to Development Areas was reduced.[1] The expenditure of the Board of Trade in providing factories fell to about half what it had been and the amount of new industrial development completed in the Development Areas in the years 1948 to 1950 was only 17.2 per cent of the national total (see Table I), although the population in the Areas was 18.3 per cent of the total population.

This trend was continued after the change in government in 1951, as is shown by the proportion of new factory building taking place in the Development Areas in the early 1950s. The Conservatives were, in principle, anxious to reduce the amount of controls on the economy. In line with this, building licences were abolished in 1954. This should not have greatly affected the Government control over the location of new factory building, since the Industrial Development Certificate remained in operation; but it appears that IDCs were fairly easily obtained at this time even for new development in the South-East and Midlands. Regional policy was more or less in abeyance.

[1] A. J. Odber, 'Regional Policy in Britain', Part 6 in *Area Redevelopment Policies in Britain and the Countries of the Common Market*, US Department of Commerce and Area Redevelopment Association, 1965, p. 338. Odber's paper provides an excellent critique of British policy to 1963.

This period of 'free wheeling', as Odber has called it, was only possible because the boom in the traditional industries continued.[1] Unemployment, though above the national average in Scotland, Wales and the Northern Region, continued at a very low level compared with previous experience. The coal industry had difficulty in producing sufficient output to meet market demand, and the Ridley Committee had foreseen the need for its production to rise to 260 million tons a year by 1961 if a national fuel shortage was to be avoided.[2] The boom in ship-building continued with yards unable to meet demand and fear of a steel shortage was a factor which recurred more than once during the period.

TABLE IV

INDICES OF INDUSTRIAL PRODUCTION

1956=100

	1954	1956	1958	1960	1962	1964	1966
Mining & Quarrying	101	100	95	89	90	90	82
Shipbuilding & Marine Engineering	85	100	93	79	81	70	69
Metal Manufacture	91	100	92	111	99	118	115
Textiles	104	100	90	99	95	105	106
All Manufacturing Industry	95	100	101	116	116	131	138

Source: Annual Abstract of Statistics.

In consequence it was not surprising that unemployment remained low and the regional economies buoyant. Wales's economy grew more rapidly in the early 1950s than Britain's and steel was undoubtedly largely responsible. Northern Ireland's GDP also grew slightly faster than the United Kingdom's up till 1958 and Scotland kept pace with the United Kingdom at least until 1954.[3]

Governments may, perhaps, be excused for supposing during this period that the regional problem was virtually solved. In fact, however, though policy measures immediately after the War had

[1] A. J. Odber, op. cit., p. 339.
[2] Report of the Committee on National Policy for the Use of Fuel and Power Resources, Cmd. 8647, HMSO 1952, para. 40.
[3] E. T. Nevin et. al., The Structure of the Welsh Economy, University of Wales Press 1966. Economic Development in Northern Ireland (Wilson Report), Cmd. 479, HMSO Belfast 1965. G. McCrone, Scotland's Economic Progress 1951-60, George Allen & Unwin 1965. This question is examined in greater detail in Chapter VI.

116

achieved considerable success, the economies of the Scottish, Welsh and Northern regions were still heavily dependent on their traditional industries. Immense tasks remained if their infrastructure and environments were to be recreated to stimulate new economic growth. The continued boom in the traditional industries had not solved the problem, but only masked it for a time.

The surprising fact was that a decline in the traditional industries was almost totally unforeseen. Subsequent analysis shows that the growth of Scottish Gross Domestic Product began to lag behind the United Kingdom rate after 1954, but it was in 1958 that the problem really became serious. The boom in the traditional industries at last collapsed. Ship-building had caught up with the backlog of demand and the international market became highly competitive. In this situation the British yards, which were insufficiently modernized, plagued by labour trouble and probably poorly managed, were not well placed to withstand foreign competition, especially from Japan. Coal began to feel the effects of competition from other fuels, especially oil.

But added to these secular trends, which should perhaps have been foreseen, were the effects of stagnation in the British economy as a whole. After a period of rapid economic growth up to 1951 and moderate growth thereafter, culminating in the investment boom of 1954–5, the economy had to slow down because of inflationary pressures and the threat to the balance of payments. There followed in succession the credit squeeze and autumn budget of 1955, the post-Suez measures of 1956 and the Thorneycroft 7 per cent bank rate of 1957. In the absence of measures to prevent it, these deflationary policies could be expected to bear particularly heavily in the problem regions for precisely the same reasons as they had suffered most heavily in the pre-war slump.

The combined effect of the secular decline and the trough of the trade cycle hit coal and ship-building most seriously, though steel output also fell well below capacity. Coal output fell from 223 million tons in 1957 to 215 million in 1958; but consumption in 1958 was only 208 million tons, so that stocks at the end of the year rose to 20 million. In 1959 output fell further to 206 million tons; but demand was down to 190 million, so that stocks during the year reached the unprecedented level of 50 million tons. A similar situation affected ship-building. For the first time since the War the number of ships afloat exceeded requirements. It was not surprising, therefore, that the output of ship-building fell back to its 1954 level in 1959 and in 1960 was some 22 per cent below the

117

post-war peak of 1956 (see Table IV). Traditional textiles, too, suffered during this period and, even allowing for the continuous expansion of synthetic fibres, the output of the textile group of industries as a whole did not regain its 1954 level until 1964.

As a consequence of this worsening situation, it became necessary once again to give greater priority to regional policy. Control over Industrial Development Certificates was accordingly tightened up. The steel industry which had been planning a new strip mill project, originally to be sited in the Midlands, found its plans subject to much canvassing from hard hit regions. At length, as a result of personal intervention on the part of the Prime Minister in 1958, the project was split, one strip mill being set up at Llanwern in South Wales and another at Ravenscraig in the Central Belt of Scotland. There is little sign that the economic implications of this were seriously considered, the decision was due mainly to political and social considerations. Experience has shown that in consequence neither project was large enough to enjoy the economies of scale which the large integrated works on the Continent now enjoy, and in the case of the Scottish mill especially, which was situated inland, the siting was also poor. It is questionable if this type of policy is really in the interests even of the regional economy.

But apart from according regional policy a higher priority, it became clear that some amendment to the legislation was also required. In 1955–6 the Estimates Committee had pointed out that some of the Development Areas might, in their opinion, be descheduled and certainly in some cases unemployment in the Development Area was lower than in the surrounding region. On the other hand, the 1958 situation showed that there were other hard hit areas which were not scheduled. The Western Isles, for instance, reached unemployment of over 30 per cent at one point and in Anglesey it was 11 per cent, yet neither of these had been scheduled as Development Areas.

The Government's answer was the Distribution of Industry (Industrial Finance) Act of 1958. This Act kept the existing Development Areas, which despite their earlier health were now needing continuing assistance, but added to them certain smaller development 'places' where the Treasury's power to give loans or grants on the advice of DATAC could be extended. Such loans and grants were to cover any form of trade and were no longer limited to industry as had previously been the case.

The criterion for selecting these additional development places was the existence of a high rate of unemployment which was likely to persist. There was, therefore, a tendency to tie policy measures more closely to unemployment than had previously been done. This was an indication that regional policy was being regarded primarily from a social point of view, and the Board of Trade admitted as much in evidence.[1]

Yet, if there is a criticism of regional development policy up to this time, it is that the economic aim of stimulating sound economic growth in the regions had not been sufficiently followed up. As has been pointed out, such objectives were mentioned in the Barlow Report and in the White Papers on Employment Policy and the Distribution of Industry. Yet the research recommended by the Barlow Commission had not been undertaken and policy had stopped far short of reorganizing the basic economic structure, the infrastructure and modernizing the environment of the regions in such a way as to promote growth. The problem regions still had their economies based on the problem industries and their urban environments still suffered from the squalid conditions inherited from the nineteenth century. Nothing less than a complete refashioning of their economies was necessary if they were really to enjoy healthy economic growth.

---

[1] See, for instance, Second Report of the Select Committee on Estimates, Session 1955/6: The Development Areas, HMSO, p. viii and p. 264.

CHAPTER V

REGIONAL POLICY SINCE 1960

The year 1960 marks a natural dividing line in the development of post-war regional policy for a variety of reasons. First, the regional problem, which had been deteriorating during the latter years of the 1950s, was now to go through a more critical phase than at any time since pre-war. Second, the Distribution of Industry Acts, which had been the basis of post-war policy since 1945, were repealed and replaced by the new Local Employment Act of 1960. This Act, though it has been substantially strengthened and amended since, still remains the foundation of regional policy in 1967. Thirdly, owing no doubt to the greater severity of the problem, regional policy in the 1960s was accorded a much higher degree of priority by the Government than it had been in the 1950s, and was indeed prosecuted with more vigour than at any time since the years immediately after the War.

During the course of the 1960s, there were some important changes in official thinking on the regional problem. Foremost amongst these was the greater emphasis which came to be put on economic factors. This was not apparent at the start of the period; indeed, the 1960 Act largely ignored economic factors, and in this adopted a more extreme view than the legislation which went before it. But the whole question of economic growth was at this time receiving much greater attention than ever before both because of Britain's low rate of growth when compared with other European countries and because of increasing frustration over the stop-go cycle. It was perhaps natural, therefore, that the regional problem should also be increasingly seen as a problem of economic growth. Attention was directed to ways of promoting regional expansion and to the contributions which the regions might make to the achievement of a higher national rate of growth. This change in attitude began to emerge in 1963, and was revealed in the first tentative steps to establish growth areas and to start regional economic planning. This was the first attempt to relate economic planning to physical and transport planning; and the importance of creating an environment conducive to growth and the role which new towns, urban renewal or infrastructure could play in creating this environment began to be recognized.

Very little of this was original. As was shown earlier in this book, the importance both of promoting sound economic growth based on the areas capable of expansion, and of economic planning or the links between regional economic and physical planning, had all been emphasized by the Barlow Report some twenty years before.[1] But the apparent success of post-war policy, followed in 1958 and 1960 by a preoccupation with the social aspects of the problem, had caused them to be ignored.

The development of policy in the 1960s took place in three phases: first, the Local Employment Act of 1960; second, the Budget and Local Employment Act of 1963, which amended and greatly strengthened the 1960 measures; and third, the changes which were introduced by the Labour Party after the change of government in 1964. The changes in the legislation were numerous and often complex. To adhere to a strict chronological exposition, therefore, would be confusing. The following sections take each group of measures in turn and explain their evolution up to the time of writing.

I. THE SCHEDULED AREAS

The 1958 legislation amending the old Distribution of Industry Acts had borne the marks of haste rather than a carefully thought-out policy. Something had had to be done to meet the needs of a sudden deterioration in the situation, but the addition of new localities to the old Development Areas had been unsatisfactory. The new additions had the advantage of DATAC loans, but they did not have industrial estates and could in some respects, therefore, be regarded as second-class Development Areas. Many were small and not particularly suited to industrial development. At the same time, it was thought that the old Areas no longer defined very clearly the parts of the country in greatest need.

Thus, in many ways the most important change introduced in the 1960 Act was the rescheduling of the areas qualifying for assistance. The old Development Areas were abolished. Since their original designation in 1945 these had been altered only by the inclusion of additional areas in the late 'forties; and, while areas

[1] *Royal Commission on the Distribution of the Industrial Population*, Cmd. 6153, 1940. See Chapter III.

could have been withdrawn, all changes required Parliamentary approval. Experience of the late 1950s, when many other areas suffered unemployment, led to the view that this system was too inflexible. The new legislation, therefore, gave the Board of Trade power to schedule what were known as 'Development Districts', which were to be based on the Local Employment Exchange area. These Districts could be scheduled or descheduled by the Board without Parliamentary approval for changes, but the Board was to base its policy on an unemployment criterion. As defined in the Act, Development Districts would be: 'Localities in which, in the opinion of the Board, a high rate of unemployment exists or is imminent and is likely to persist.'[1]

In practice the Board adopted $4\frac{1}{2}$ per cent of the insured population unemployed as the critical figure; but it was allowed latitude in its decisions, and it therefore showed no hesitation in adding areas to the list, if it thought unemployment was likely to rise, or in striking them off, if recently announced expansion plans seemed likely to lower it.

The area of the country thus scheduled included the greater part of the old problem areas, South Wales, the North-East of England, West Cumberland, Merseyside and part of Central Scotland. But it also included a lot of additional areas. Indeed, there was scarcely a region in the country which did not have some odd little pockets of $4\frac{1}{2}$ per cent unemployment, even if the unemployed were of little significance in total numbers. Even the South-East, therefore, had for a while some such Districts which came within the scope of the legislation. The most important additions were some predominantly rural areas which, although suffering from unemployment, had not been included in previous legislation. The most significant of these were Cornwall and North Devon in the South-West, part of North Wales, virtually the whole of the Highlands and Islands of Scotland, except Perthshire, and a large section of North-East Scotland around Aberdeen. All these areas had been in difficulties for some time and they had been considered carefully in the 1948 White Paper;[2] but they had not been included as Development Areas at that time on the grounds that the latter were industrial areas, and that measures appropriate for them would not also be appropriate for rural areas. As we have seen, an exception had been made of the Highlands of Scotland, but only to the extent that a small area around Inverness and the Cromarty Firth

[1] *Local Employment Act, 1960*, p. 1.
[2] *Distribution of Industry*, Cmd. 7540, HMSO 1948.

MAP 4

THE DEVELOPMENT DISTRICTS IN 1966

was scheduled as a focus for industrial development.[1] The new policy was, therefore, a major departure from the earlier approach which had contained some elements, albeit inadequately developed, of the growth area idea.

The geographical extent of the Development Districts varied substantially from one time to another, depending on the level of activity in the economy as a whole and the percentages of regional unemployment which resulted. It also depended in part on the optimism or pessimism of the Board of Trade in forecasting the impact of new developments undertaken in certain areas and the prospects of increased unemployment in others. Thus, the percentage of the country's total population covered by Development Districts was 12.5 in 1961 but fell to 7.2 in 1962 and rose again to a maximum figure of 16.8 in 1966. The areas covered at this latter date are shown in Map 4.

This type of system had two serious disadvantages. First, the frequent changes in the coverage of Development Districts was bewildering, upset industrialist's plans for expansion and made long-term planning by public authorities difficult. For instance, areas such as Plymouth, Merseyside, Llanelly and Bathgate were all included initially as Development Districts, then in 1962 they were either taken off the list or stop-listed, which meant that for the time being further development would not be encouraged to go there. Shortly afterwards, all except Plymouth were added to the list again. Thus a firm might become interested in a particular Development District, and start working on plans to build a factory there, only to find at the crucial stage that the area was descheduled, that the assistance it intended to apply for was no longer available and that the IDC system might even be used to prevent its plans being realized there. Alternatively, a firm might set up in a Development District intending in a few years' time to extend its activities if all went well; yet by the time it was ready to build the extension the District might be descheduled, with the result that the firm would not only lose the benefits of any assistance but perhaps have difficulty in obtaining permission for the extension.

This was obviously highly unsatisfactory, but the second disadvantage of this system was possibly more fundamental. This concerns the use of unemployment percentages as the criterion for scheduling Development Districts. Unemployment is a measure of social distress and of the additional work needed to bring about

[1] See p. 109 above.

full employment; but it is not necessarily related to an area's economic potential for development. As has been shown in the last two chapters, both the Special Area Commissioners and the Barlow Commission recognized that there were some locations where it was almost impossible to create new employment and cited some remote mining villages as the clearest examples of such places. In these cases it had been held that some labour movement was both inevitable and desirable; and that the aim of policy should be to prevent long-distance inter-regional migration by regrouping the population within the region around the industrial focal points which were capable of development. Thus the Barlow Report held that industry should be located at key points as near as possible to the areas of high unemployment and the post-war White Paper, as shown in the last chapter, emphasized the coherent economic nature of the Development Areas.

This approach, though expressed in the post-war legislation, had perhaps not been pushed very far, but it was dropped altogether in the 1960 Act. Emphasis on the unemployment percentage of a local Employment Exchange area meant that the worst areas were often the ones with the least chance of development. Yet these were the Development Districts which were given the greatest priority. Often sites more suitable for development might be found not far away, even within travel-to-work distance. But unless they, too, had 4½ per cent unemployment they were unlikely to be scheduled, and firms might even be discouraged from expanding there. Thus, the effort to steer development to Development Districts might fail, because the locations were unsatisfactory; yet expansion elsewhere in the region, which could succeed and would assist the Development Districts, was not encouraged.

The faults in this policy arose, perhaps, from giving more emphasis to its social than its economic aspects, from being concerned with providing employment rather than stimulating economic growth. If priority is given to growth it becomes necessary to view the region as a whole rather than think simply in terms of unemployment blackspots. It will then be seen that the promotion of industrial growth will require some regrouping of population and that assistance, if given, must be sufficiently permanent to make planning possible.

These criticisms were met to some extent for two of the worst problem areas with the publication in the autumn of 1963 of the White Papers on Central Scotland and North-East England.[1] These

[1] Central Scotland: A Programme for Development and Growth. Cmnd. 2188, HMSO.

125

documents are in part a first step towards regional planning and in part an attempt at a growth area policy; they are, therefore, examined more closely in later chapters. The important feature here is the way they modified the scheduling of assisted areas.

The two sub-regions in question had suffered particularly severely since 1958, and especially in the 1962–3 recession, when unemployment had reached its highest level since the war. Conditions in the North-East had resulted in the appointment of Lord Hailsham as Minister with special responsibility for the area. In Scotland, the Toothill Committee's Report in 1961 had given emphasis to the promotion of faster economic growth and the ways and means by which this might be achieved.[1]

The White Papers adopted this approach in that they too put the emphasis on stimulating viable growth. For this purpose they designated eight growth areas in Central Scotland and a growth zone in North-East England. To these areas were to apply all the benefits currently available for Development Districts and notice was given that these would be retained regardless of the level of unemployment which might subsequently prevail there. Furthermore, the areas were to be built up as centres of economic growth by a programme of public investment which was outlined in the White Papers. But this approach was, of course, only applied to two areas, Central Scotland and the North-East. Moreover, it left the scheduling of Development Districts still dependent on the unemployment criterion except where this was modified by growth areas. It was, therefore, an odd compromise.

The final change was made after Labour came to power, when the 1966 Industrial Development Act abolished the Development Districts and replaced them with new Development Areas (see Map 5).[2] These were by far the largest areas yet scheduled, comprising the whole of Scotland except Edinburgh, the Northern Region plus the Furness peninsula, Merseyside, almost the whole of Wales save some pockets along the North Coast and around Cardiff in the South, and Cornwall and North Devon in the South-West. They thus included over 40 per cent of the land area of Britain and 20 per cent of the population compared with 16.7

Edinburgh, November 1963. *The North-East: A Programme for Development and Growth*, Cmnd. 2206, HMSO London, November 1963.
[1] *Report of the Committee of Inquiry into the Scottish Economy*, Scottish Council (Development and Industry) 1961.
[2] *Investment Incentives*, Cmnd. 2874, January 1966. Industrial Development Act 1966, HMSO.

MAP 5

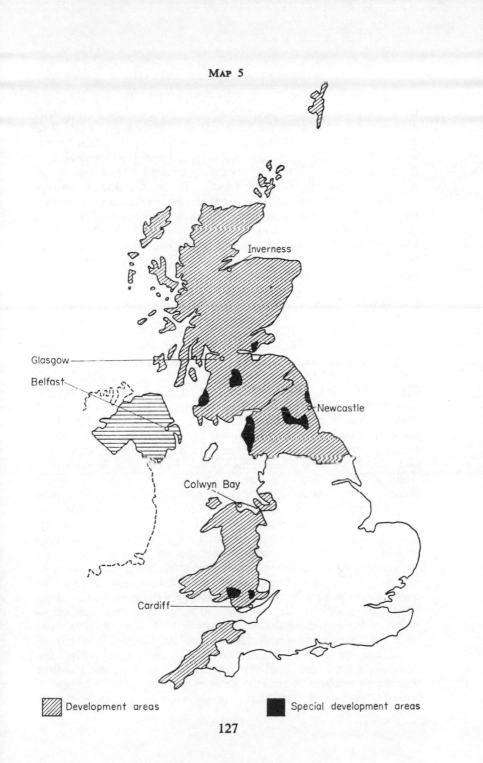

Development areas

Special development areas

per cent for the Development Districts in 1966. These areas could be amended as the need arose, but they were not based on a strict employment criterion as the Development Districts had been. This would, therefore, avoid the disruptive effects on industrial investment which frequent changes in the scheduled Development Districts had caused. Moreover, since they covered wide areas, industry was now able to select the location it considered most suitable for the development in the problem regions instead of being limited merely to the worst unemployment blackspots if it wanted the benefit of assistance. In the long run this seems to offer a better basis for sound regional economic growth, and industry might now be expected to tend towards the natural growth points in the regional economy. Thus, although this new policy is far from being an explicit growth area policy, it appears to contain some of the latter's advantages.

However, in the autumn of 1967 a further modification was made to this system. The closure of coal mines, hastened no doubt by the 1966–7 economic squeeze, produced severe unemployment in a number of coal-mining areas at a time when there seemed little prospect of new development to absorb the available labour. The Government accordingly designated these places as 'Special Development Areas' with the intention of giving them special priority. The places in question are shown on Map 5. They bear some similarity to the old pre-war Special Areas, consisting of certain coalfields in Scotland, the North-East, West Cumberland and Wales. All these places were already in the 1966 Development Areas and received all the benefits to which the legislation entitled them, but this new status gave them especially favourable terms: a 35 per cent building grant, assistance to cover operating costs and Board of Trade factories available rent free for five years. Clearly, this legislation was the result of acute social distress and political pressure. Its economic effects cannot yet be assessed as it only came into effect as this book was completed, but it would seem to repeat the failings of the Development Districts and is likely to conflict with a growth area policy. Indeed, it is a step away from a growth area policy back to the old blackspots approach exemplified in the earlier legislation. It may be that some of these areas have the potential to enable them to be transformed into growth areas, but for most of them, particularly the Welsh valleys, the Northumberland and Durham moors and the Ayrshire coalfield this seems unlikely. Certainly their growth potential was not a criterion considered in designating them and the transformation of any of them into growth areas would require much public investment and planning, neither of which have so far been attempted.

II. THE USE OF CONTROLS

The 1960 Local Employment Act made no alteration in the measures to control new industrial development. The Industrial Development Certificates, established under the 1947 Town and Country Planning Act, remained. IDCs had to be obtained from the Board of Trade for any industrial development over 5,000 square feet before local planning permission could be granted; and the control was used to restrict development outside the Development Districts, especially in the Midlands and the South, in favour of locations within them, or in Northern Ireland. The effect of this, however, depends upon the strictness with which the system is enforced, and there is little doubt that in the 1960s it was applied with much greater stringency than during the early or mid-1950s.

This control has been regarded by the Board of Trade as their most effective weapon of regional policy. The Labour Government, on assuming office, extended its use to all factory development in excess of 1,000 square feet. But it is questionable if development of this size is potentially mobile on any appreciable scale. The results of this extension of the control cannot have been encouraging, because under the Industrial Development Act of 1966 the exemption limit was raised again to 3,000 square feet and 5,000 square feet outside the Midlands and South-East. At the same time, however, the system was extended to include buildings used for storage and for scientific research in the course of business.

Industrial development, however, is only a part of the national economy, and indeed accounts for only some 50 per cent of economic activity as measured by its contribution to GDP. In particular, during the early 1960s, regional policy was criticized for leaving office development subject to no restraint save the normal local authority planning permission.[1] The nation's office employment is, after all, much more mainly concentrated in the

[1] NEDC, *Conditions Favourable to Faster Growth*, HMSO 1963, pp. 19–20. A. J. Odber, 'Regional Policy in Great Britain', in *Area Redevelopment Policies in Britain and the Countries of the Common Market*, US Dept. of Commerce 1965, p. 386.

South-East than is its manufacturing production. Indeed, a White Paper published in 1963 showed that of about 40,000 jobs created annually in the London conurbation only 20 per cent were in manufacturing industry.[1] At least 15,000 new office jobs were being created annually in Central London alone. Office growth was probably the main culprit in causing congestion in the capital and overloading its public services, and the main source of employment growth. Its exclusion from regional policy, therefore, seemed absurd.

In 1963 the Location of Offices Bureau was set up to tackle the congestion aspects of this by trying to encourage office development to move from the centre of London to the periphery, but this was of little significance for regional development. Accordingly, the Labour Government, on coming to power, required all new office development in London to obtain Board of Trade permission as from November 5, 1964. This was subsequently formalized by the Control of Office and Industrial Development Act 1965. Under this Act the building of offices with a floor space in excess of 3,000 square feet could only be undertaken in the London Metropolitan Region if an Office Development Permit is first obtained from the Board of Trade. The Act gave the Board power to designate further areas outside the London Metropolitan Region which would also be subject to control as the need arose. The Birmingham conurbation was brought under control in August 1965, and in July 1966 the control was extended to the whole of the South-East, East Anglia, the West Midland and the East Midland Planning Regions.

The Board have exercised their power of control with greater stringency in the Greater London Area than elsewhere. But, before issuing an Office Development Permit for any of the controlled areas, they have required applicants to satisfy them on three main counts: first, that they could not carry out the type of activity for which the accommodation is required in another area; second, that no satisfactory alternative accommodation was available, and third, that the development was essential in the public interest.[2] In the period covered by the first report, the Board refused permission in 327 cases in the London Metropolitan Region and issued 252 permits. Of this, the Greater London Council Area accounted for almost two-thirds of the refusals and a slightly smaller proportion

[1] *London, Employment: Housing: Land*, Cmnd. 1952, 1963.
[2] Annual Reports of the Board of Trade 1966 and 1967: Control of Office and Industrial Development Acts 1965. HMSO.

of the permits. In the West Midlands conurbation there were fourteen refusals and forty-three permits issued. In the second year the number of permits increased considerably to 407 for the London Metropolitan Region. No figures for refusals were given in the second report; but, as the report itself says, these have ceased to be particularly meaningful, one of the effects of the Act being to discourage firms from putting in applications which have little chance of success. Clearly, it is impossible to make an assessment of the effects of these measures in the short time they have been in operation. For this it will be necessary to wait a number of years to see whether any detectable changes emerge in the regional pattern of office development. The legislation is at least assisted by the very wide differences in rents, for as has recently been shown, London rents per square foot are around three times the levels found in provincial cities.[1]

III. GRANTS, LOANS AND FINAL INDUCEMENTS

(a) *Special Loans and Grants*
The 1960 Act continued the system, already described in the last chapter, whereby firms in the scheduled areas could obtain special loans or grants for expansion schemes on the advice of an advisory committee. This had been a Treasury Committee (Development Areas Treasury Advisory Committee) and the extent of the assistance provided in the 1950s had been extremely small. The activities of the Committee, however, had been seriously limited by the two conditions (a) that projects for which assistance was asked must be financially sound and (b) that the firms must be able to show that they could not raise the money from other sources. In practice it was rare for a firm to be able to demonstrate the commercial soundness of a proposed scheme and yet be unable to obtain finance on any terms.

Under the 1960 Act the advisory committee was transferred to the Board of Trade as the Board of Trade Advisory Committee (BOTAC) and the condition requiring firms to demonstrate their inability to raise money from other sources was removed. This greatly increased the Committee's ability to provide assistance and the much larger sums made available in the 1960s give evidence of this (see Table I). Over the period April 1960 to March 1967,

[1] *The Economist*, August 13, 1966. City centre rents were around 70s per square foot in London compared with around 20s for Glasgow, Newcastle, Manchester and Birmingham. Rents within two miles of the centre ranged from 40s in London to around 17s for the other cities.

131

£82 million was provided by BOTAC in loans and £6.7 million in special grants.

In providing assistance, however, BOTAC have been required to have regard to the estimated employment likely to be created. On average the Estimates Committee found that the cost per job of assistance provided worked out at just under £1,000. The Committee considered projects where the cost per job was up to £1,500 as reasonable, and would only exceed £2,500 in very exceptional circumstances.[1] The system has the advantage of flexibility and it can be used to discriminate in favour of particular types of development such as labour-intensive industry or particular areas. In the early 1960s, for instance, the Committee were certainly prepared to provide more generous assistance to firms who undertook to set up in Development Districts where the unemployment was particularly severe. The high costs per job of some Scottish projects were thus explained to the Estimates Committee. And the assistance given to the new motor industry factories in Scotland and the North-West greatly exceeded the normal cost per job because these were judged to be projects of unusual political and economic importance.[2]

The disadvantage with this system is that no firm knows what assistance it can expect without embarking on negotiations which may be lengthy. The inducements offered are, therefore, not clearcut, and the advantage of location in a Development District or Area cannot be advertised in precise comprehensible terms. Negotiations for assistance have been known to take two years, though this is uncommon, and they can seldom be speedy enough to help the firm which has to take a quick decision.

There is also a danger that too much attention is paid to costs per job. Not only was this rather a phoney figure as estimated by BOTAC, being made up by addition of both loans and grants, but it neglects inter-industry linkages. Highly capital-intensive projects, which might fail the cost per job rule, may nonetheless provide the steel, the power or the intermediate products without which a whole range of other industries cannot operate. For all these reasons, though the BOTAC special loans and grants are still available, increasing importance has been given to various standard grants and inducements and the employment criterion on these has been relaxed.

[1] Seventh Report from the Estimates Committee 1962/3: *Administration of the Local Employment Act 1960*, HMSO 1963, p. 47.
[2] *Ibid.*, p. 56.

(b) *Building Grants*

An innovation under the 1960 Act was the offer of a building grant. The purpose of this was to give firms who decided to build their own factories in a Development District the same advantages as those who rented a Board of Trade factory at a favourable rent. Naturally a number of large or specialist firms would require factories built to special requirements or on special sites and might prefer to do the construction themselves. The building grant was not available automatically but only after consulting with BOTAC; moreover, the formula by which the grant was determined was complicated and raised some criticism. Firms were entitled to claim 85 per cent of the difference between the cost of building a factory and its value once completed. As compared with a straight percentage payable on the cost of construction, the advantage claimed for this system was that its effect would be greater the more depressed the region and hence the lower the current market value of factories. In some parts of Scotland, for instance, where market values were particularly low, the grant payable under this system might come to 28 per cent of construction costs compared with only 12 per cent in more prosperous areas and a national average of 17 per cent in the Development Districts as a whole.[1] Nevertheless, the complicated nature of the formula, expressed as it was in terms of two figures neither of which could be discovered without lengthy investigation, meant that the benefits of the grant were obscure except to the really curious. Its effect as an inducement was, therefore, diminished.

These faults were recognized in the 1963 legislation. The Government was at that time introducing a system of standard grants and inducements and it therefore replaced the 1960 building grant with a new one payable at the standard rate of 25 per cent of actual construction costs including essential services, fixtures, etc. For most areas this was more generous than the old system which, as has just been shown, worked out at an average of 17 per cent over all the Development Districts; but it was rather less generous in the most severely depressed Districts where values were particularly low and where the flexibility of the old system had enabled more generous grants to be given than elsewhere.

Against the loss in flexibility, however, there was an immense gain in simplicity. Moreover, if the old system favoured depressed areas whose condition was particularly hopeless, the new one was much more generous than the old one had been to growth areas

[1] *Ibid.*, p. 100, 164.

133

whose future prospects caused the value of property to be relatively high; it was, therefore, in keeping with the gradual movement towards a growth area policy.

At the present time these building grants still exist, but the 1966 Industrial Development Act, while retaining the standard rate at 25 per cent payable in the new Development Areas, made provision for it to be raised to 35 per cent in exceptional circumstances and this rate is applied to the Special Development Areas. The grants still require BOTAC approval and the Committee will, therefore, have to judge whether in particular cases it should be paid at 25 or 35 per cent. The increasing use made of these grants may be seen from Table I. It is particularly interesting that the sum spent on them jumped from £3 million in 1963–4 to £10 million in 1964–5. This may partly be accounted for by the 1964 boom in the economy, but is no doubt also due to the change in the system. From that time there has been a steady increase in the annual total to £21 million in 1966–7.

(c) *Plant and Machinery*
No standard grants or inducements for investment in plant and machinery were provided in the 1960 Act, and firms were therefore obliged to rely entirely on the special loans or grants obtainable from BOTAC which have already been described. However, the need for a standardized system of grants and inducements, whose advantages would be readily understood, had impressed the Government and the measures were introduced in the Finance and Local Employment Acts of 1963.

Grants were offered for new plant and machinery in the Development Districts at the rate of 10 per cent of costs. The grants were subject only to the condition that as a consequence of the investment employment would be created in the Development Districts. £2 million was spent on these grants in the remainder of the year 1963–4 and thereafter they accounted for about £6 million a year until they were replaced in the 1966 Industrial Development Act.

The most important innovation of the 1963 legislation, however, was the provision for 'accelerated depreciation'. This scheme entitled manufacturing industry in the Development Districts to amortize investment in plant and machinery against profits at whatever rate it chose. If it wished, a firm could thus reduce its tax liability to zero until it had recovered the full cost of its capital equipment. As the Chancellor said in the budget speech: 'He need not pay a penny piece of taxation until he has written off his entire investment in plant and machinery.'[1]

What this amounted to was an interest-free loan from the Inland Revenue giving the firm increased liquidity. If a firm decided to reduce its declared profits to zero in the first year by amortizing its new investment at an accelerated rate, it would escape tax liability in that year. In subsequent years, however, profits would be higher than they would have been if amortization charges had been spread, and the tax liability in those years would therefore be proportionately greater. In the end the total tax payments would be exactly the same, but accelerated depreciation gave the firm the right to delay its tax payments until it had recovered the whole cost of its investment.

The scheme proved popular with industry and was probably the most effective of the measures introduced in 1963. Its main drawback was that a firm had to be earning profits at a sufficient rate to cover the accelerated depreciation. This would probably pose no problem for the large established firm; but the small firm setting up a new business which might well go through a lean period in the early years, even if it became highly profitable later, got little help from this measure.

In 1966, however, both the 10 per cent grants for plant and machinery and accelerated depreciation were replaced. The Labour Government had introduced a number of major tax changes in the economy, the most notable of which was the new Corporation Tax. A side effect of this had been to reduce the value of the incentives for regional development which had been in operation since 1963. With Corporation Tax at 40 per cent compared with the old 56 per cent for income tax plus profits tax, the value of any tax exemption was diminished.[2]

It was, therefore, necessary to redress the balance. But rather than tinker with the system the Industrial Development Act of 1966 made drastic changes. Not only were accelerated depreciation and the plant and machinery grants abolished, but so were the investment allowances which had been available at the rate of 30 per cent on plant and 15 per cent on buildings throughout the

[1] Hansard. April 3, 1963, No. 587, p. 482.
[2] The position is explained in detail in W. Black, N. Cuthbert and J. B. Simpson, 'Investment Incentives and the 1965 Finance Act: Regional Implications', *Scottish Journal of Political Economy*, Feb. 1967, p. 12; and in P. A. Bird and A. P. Thirlwall, 'The Incentive to Interest in the New Development Areas', *District Bank Review*, June 1967, p. 12.

country, whether in Development Districts or not. Initial allowances were raised from 5 per cent to 15 per cent on all industrial buildings and remained at 30 per cent for plant not qualifying for a grant; these rates applied to all areas.

The main change, however, and the one of principal importance for the new Development Areas, was the introduction of investment grants. These grants were to be paid at the rate of 20 per cent generally and 40 per cent in Development Areas, but later in 1966 these figures were temporarily raised to 25 per cent and 45 per cent respectively. Unlike previous systems, these grants are in no way limited by employment created or the commercial soundness of the investment.

The old system had been criticized for being complicated, in that the precise advantages of free depreciation required a sophisticated type of calculation. By contrast the new system seemed much more clear-cut than it actually was. At first sight a cash grant of 45 per cent on new investment in the Development Areas seems extremely generous. But this does not take into account the effects of taxation nor that there is at present a fifteen-month lag in the payment of grants which it is hoped eventually to reduce to six months. These effects are examined in Chapter VIII and it is shown that the new system gives only marginally more incentive for a firm investing in the Development Areas than was available under the old 1963 system before the introduction of the Corporation Tax.

(d) *Regional Employment Premium*

The most recent incentive introduced to encourage expansion in the Development Areas is the Regional Employment Premium. In contrast to all previous incentives, which were designed to reduce capital costs, even if governed by an employment criterion, the REP is the first to subsidize labour costs directly. The premium is paid by using the Selective Employment Tax machinery. Under Selective Employment Tax an employer in manufacturing industry was able to claim back the full value of the tax paid on his employees plus a premium of 7s 6d per man per week with smaller sums for women and juveniles. The introduction of REP enables manufacturing employers in the Development Areas to claim a further sum of 30s per man per week. The position was modified by the post-devaluation measures in the autumn of 1967 which abolished the 7s 6d SET premium for employees outside the Development Areas. The latest position is, then, that a manufacturing employer in a Development Area receives a total premium of 37s 6d per man per week in addition to the reimbursing of his tax, while a similar employer outside the Development Areas only has his tax reimbursed.

It is expected that the REP will cost about £100 million in a full year, which will be distributed among the Development Areas as follows: Scotland £40 million, Northern Region £28 million, the North-West £18 million, Wales £12 million and the South-West £1.6 million.[1] In addition, the SET premium payable to Development Areas could cost about £25 million. The combined effect may amount to a subsidy of around 8 per cent of the wages bill. The premium is payable on all labour employed in manufacturing industry in the Development Areas and is not limited to schemes for expansion, as all previous inducements were. At the same time, it is important to notice that SET, which is designed to penalize the services sector, had hit some of the Development Areas extremely hard. The rural parts of the Development Areas, the Scottish Highlands, Cumberland and Westmorland, Wales and Cornwall, for example, all depend heavily on tourist business. SET, therefore, penalized them heavily, and REP, which is limited to manufacturing, is of little benefit to them.

The merits of this type of incentive are fully discussed in a later chapter. The idea of a labour subsidy, however, is not new and from time to time it has been advocated on the grounds that, since labour was the excess resource of the problem regions, a labour rather than a capital subsidy was what was required. A scheme for a wage subsidy had been examined by the Hall Committee on Northern Ireland but was rejected on the grounds that, once introduced, it would be impossible to remove and that it should not be the purpose of regional policy permanently to prop up industry which was not viable economically.[2] Recently a scheme for a regional payroll tax, variable according to a strict formula, had been outlined by Mr Colin Clark.[3] His scheme would have provided for a whole range of variable rates from London at one extreme to the Hebrides at the other.

The case for the REP scheme, however, was not based primarily on the need for labour-intensive industry. Rather it was seen as

[1] Hansard, November 9, 1967.
[2] Report of the Joint Working Party on the Economy of Northern Ireland, Cmnd. 1835, London, HMSO, p. 314.
[3] Colin Clark, 'Industrial Location and Economic Potential', Lloyds Bank Review, October 1966.

an extension of Keynesian techniques of economic management to the regional level. The injection of £100 million or £125 million into the economies of the Development Areas need not be regarded as a cost to the community at large, since the expansion thus stimulated could employ resources which would otherwise be idle. Therefore, it need not produce inflationary pressure or require a cut-back in output elsewhere. Moreover, since the particular form of the scheme would lower production costs for manufacturing industry in the Development Areas, it would have something of the effect of a regional devaluation, improving the competitive position of regional production and tending to stimulate exports with consequent gain to the balance of payments.

(e) *Other Grants—Labour Training*

Various other forms of financial assistance have been provided by the legislation. Local Authorities, for example, have been able to obtain grants to assist with the reclamation of derelict areas. These were normally at the rate of 50 per cent of cost, but were raised in the budget of 1963 to 85–90 per cent. The housing of key workers for new industrial projects has been recognized as a valid expense of regional development.

Much the most important item, however, has been labour training. The expansion of new industries in the Development Areas involves a changing industrial structure and a need for new skills. In some cases firms might even find the labour surplus of the Areas an illusion, because, as far as the type of labour they required was concerned, there might be an acute shortage. The re-employment of the labour surplus, therefore, could not be accomplished without an extensive retraining programme.

Accordingly, the 1963 budget set aside £10 million for a retraining programme over a period of years, and greater emphasis was placed on this after the Labour Government came to power. The 1964 Industrial Training Act empowered the Minister of Labour to set up Training Boards for different branches of industry and Commerce. The purpose of these Boards was to ensure that sufficient training was undertaken and to help finance it by grants paid out of levies imposed on industry. Finance is also provided by the Government to assist the Boards and grants are paid to assist employers in installing machinery for training purposes.

These arrangements are concerned primarily with on-the-job training. Where more skill is required, such as would normally be provided by an apprenticeship scheme, retraining can be undertaken in a Government Training Centre and the number of these throughout the country has been increased rapidly from thirteen in 1963 to thirty-eight in 1967 handling 13,000 workers a year. By 1969 there will be forty-eight centres catering for 21,000 workers. Fees for employees under training from firms in Development Areas may be waived.

For firms in Development Areas financial assistance towards the cost of training was doubled in 1967 and is now paid at the rate of £10 per week for men and £7 for women; juveniles under 18 being paid for at the rate of £5 and £4, male and female respectively. Grants are limited to training which lasts more than two weeks and less than fifty-two weeks. Firms renting temporary accommodation for training purposes may obtain a grant to cover half the cost of the rent and rates for a period up to two years and half the cost of adaptations to the building. In addition, Development Area firms may be repaid half the cost of tuition fees for managerial, supervisory and technical staff who undertake approved instruction courses.

(f) *Northern Ireland*
The position of Northern Ireland has been rather different from that of any of the problem areas in Great Britain, because regional development has been partly the responsibility of the Northern Ireland legislature. The use of Industrial Development Certificates in Britain does, of course, favour Northern Ireland in the same way as it favours the Development Areas, but most of the grants and other inducements are locally determined and locally administered. In general, these inducements have been on a more generous scale than in the Development Areas in Great Britain and there has been the added advantage that decisions may be taken on the spot with much less delay.

Prior to 1966 Northern Ireland benefited from the same tax allowances as Britain. Investment and Initial Allowances were paid in the same way as throughout Britain and the accelerated depreciation available for the Development Districts also applied to Northern Ireland. But the grants were more generous. The Capital Grants to Industry Acts provided standard grants of 33⅓ per cent on both buildings and plant and machinery in place of 25 per cent and 10 per cent available in British Development Districts after 1963. The equivalent of the special grants or loans available from BOTAC was and still is provided under the Industries Development Acts. These grants or loans are administered by an advisory committee which must be satisfied that the projects are commercially viable and that they will provide employment in Northern Ireland. In line with the changes made in Britain in 1966, this legislation was replaced. The Capital Grants to Industry Acts were replaced by an Industrial Investment Act which, as in Britain, gave standard investment grants at the rate of 40 per cent. Unlike Britain, however, these applied to buildings as well as plant and machinery. In due course the rate was raised to 45 per cent to keep in step with the rise in the rate for the British Development Areas. Together with the introduction of these grants went the abolition of the tax allowances and, in particular, accelerated depreciation.

The effect of all these changes was not altogether to the advantage of Northern Ireland, since the discrimination in favour of the province compared with British Development Areas was reduced. The grants on plant and machinery at 45 per cent are not only on a par with those available for the Development Areas, whereas the previous systems had been more generous, but the rate of return, at 10.7 per cent, is lower than under the old system of 33⅓ per cent grants plus accelerated depreciation.[1] Prior to 1965 this had given a return of 11.8 per cent which had risen to 12.2 per cent in 1966 after the introduction of Corporation Tax.[2]

In practice, however, the Northern Ireland Government have been able to retain their discriminatory advantage over the British Development Areas by supplementing the standard grants with the special grants under the Industries Development Act which may, of course, if desired, be offered on more generous terms than in Great Britain. In advertising the advantages of a location in Northern Ireland they have stated that the combined grants will normally be at the rate of 50 per cent of capital cost provided that employment is created. Moreover, on buildings the Irish grants remain more generous than the British: 45 per cent under the Industrial Investment Act instead of 25 or 35 per cent in Britain. They are also able to offer a generous derating system. The other incentives are the same in Northern Ireland as elsewhere. The Regional Employment Premium is available and assistance is provided with labour training. On balance, therefore, the combined

[1] W. Black, N. Cuthbert and J. V. Simpson, 'Investment Incentives and the 1965 Finance Act: Regional Implications', *Scottish Journal of Political Economy*, Feb. 1967, p. 26.
[2] *Ibid.* The introduction of corporation tax increased the value of grants and reduced that of tax allowances. This had the result of raising the inducements to attract industry to Northern Ireland and reducing them in the Development Districts in Britain.

inducements to attract industry to Northern Ireland remain more generous than for the Development Areas.

IV. INDUSTRIAL ESTATES AND BOARD OF TRADE FACTORIES

As the last chapter has shown, Industrial Estates and Board of Trade Factories accounted for the largest part of government expenditure on regional policy in the period up to 1960. Factories built speculatively in advance of requirements had played an important part after the War, but these were stopped in 1948 and only started again in 1959. Factories built to order, however, were built steadily throughout the period.

The 1960 Act changed the situation in various ways. First, the redefinition of assisted areas with the replacement of Development Areas by Development Districts resulted in some of the industrial estates now no longer being in assisted areas. The Board of Trade retained responsibility for these, but extensions to existing factories were only undertaken at a rent which fully covered costs.

Secondly, the replacement of Development Areas by Development Districts made the old system of management impossible. Separate industrial estates companies had previously existed for each of the major Development Areas. With the small size of Development Districts and their more scattered nature, this arrangement could no longer work. The companies were therefore replaced by three Industrial Estates Management Corporations, one each for England, Scotland and Wales. This structure has been retained for the new Development Areas. In Northern Ireland industrial estates and building of government factories are the responsibility of the Ministry of Commerce. The whole province has always enjoyed the same status similar to that of a Development Area in the United Kingdom, so that no re-arrangement in the management of industrial estates has been required.

Board of Trade expenditure on factory building for rent and sale was high, £21 million, in the boom conditions of 1960, but rose again to around £13 million from 1964 onwards. The Labour Government has put much emphasis on this measure; thirty-two advance factories have been built since 1964 and a further ninety-two are projected or under construction. Several of these have been constructed in remote locations, which seemed somewhat at variance with the general move under the Conservatives towards a growth area approach; and it is perhaps not surprising, therefore, that tenants have sometimes been slow of coming forward. Thus, of the thirty-two advance factories completed since 1964 only twenty-one were occupied by the end of May 1967. Two in Cornwall had lain empty for six months and five of Scotland's thirteen were still unoccupied. Undoubtedly, government factories have been and will remain one of the most important weapons of regional policy. But the lesson of the last few years, like the lesson of Development Districts, is that unemployment alone is not a suitable criterion by which to measure an area's potential for economic development; and even if factories are provided there are certain locations to which it is very hard to attract new industry.

V. REGIONAL PLANNING

One of the more important developments in regional policy in the years up to 1967 was the creation of a system of regional planning. This is still in its infancy, and it cannot yet be said to have had a significant effect on the regional problem. A full description of the machinery and a discussion of its development is, therefore, left to a later chapter in Part III of this book. At this stage it is sufficient to note how it fitted in with the general development of regional policy measures in the 1960s.

The 1960s witnessed a gradual development of economic planning both at the national and regional levels. At the national level, the Conservative Government had set up the National Economic Development Council. This body, in attempting to plan a faster rate of growth for Britain, raised a number of important regional issues; and their concern over the economic aspects helped to bring about a new approach to regional policy. At the regional level, the first steps towards planning were taken in the White Papers on Central Scotland and North-East England.[1] These documents, while not attempting to set detailed output targets for the areas in question, did try to co-ordinate public investment expenditure and to develop a link between physical and economic planning. A similar approach, though more detailed, was followed in the Wilson report on Northern Ireland.[2]

The Labour Government were, however, much more firmly committed to economic planning in all its forms than the Conservatives had even been. Whilst in opposition, Labour spokesmen had frequently criticized policy documents produced by the Con-

[1] *Op. cit.* Cmnd. 2188 and 2206.
[2] *Economic Development in Northern Ireland*, Cmnd. 479, HMSO Belfast 1965.

servative Government, both at the regional and at the national level, as not being 'proper planning'. Notably this criticism was made of the White Papers referred to above. Presumably this was because they did not contain a blue-print of all aspects of the economy's development and appeared in a rather piecemeal fashion. It is fair to say that some sections of the party credited planning with remarkable ability to solve the regional problem. Yet they seldom appeared to have a precise idea of what it would involve. Their support for it was perhaps as irrational as some Conservatives' aversion to it.

However, within a few weeks of assuming office, the Minister for Economic Affairs made a start with devising a framework of regional planning. England was divided into eight planning regions which, with the addition of Scotland, Wales and Northern Ireland, makes a total of eleven. Regional Planning Councils were set up, supported in each case by a Planning Board of Civil Servants (see map on p. 229). Only one region, Scotland, may be said to have an economic plan so far, and it, like the National Plan, has no longer much application in any operational sense, but studies have been prepared for each of the other planning regions. These documents are largely in the form of surveys or draft strategies for development. The English Regional Planning Councils have no executive power, and their function must therefore be regarded as advisory. This means that their reports may be less inhibited than if they had the power to implement them; but it also implies that there is no commitment to carry out their recommendations. They therefore have much the same status as the reports of any government advisory committee.

The role of regional planning is obviously still largely experimental, and it would be surprising if it did not undergo drastic change in the next few years. A proper integrated system of regional plans all dovetailing with the National Plan is, as Chapter XI argues, impossible in the present absence of statistics and appropriate expertise. Regional planning up to 1967 must be regarded as the start of something which is potentially of the first importance, but it cannot be claimed that it has yet had any major impact on the regional problem.

VI. THE POLICIES IN PRACTICE

There is no doubt that increasing priority was given to regional policy in the 1960s and that by 1967 a wider and more effective range of measures existed than at any time in the past. In 1960 policy had depended on the scheduling of Developments Districts, discrimination in their favour by IDCs, the offer of a building grant and BOTAC loans and grants. 1963 saw the strengthening of the building grants, the offer of a grant for plant and machinery and accelerated depreciation. In the autumn of the same year the first steps were taken towards regional planning and a growth area policy. Since the Labour Government came to office the Development Districts have been replaced by the new Development Areas, investment grants have replaced previous assistance for investment in plant and machinery, controls over office development have been instituted and over industrial development strengthened, and a system of regional planning has been started. These are substantial developments in policy for a short period of seven years. Quantitatively their importance is shown by the statistics of public expenditure, Board of Trade factory space and the proportions of new development taking place in different parts of the country. Qualitatively it may be seen in the changing approach to the regional problem and the frequent reshuffling of measures to find a more effective combination.

Public expenditure on loans, grants and the provision of factories, which had been small in the 1950s, rose substantially in the 1960s. There was a drop during the 1962–3 recession, but by 1966–7 the annual total was around £55 million (see Table I). This does not include accelerated depreciation. The replacement of this by the new investment grants was expected to cost about £40 million for the higher rate paid in the Development Areas when the 25 per cent payable throughout the country is excluded.[1] In the event, according to figures recently published by the Board of Trade, the investment grants in Development Areas cost £142 million in 1967, of which some £65 million may be accounted for by the higher rate.[2] The regional employment premium plus the retention in the Development Areas of the small Selective Employment Tax premium may cost another £125 million in a full year. The present total expenditure is thus very roughly running at an annual rate of £230–£240 million; and, even allowing for the £30 million of this which is in the form either of returnable loans or Board of Trade factories built for sale or to rent, it is still a substantial sum and a large increase on anything spent previously on

[1] *The Development Areas: A Proposal for a Regional Employment Premium*, Department of Economic Affairs, HMSO 1967, p. 9.
[2] *Board of Trade Journal*, March 1968, pp. 691–4.

TABLE

ASSISTANCE OFFERED TO DEVELOPMENT DISTRICTS

Expenditure in £000

	Year ending March 1960/61	1961/62	1962/63	1963/64	1964/65	1965/66	1966/67	Total 1/4/1960–31/4/1967
I. Loans	23,491	16,361	4,589	18,959	10,429	9,569	13,248	82,772
Special Grants	2,734	1,171	1,753	742	632	450	444	6,715
Building Grant	3,306	1,056	4,365	2,991	10,027	13,823	21,117	36,137
Plant and Machinery	—	—	—	1,961	6,790	6,075	6,257	20,192
II. Total Grants	6,040	2,227	6,118	5,694	17,449	20,348	27,818	83,044
III. Factory Building for rent and sale	21,010	5,450	5,367	5,558	12,730	12,338	14,365	64,839
(No. of factories)	74	50	53	85	130	114	120	—
IV. Total Expenditure	50,541	24,038	16,074	30,211	40,608	42,255	55,431	230,635
Grants as % of Total	12	9.5	38	19	43	47	50	—
Estimated Employment Created	57,400	27,600	27,100	41,800	60,243	92,491	86,183	370,756

Source: Annual Reports of the Board of Trade on the Local Employment Acts.

145

regional policy. A word of caution, however, must be given on the interpretation of these figures. Owing largely to the operation of the tax system, much of what is spent returns to the Government and the true value of the incentives is not nearly as high as it at first appears to be. These questions are discussed in Chapter VIII.

Board of Trade factory space also showed an increase. Whereas between 1955 and 1960 the Board had increased its factory space by 4 million square feet for an employment of 15,000 workers, between 1960 and 1967 its factory space rose by 10 million square feet, employment by 43,000 and tenant firms by ninety-one.

The effect of the policies may be seen in the proportion of industrial development going to the problem areas (see Table II). In absolute terms the figure for Development Districts is, of course, affected by the changing coverage of the Districts. And whereas in 1962 these covered only 7.2 per cent of the national population, the 1966 Development Areas covered 20 per cent. But it is much more significant that, as shown by the statistics of IDCs granted, the proportion of the nation's new employment going to these areas substantially exceeded the ratio of their population to the national total. Throughout the whole history of British regional policy, the immediate post-war years were the only other period in which this situation applied. Of course, this does not of itself mean that the regional problem was being overcome or that disparities in income levels or unemployment were diminished; for undoubtedly the problem regions were also suffering an above average fall in employment from their declining industries. But it does indicate that the measures were producing a greater effect than in the past.

As regards the type of measures in operation the period saw an increasing awareness of the economic as opposed to the social aspects of regional development. This was particularly stressed in the Toothill Report, by NEDC and in the National Plan as well as by other authors.[1] The Development District system introduced by the 1960 Act exemplified the extreme of a policy based purely on the social criterion of unemployment. Previous measures had never gone so far as this, and, as other chapters have shown, there were occasional indications both in the Barlow Report and in post-war legislation that the need for a growth area approach had been recognized. As a result of criticisms and of the increasing

[1] Report of the Committee of Inquiry into the Scottish Economy, *op. cit.*, NEDC, *Conditions Favourable to Faster Growth*, Chap. 14, HMSO 1963; *The National Plan*, pp. 84–97, HMSO 1965.

TABLE II

REGIONAL PROPORTION OF INDUSTRIAL BUILDING*

	Employees in Manuf. as % of GB 1966	Area as % of GB							Estimated Additional Employment as % of GB						
		1960–1961	1961–1962	1962–1963	1963–1964	1964–1965	1965–1966	1966–1967	1960–1961	1961–1962	1962–1963	1963–1964	1964–1965	1965–1966	1966–1967†
South-East ⎱ East Anglia ⎰	27.0	23.5	27.4	26.0	18.9	18.6	21.1	22.4	10.0	12.9	9.0	8.1	5.5	16.1	15.9
Yorks, Humberside ⎱ East-Midland ⎰ West-Midland	23.7	19.3	18.0	16.7	16.8	17.2	24.8	24.8	22.7	23.7	29.3	19.9	18.3	9.1	12.6
South-West	4.6	7.0	4.8	5.9	6.4	7.0	5.3	5.7	9.1	5.4	6.9	4.9	6.8	4.4	5.5
North-West	15.5	14.3	10.9	12.4	13.8	14.1	16.0	12.4	14.7	9.6	8.9	14.9	15.6	22.2	12.8
Northern	5.2	5.0	13.1	7.8	12.9	11.9	9.0	10.9	5.9	16.8	10.5	19.7	22.1	15.7	15.8
Wales	3.6	6.1	4.7	6.3	3.5	5.6	7.7	11.3	9.0	7.3	7.9	4.0	6.5	7.6	15.6
Scotland	8.5	9.3	6.8	11.6	12.8	11.6	16.1	12.5	13.7	9.7	12.9	16.7	13.0	20.2	16.1
In Development Districts/Area	—	—	13.3	16.7	30.1	27.5	31.6	36.0	30.0	24.5	20.7	43.4	41.3	52.5	51.0
Populations of Development Districts/Areas as % of UK total	—	—	—	—	—	—	—	—	12.5	7.2	12.5	14.8	15.0	16.8	21.0

* Year ending March 31st.
† In 1966–7 industrial building was extended to include space for storage, canteens, etc., making the figures not exactly comparable with earlier years.
Source: Annual Reports of the Board of Trade on the Local Employment Acts.

emphasis on economic growth, the Development District system was modified, first in 1963 by the introduction of growth areas, and then in 1966 by the replacement of the whole system by broad Development Areas. But there still seems to be some uncertainty about the objectives: the new Development Areas are not necessarily incompatible with a policy of concentration and building up centres of growth, but the precise aim of policy in this respect is not clear. The case for concentration and the part that growth areas might play needs further consideration.

The role of regional planning also needs clarification. The period has seen the gradual acceptance of regional planning as an instrument of policy and the first steps in its adoption. But it has had little impact so far on the problem and its role is not yet clear.

Since 1960 the inducements offered to attract firms to the problem areas have also been greatly increased. The alterations have been so frequent as to be bewildering and have not always made as much difference in the scale of what was offered as appeared at first sight. The increasing proportion of development going to the Development Areas may be largely a consequence of these inducements. But little has been done to evaluate the merits of different types of inducement or to elucidate the principles according to which they should be developed.

There are, therefore, a number of topics which require further investigation if the effectiveness of regional policy is to be improved. These are the subjects of Part III of this book. First, however, it is necessary to have a close look at the progress of the regional problem as measured by various indicators of regional disparities to see what achievements may be claimed for policy.

CHAPTER VI

CHANGES IN REGIONAL DISPARITIES

Regional policy has now been in operation in Britain for over thirty years; yet regional differences still remain and the problem regions are approximately the same ones as in 1934. Some might think this is a clear indication of failure. But the success or failure of a policy can only be measured against what would have happened without it; and it is plain that, in such a case, the regional imbalance of the British economy would be substantially worse than it is today.

In comparing the present situation with pre-war, one must distinguish between the effects of the regional measures and of the change in the aggregate level of economic activity in the economy as a whole. It is clear that the latter has immense regional implications in two quite separate ways. First, some industries are by nature more sensitive to swings in the trade cycle and there is evidence, as Thirlwall has shown, that these have an above-average concentration in the problem regions.[1] Secondly, in times of boom there is a greater volume of industrial expansion and consequently a greater amount of potentially mobile development which can be steered by regional policy measures. Moreover, it is in times of boom also, when labour shortage in the prosperous regions becomes acute, that firms start to consider locations in other regions as a means of getting the labour they require. Indeed, availability of labour has been shown to be the most important factor in influencing the movement of firms to the problem regions.[2] Thus the pursuit of a high level of economic activity in the economy as a whole is crucial to the success of a regional policy.

[1] A. P. Thirlwall, 'Regional Unemployment as a Cyclical Phenomenon', *Scottish Journal of Political Economy*, June 1966, p. 205 ff.
[2] G. C. Cameron and B. D. Clark, 'Industrial Movement and the Regional Problem', *University of Glasgow Social and Economic Studies*, Occasional Paper No. 5, Oliver & Boyd 1966.

To a large degree this explains the difference in the pre-war and post-war situations of the problem regions, though, of course, the destruction brought about by the War and the consequent boom in the traditional industries is also an important factor. At the same time, regional policy has itself had considerable effect, especially during the two periods immediately post-war and during the 1960s, when it was applied with some determination. In the years 1945–7 over half of the new industrial building was set up in the Development Areas, although they held only 19 per cent of the country's population; and in the 1960s the proportion of new development started in the Development Districts and Development Areas was in many years well above the population ratio, as measured by employment created, rising from 30 per cent in 1960 to 51 per cent in 1967 (see Table II in the last chapter).

How much was this due to policy? The fact that the periods of most rapid relative expansion in the problem areas were also periods when policy measures were most rigorously applied gives some *prima facie* evidence that they were effective. But it would be a mistake to imagine that all development in the problem regions is the result of regional policy and that without these measures new developments would all be concentrated in other areas. One survey shows that around two-thirds of the growth in employment in Development Districts was accounted for by indigent firms, who may perhaps have been encouraged by the offer of grants or tax allowances, but would be unlikely to transfer in any event to another region.[1] Of the companies which moved into Development Districts, the same survey shows that between 10 and 20 per cent of the employment created was by firms which would have chosen to move into a Development District location in any case.[2]

Other examples may be given: the largest proportion of American firms setting up in this country have chosen to locate in Scotland; and the successful industrial expansion of electronics and other industries in the East of Scotland, even though for most of the time it was not an assisted area, shows that perfectly healthy expansion can take place in the region even without assistance. During the period of the Cameron and Clark survey, it seems that the development which was steered to the problem areas by the legislation and would not have come otherwise amounted to rather less than a third of the development taking place in these areas.

[1] G. C. Cameron and B. D. Clark, *op. cit.*
[2] *Ibid.*

But even this may be an over-estimate, since in the absence of policy the shortage of labour and other resources which would have resulted in the congested regions might well have forced firms to consider locations elsewhere. Nevertheless, if all the development taking place in the problem regions was not a direct consequence of policy, policy still did account for a significant proportion; without this, the state of the regions would have been much worse than it was.

It would be a mistake, too, to imagine that the problem of the Development Areas was one of stagnation in the sense that a paltry amount of development was taking place. It is true, as will be seen later, that the growth of employment was disappointing and that Scotland's gross domestic product in particular grew very little in the second part of the 1950s. But these are overall figures made up of both expanding and contracting industries. Generally speaking, the problem areas have a higher concentration of declining industries than the nation as a whole, and this masks much of the expansion which is taking place in other sectors. To achieve the same overall growth rate as the rest of the country, therefore, the problem regions would have to achieve a rate of growth in the expanding sectors which is above the national average. This implies that they must also achieve a more rapid rate of structural change in their economies, and there is some evidence that this has actually been the case (see Chapter VII). It is noteworthy that the rate of growth of labour productivity has been more rapid in Northern Ireland, Wales and Scotland than it has been in the United Kingdom as a whole, at any rate throughout much of the period. This seems to be associated with a movement of the labour force from low productivity declining industries to capital intensive growth industries at a faster rate than in the national economy. Thus, though the growth rate may not be adequate overall for the problem regions, the problem is not so much occasioned by stagnation as by the need for an above-average rate of structural change.

THE PERFORMANCE OF THE REGIONS TO 1966

Bearing these difficulties in mind, one may attempt to measure the achievements of regional policy by means of the normal yardsticks of unemployment, disparities in income levels and rates of economic growth. Regional statistics are still far from adequate and it is therefore impossible to do as detailed an assessment as one

151

would wish, but it is possible to see whether regional disparities have increased or diminished.

(a) *Unemployment*

Unemployment is the traditional yardstick for measuring the severity of the regional problem. It was the existence of unemployment which brought British regional policy into being; and, as has been seen, throughout much of the time, problem areas have been defined by means of an unemployment criterion. The details of regional unemployment are given in Tables I and II. It is rather difficult to find an adequate means of comparing unemployment in problem areas over a series of years with that in the rest of the country. This is because the problem areas were themselves redefined on several occasions, and particularly under the 1960 Act were subject to continuous modification. Table I shows unemployment for each of the six regions which have contained scheduled Development Areas or Districts in selected years during the postwar period. It is clear that unemployment in Northern Ireland was much more severe than in any other region, but it reached its height in 1958 and since then the percentage seems to be falling. Of the other regions, Scotland, Wales and the Northern Region suffered much higher rates than the rest of the country, the average rate for these three regions varying between 160 and 180 per cent of the national rate from 1955 to 1966. In the case of Scotland and Wales, it was hard to discern any trend either for better or worse, the disparity in unemployment rates between these two regions and the country as a whole remaining much the same throughout the period. The Northern Region, however, does appear to have suffered from a worsening situation. Indeed, unemployment in the Northern Region was virtually down to the national level in the early 1950s but deteriorated again sharply after 1958.

These figures for planning regions do not give an entirely satisfactory comparison between problem areas and the rest of the country in that problem areas do not exactly correspond with regions. In particular, both the North-West and the South-West contain scheduled problem areas, although in each case the greater part of the region has never been scheduled. There is little point in trying to draw conclusions from the unemployment rates of Development Districts, since these were constantly altering in coverage throughout the period and the comparison is thereby invalidated. Indeed, since the scheduling of Districts was based on the unemployment criterion, an improvement or a worsening in the situation resulted in Districts being added to or taken off the schedule. The progress achieved by regional policy is, therefore, more likely to be shown by the coverage of the Districts than their unemployment rates. As was seen in the last chapter, the extent of the Development Districts varied immensely during the period.[1] After the fairly substantial amount of development which was induced to go to the problem areas in 1960, the Board of Trade descheduled a number of areas including Merseyside, Plymouth, Bathgate, Llanelly. The coverage of Development Districts by 1962 had therefore fallen from 12.5 per cent in 1960 to 7.2 per cent of the population. Then, when this proved over-hasty and the economy went into the 1963 recession, most of these areas were added to the list again so that by 1966 16.8 per cent of the population was covered. It may be wrong to regard this increase as evidence of a deterioration in the situation, because the Board of Trade was no doubt sensitive to the criticism of its earlier over-hasty delisting and may, therefore, have tended to be more generous in interpreting the criteria for scheduling areas. After all, unemployment rates in the Development Districts fell during 1965 and 1966 (see Table II). Nonetheless, it certainly cannot be claimed from these figures that policy measures were having any success in narrowing the gap between the problem areas and the rest of the country.

It is also possible to get figures for the new Development Areas, as defined in the 1966 White Paper, covering the ten years back to 1956.[2] These show (Table II) that the situation has tended to be worse in the 1960s, and indeed from 1958 on, than it was earlier. This is no doubt largely because the rapid decline in the traditional industries did not really get underway until 1958. The worst periods were the recessions of. 1958–9, 1962–3 and 1967. This illustrates that one reason for greater severity in the regional problem since 1958 is simply that since that time deflationary measures have had to be imposed more frequently and ruthlessly to correct chronic balance of payments deficits and this has seriously aggravated the regional problem. It is interesting to note, however, that whereas the Development Areas had their highest unemployment rate in 1963, the country as a whole has had a higher unemployment rate in 1967. This suggests a modest measure of success for regional policy, in that by 1967 the measures were

[1] See p. 146 above.
[2] Development Areas as defined in *Investment Incentives*, Cmnd. 2847, January 1966.

TABLE 1

UNEMPLOYMENT RATES IN THE PROBLEM REGIONS
(as a percentage of insured employees)
Annual Average Rates

	1949	1955	1958	1960	1962	1963	1964	1965	1966	1967
United Kingdom	1.5	1.1	2.1	1.6	2.1	2.6	1.8	1.5	1.6	2.5
South-West	1.4	1.2	2.2	1.7	1.8	2.1	1.6	1.6	1.8	2.5
North-West	1.7	1.4	2.7	1.9	2.6	3.1	2.1	1.6	1.5	2.5
Northern	2.6	1.8	2.4	2.8	3.8	5.0	3.4	2.6	2.6	4.0
Wales	4.0	1.8	3.8	2.7	3.8	3.7	2.6	2.6	2.9	4.1
Scotland	3.0	2.4	3.7	3.6	3.8	4.8	3.7	3.0	2.9	3.9
Northern Ireland	—	6.8	9.3	6.7	7.5	7.9	6.6	6.1	6.1	7.7

Source: Abstract of Regional Statistics.

TABLE II

UNEMPLOYMENT IN THE DEVELOPMENT AREAS 1956-67
at Mid-June

	1956	1958	1959	1960	1961	1962	1963	1964	1965	1966	1967
Scottish	2.2	3.7	4.1	3.4	2.9	3.5	4.6	3.5	2.7	2.6	3.8
Welsh	2.2	4.1	3.8	2.5	2.4	3.0	3.4	2.4	2.5	2.6	4.1
Northern	1.4	2.2	3.0	2.5	2.0	3.2	4.3	2.9	2.1	2.0	3.6
Merseyside	2.0	3.6	4.2	3.1	2.7	3.9	4.9	3.4	2.4	2.0	3.1
South-West	1.8	2.8	2.5	2.8	1.8	2.2	3.1	2.4	2.6	2.3	3.4
All Development Areas	1.9	3.3	3.7	3.0	2.5	3.4	4.3	3.1	2.5	2.3	3.6
Development Districts (annual average)	—	—	—	—	3.9	3.7	5.0	5.1	3.8	3.0	—

Source: Ministry of Labour Gazette and Annual Reports of the Board of Trade on the Local Employment Acts.

sufficiently developed to shelter the problem areas from the defla- ⟍ flationary measures more effectively than was possible in 1963.

Unemployment is, however, only one aspect of the labour surplus in the problem regions. Another possible measure is the activity rates. As was shown in the introduction to this book, for most of the problem regions activity rates have been markedly below the national level.[1] But while activity rates are all important indicators of the nature of the regional problem, no very significant trends could be deduced from them. Activity rates in the Northern and North-West regions were found to be slightly lower in 1966 than in 1961. In the United Kingdom as a whole and the other problem regions they were fractionally higher. However, the male activity rate was lower in 1966 than in 1961 in the UK and all the problem regions except Northern Ireland; the female rate was higher in all regions except the North-West.[2]

(b) *Migration*

Unemployment and activity rates are, however, only one aspect of this problem. So long as employment opportunities exist in some part of the country migration will tend to prevent regional unemployment from rising to intolerable levels. Table III shows that Northern Ireland, Scotland, Wales, the Northern Region, the North-West and Yorkshire and Humberside have all suffered a loss in net migration during the period 1951 to 1966, but for some of these the loss was small. For most regions the loss in the last five years 1961–6 was much less than in the preceding two periods and Wales changed from a net loss to a net gain. The exception was Scotland, whose annual loss in net migration rose from about 25,000 in the mid-'fifties to 47,000 in 1965. At this latter figure it exceeded the rate of natural increase and for the first time' since pre-war the Scottish population fell in numbers in 1964 and 1965. Over the five years 1961–6 the emigration exactly equalled the natural increase of the Scottish population. After Scotland, Northern Ireland suffered the heaviest rates of emigration. But Northern Ireland has an exceptionally high rate of natural increase and this exceeded the emigration by a comfortable margin.

The experience of the regions receiving population inflow is also interesting. The South-West had a small net immigration, 0.4 per cent of the population, in the five years 1951–6. This rose to 2.8 per cent in 1956–61 and 3.1 per cent in 1961–6. This gives the

[1] See p. 20 above.

[2] Detailed figures may be found in the *Abstract of Regional Statistics*.

TABLE III

GAIN AND LOSS FROM MIGRATION

Actual Change in 000s and rates expressed as % of total regional population

	1951–6				1956–61				1961–6			
	Net Migration		Natural Increase	Total Change	Net Migration		Natural Increase	Total Change	Net Migration		Natural Increase	Total Change
	Actual Change	%	%	%	Actual Change	%	%	%	Actual Change	%	%	%
South-East	+111	0.7	1.9	2.7	+360	2.2	2.5	5.3	+167	0.9	3.1	4.1
East-Midlands	+ 12	0.4	2.5	3.1	+ 35	1.2	3.0	4.7	+ 44	1.3	3.8	5.1
West-Midlands	− 3	—	2.8	2.9	+ 54	1.2	3.4	5.2	+ 55	1.1	4.4	5.5
Yorkshire and Humberside	− 47	−1.0	1.9	1.0	− 56	−1.3	2.4	1.7	− 3	−0.1	3.1	3.0
South-West	+ 12	0.4	1.4	1.9	+ 91	2.8	1.8	5.8	+108	3.1	2.4	5.2
North-West	− 60	−0.9	1.6	0.8	− 60	−0.9	2.1	1.7	− 13	−0.2	3.0	2.9
Northern Region	− 47	−1.5	2.9	1.5	− 30	−0.9	3.3	2.9	− 37	−1.1	3.3	2.1
Wales	− 25	−1.0	1.5	0.7	− 22	−0.8	1.7	1.5	+ 5	0.2	2.4	2.7
Scotland	−140	−2.8	3.0	0.4	−142	−2.8	3.6	1.4	−194	−3.8	3.8	0.0
					1951–61							
Northern Ireland	—	—	—	—	− 93	−6.8	10.7	3.7	− 38	−2.7	6.9	4.2

Source: Annual Abstract of Statistics.
Abstract of Regional Statistics.
Digest of Scottish Statistics.

156

South-West by far the highest rate of population inflow in the last five years and a high rate of population growth. The two Midland regions have received a steady inflow during the last ten years, and though this is a lower percentage rate than for the South-West, in absolute terms it is large. Both regions have a high rate of population growth.

Most significant, however, is the change in the experience of the South-East. As the Table shows, this region had heavy net immigration in the five years 1956–61, very heavy in absolute terms. In the last five years, however, it has been greatly reduced. Indeed, taking the years of the 1960s, individually, it can be seen that the inflow of population to the South-East has been eliminated. From a net inflow of 101,000 in 1961–2 the figure was reduced to 32,000 in 1963–4 and a net loss of 1,000 in 1965–6.[1] Moreover, throughout the 1960s there was a net loss to other regions of England and Wales; the inflow came from abroad or from Scotland and Ireland. Obviously the drop in population inflow to the South-East is in considerable measure due to the restrictions imposed on immigration from the Commonwealth. But that there was a net outflow from the region to the other regions of England and Wales is striking evidence of the effects of regional policy.

(c) *Regional Economic Growth*
Unemployment and migration are, of course, only symptoms of an inadequate rate of regional economic growth. They merely indicate that economic growth was inadequate to utilize the labour resources available in the region. It is therefore important to measure regional rates of economic growth to find out in what respects the regions lagged. The statistics available for this purpose are, unfortunately, highly inadequate. The standard national accounting aggregates are not available for regions and one has to be content with estimates of gross domestic product for Scotland, Wales and Northern Ireland covering part of the period. Indices of industrial production are also available for these three regions, but for the rest one has to make do with Inland Revenue data on personal incomes and the growth of employees in employment.

Starting with gross domestic product, the figures show that Wales has enjoyed a faster rate of economic growth than the United Kingdom in the period up to 1954 and for the remainder

[1] First Report of the South-East Economic Planning Council, *A Strategy for the South-East*, HMSO 1967, pp. 72 and 86.

157

REGIONAL POLICY IN BRITAIN

of the period she has kept pace with the British figures. Scotland, on the other hand, more or less managed to keep pace with the United Kingdom up to 1954, but in the latter part of the 1950s her growth fell to only half the British figure. As a consequence, GDP per head which had been 92 per cent of the British figure in 1957 fell to 88 per cent by 1960. Northern Ireland fared rather better and managed to outstrip the United Kingdom in certain parts of the period.

A substantial part of the disparity between GDP per head in the problem regions compared with the United Kingdom as a whole is, of course, explained by the lower proportion of the population in employment, both through higher unemployment and lower participation rates. In Scotland's case, for example, it has been estimated that this factor accounts for about half the difference between Scottish and United Kingdom GDP per head. Thus, Scotland's GDP per head of total population in 1960 was 88 per cent of the United Kingdom average while GDP per person in employment was 94 per cent of the United Kingdom level.[1] For Wales the contrast was even more remarkable, GDP per head of total population in 1964 being 91 per cent of the United Kingdom level while GDP per person employed was 106 per cent.

The index of industrial production covered only some 50 per cent of the economic activity making up GDP. The figures show the same trend (Table V) but since an official series is regularly published for Scotland it is possible to bring the comparison forward into the 1960s. It will be seen that Scotland did much better in the 1960s than she had done in the last part of the 1950s. Not only did her growth of industrial production keep pace with the United Kingdom but at times was slightly higher. By this time some of the declining industries had acquired more stability and big new projects, such as the motor industry plants, were beginning to get under way. The contrast between the 1960s and the second half of the 1950s in Scotland does seem to offer evidence of the effects of the new regional policy after 1960. Nevertheless, while the faster growth of the Scottish economy in the 1960s was certainly an achievement, it was probably still inadequate to narrow the disparity, which had widened in the 'fifties, between Scotland's GDP per head and that of the United Kingdom.

[1] G. McCrone, *Scotland's Economic Progress 1951–60*, George Allen & Unwin, 1965, p. 32. E. T. Nevin *et al.*, *The Structure of the Welsh Economy*, University of Wales Press 1965.

TABLE IV

GROSS DOMESTIC PRODUCT BY REGIONS

| | GROWTH Index: 1954=100 | | | | GDP per HEAD UK=100 | | |
	N. Ireland	Scotland	Wales	UK	N. Ireland	Scotland	Wales
1948	—	—	81	85	—	—	81
1951	95	93	87	93	65	92	84
1954	100	100	100	100	62	91	91
1958	110	105	105	107	61	90	90
1960	122	110	115	118	63	88	90
1962	129	—	119	121	63	—	88
1964	144	—	134	133	65	—	91

Sources: National Income and Expenditure, IIMSO.
Economic Development in Northern Ireland.
E. T. Nevin, et al., The Structure of the Welsh Economy, University of
Wales Press 1966.
Gavin McCrone, Scotland's Economic Progress 1951-60, George Allen
& Unwin 1965.

TABLE V

GROWTH OF INDUSTRIAL PRODUCTION BY REGIONS

1960=100

	N. Ireland	Scotland	Wales	UK
1958	86	92	89	89
1959	93	94	90	93
1960	100	100	100	100
1961	103	103	98	101
1962	107	103	103	102
1963	112	106	111	105
1964	124	114	118	113
1965	133	118	—	117
1966	136	121	—	118

Sources: Annual Abstract of Statistics.
Digest of Scottish Statistics.
Digest of Northern Ireland Statistics.
E. T. Nevin, et al., op. cit.

(d) Growth of Labour Productivity

The impact of growth upon employment depends, of course, on
the degree of capital or labour intensity of the development taking
place. It is, therefore, interesting to set alongside the growth
figures some data on the growth of employment. The contrast is
at once apparent; the problem regions had much slower rates of
employment growth than the country as a whole. Indeed, in the
1963 recession employment in Scotland, the Northern Region and

159

the North-West was actually below the 1956 level and in 1966 it was only marginally above.[1] That the growth of employment in the problem regions should lag further behind the United Kingdom average than the rate of growth of output, implies that the growth of productivity in the problem regions must have been more rapid than in the country as a whole. This is an important, if surprising, conclusion. But it is clearly supported by the evidence. Wales had a faster rate of growth of labour productivity than the United Kingdom throughout the 1950s and 1960s. So did Northern Ireland, and this despite a level of gross investment which, as a proportion of manufacturing output, was only 9.9 per cent compared with the United Kingdom's 10.9 in the period 1951–60.[2] Scotland did slightly less well in that her growth of productivity was roughly equal to the United Kingdom rate in the period 1951 to 1960. But this was achieved despite a slower growth of output as a whole and a level of gross investment in manufacturing industry during those years which was only 10 per cent of net output compared with the United Kingdom's rate of 10.9 per cent. During the 1960s, on the other hand, when Scotland's growth of industrial output was keeping pace with the United Kingdom's, her annual growth of productivity in the industrial sector was well above the British rate, 3.6 compared with 3.1 per cent.[3]

It is in many ways ironic to find that, during a period when the United Kingdom as a whole was suffering from labour shortage so that the growth of output had very largely to come from productivity increases, the regions with surplus labour resources actually achieved faster productivity growth. Had the United Kingdom achieved the rate of growth of productivity which Wales and Northern Ireland achieved, its rate of growth of output could have been substantially better than it was. Conversely, had the problem regions experienced productivity growth at only the United Kingdom rate, but retained their own rate of growth output, they would have been able to absorb a larger part of their unused labour resources.

---

[1] The actual figures were Scotland 2,122 thousand in 1956 and 2,091 thousand in 1963, the Northern Region 1,267 thousand and 1,257 thousand and the North-West 2,956 thousand and 2,930 thousand respectively.

[2] Gavin McCrone, *Scotland's Economic Progress 1951–60*, George Allen & Unwin, 1965, p. 109.

[3] See *The Scottish Economy 1965–70*, Cmnd. 2864, p. 8. No figures are available for gross domestic product in Scotland during the 1960s. The industrial sector comprises those industries covered in the Census of Production: mining and quarrying, manufacturing, construction, gas, electricity and water.

TABLE VI

GROWTH IN EMPLOYMENT
1958=100

	Scotland	Wales	Northern Ireland	Northern England	North-West	United Kingdom
1950	99.2	96.0	102.8	95.2	98.3	95.1
1954	100.8	97.8	103.2	96.9	100.2	98.1
1956	102.3	102.0	—	99.5	101.2	100.3
1958	100.0	100.0	100.0	100.0	100.0	100.0
1960	100.6	101.6	106.3	97.7	100.5	103.0
1962	101.9	102.6	106.2	100.1	101.1	105.4
1964	101.8	105.8	109.0	100.3	102.0	107.0
1966	102.8	106.6	113.3	102.8	102.7	109.0
Growth 1950–66 %	3.6	11.1	10.2	8.0	4.5	14.8

Sources: Annual Abstract of Statistics.
Digest of Scottish Statistics.
Digest of Northern Ireland Statistics.
Digest of Welsh Statistics.
The North West, HMSO 1965.
The Challenge of the Changing North, HMSO 1966.

But this apparently paradoxical situation is perhaps less surprising when the reasons for it are examined. The problem regions are typified by declining employment in labour-intensive industries, coal-mining, ship-building, cotton and linen textiles, agriculture. Yet the new growth more often than not comes from capital-intensive industries, simply because these are the growth industries of the twentieth century: strip steel mills, petrol refineries and associated products in Wales and Scotland, synthetic textiles in Wales, electronics in Scotland, motor-cars, etc. To take two extremes, the output per head in the declining Northern Ireland textile industry (mostly linen) was £491 in 1958. In the expanding Welsh synthetic textile industry it was £1,519 in the same year.[1] Increased productivity per man employed can result from the collapse of low and the expansion of high productivity sectors as well as from productivity increases right across the range of industry. In fact, the high rates of productivity growth in the problem regions are probably only an indication that their industrial structures were having to undergo more drastic and more rapid change than that of the country as a whole. The lesson for regional policy

[1] McCrone, op. cit., p. 56.

161

is that the rate of growth of output in the problem regions has to be above the national level if they are to attain the national rate of employment growth. If they are to go further and absorb their under-utilized labour resources then their rates of growth of output must be even higher still.

TABLE VII

GROWTH IN LABOUR PRODUCTIVITY*

1954=100

	Scotland	Wales	Northern Ireland	United Kingdom
1951	94.3	88.7	96.2	94.5
1954	100.0	100.0	100.0	100.0
1958	108.0	105.1	114.0	105.4
1960	113.1	112.7	121.0	113.6
1962	—	115.7	129.2	115.4
1964	—	127.4	141.0	124.9
Growth 1951–64	—	43.6	46.6	32.2

* Gross domestic product per head of occupied population excluding unemployed.

(e) *Growth of Incomes*
Another measure of regional disparity may be obtained from the Inland Revenue figures for personal income. These provide some guidance to the relative well-being of the population in different regions but they differ from the growth of output, as measured by GDP, in several important respects. First they do not measure income or output generated within a particular region, but rather income received by the inhabitants of a region from whatever source. Though income from employment is common to both, companies operating in a particular region, say, Scotland, will distribute their profits to shareholders all over the United Kingdom; similarly Scots earning investment income will derive this from United Kingdom companies operating all over the British Isles and abroad. There is therefore no reason why the profits earned by companies in Scotland should match at all closely the investment income received by Scots. In addition, the Inland Revenue personal income figures do not contain estimates of profits retained by companies, public corporations or government and naturally they only embrace those personal incomes which legally had to be declared to the Inland Revenue for tax purposes.

Bearing these qualifications in mind, some interesting results may

162

be obtained from the figures. It will be seen from Table VIII that with the exception of Northern Ireland and the South-West (of which only a small part is a problem area) the problem regions all had higher personal incomes per head in relation to the United Kingdom in 1954–5 than they have had subsequently. Not surprisingly, in view of the growth figures already analysed, Scotland lost ground between 1954–5 and 1959–60 but has since then held its position with perhaps a marginal improvement. A similar pattern emerges for Wales. On the other hand, both the Northern Region and the North-West have lost ground steadily after 1954–5. The North-West's level of income per head is, however, very high and in 1954–5 actually exceeded the United Kingdom average. Only a part of the region is regarded as a problem area, but the high income figure is probably a consequence of the high degree of industrialization in the region and its low dependence on activities such as agriculture.

TABLE VIII

PERSONAL INCOME PER HEAD AS PERCENTAGE OF UK AVERAGE

	1949/50	1954/55	1959/60	1964/65
Northern Region	90	93	87	82
North-West	100	102	98	95
South-West	82	87	88	91
Wales	81	87	84	84
Scotland	90	93	87	88
Northern Ireland	58	63	64	64

GROWTH OF PERSONAL INCOME
1954/55=100

	1949/50	1954/55	1959/60	1964/65
Northern Region	74	100	134	174
North-West	74	100	135	182
South-West	68	100	139	204
Wales	71	100	136	188
Scotland	73	100	134	182
Northern Ireland	69	100	144	204
UK	73	100	139	194

Source: Reports of the Commissioners of Her Majesty's Inland Revenue.

The figures for 1949–50 may be somewhat less reliable than the rest. They correspond less well with other studies than do the remainder of the series and it is possible, therefore, that they may be on the low side for the regions.[1] They seem to show that the gap in income levels between the problem regions and the rest of the country narrowed between 1949–50 and 1954–5 in contrast to the later period when it widened. This could well be right, since, with a prolonged boom in all the traditional industries in the early 1950s, the adverse economic structure of the regions scarcely became apparent until the mid-'fifties; and the forces which tended to drive down their prices and their profits, thus exerting a constraint on the rise in wages, were not yet apparent.

The figures for growth of personal income show the same trends. The performance of the Northern Region is the poorest followed by Scotland and the North-West. Northern Ireland and the South-West have the best performance.

CONCLUSION

Despite the fragmentary nature of the statistics they point to certain common conclusions. By the mid-1950s the regional problem was greatly diminished at least as shown by those disparities capable of measurement. Above-average unemployment in the Northern Region and the North-West was almost eliminated, the figures for Scotland and Wales were low and only Northern Ireland retained a serious unemployment problem. Personal income levels per head had also moved closer to the United Kingdom level, with only three regions more than 7 per cent below the British average. This illustrates a remarkable degree of conformity and, except for Northern Ireland, a much smaller amount of variation in regional income levels than is common for most countries. Economic growth rates had enabled Scotland and Northern Ireland more or less to keep pace with the United Kingdom, and Wales had enjoyed faster growth. Only a rather heavy rate of out-migration and a slower growth of employment indicated that much of a problem remained.

During the later part of the 1950s, however, the situation deteriorated. Wales's rate of growth fell below the United Kingdom level. Scottish growth lagged seriously and so did income

[1] A. D. Campbell, 'Changes in Scottish Incomes 1924–49', *Economic Journal* 1955, gives a Scottish figure of 92.6 of the United Kingdom average for Scottish National Income in 1948. N. Cuthbert in K. S. Isles and N. Cuthbert, *An Economic Survey of Northern Ireland*, HMSO Belfast, 1937, gives a much higher figure for 'Private Civilian Income' in Northern Ireland as a proportion of the United Kingdom level per head.

levels in Scotland, Wales, the Northern Region and the North-West; yet productivity tended to rise faster than in Britain as a whole. Unemployment therefore rose. From the mid-1950s up to 1960, therefore, regional disparities increased and the problem re-emerged. In the third period, 1960–6, income levels in the Northern Region and the North-West fell further behind the United Kingdom and net emigration from Scotland was proceeding at about twice the rate of the 1950s. Employment in the problem regions was still growing more slowly than in the country as a whole. But in many respects the impression of this latter period was that regional disparities remained much the same or in some instances diminished slightly. In terms of economic growth and income levels the regions, with the exceptions of the Northern and North-West, did rather better than the United Kingdom.

To what extent may these trends be accounted for by regional policy? In the early period the improvement compared with pre-war was due to three factors: the high level of domestic demand; the boom in the traditional industries; and the determination with which regional policy had been implemented in the early post-war years. What importance to attach to each it is hard to say; but the importance of the boom in the traditional industries was shown when it came to an end around 1957.

The middle period was one in which regional policy measures were not rigorously applied, the boom in the traditional industries came to an end and throughout much of the time from 1955 to 1958 the economy was under restraint and growth rates rather stagnant. Again these factors jointly were responsible for the re-emergence of the regional problem. The problem regions were, however, distinguished by their failure to pick up properly when the recession in the rest of the country came to an end in 1959.

The interesting feature of the third period was that the decline of the traditional industries continued but regional policy measures were greatly stepped up. As a result the regions did better than in the late 1950s, though not well enough to narrow the gap between them and the rest of the United Kingdom to any substantial extent. This is clearly due to regional policy. Because of it, growth occurred in the problem regions which would only have produced inflationary pressure if allowed to take place elsewhere. As a result, the United Kingdom's gross domestic product reached a higher level than it would otherwise have done. But if regional policy thus demonstrated its effectiveness, the gaps in income and employment still remain to be reduced. Yet as time goes on, the

165

structure of the problem regions is gradually becoming more favourable; the declining industries cannot decline for ever, and new industries are playing a larger part in the regional economies. As this process continues the problem should get easier. But if regional policy has achieved some results, many of the measures are still new and much remains to be learnt about their effectiveness. It is to increase this effectiveness that is the next task.

PART III

AN APPRAISAL OF POLICY
MEASURES

CHAPTER VII

STRUCTURAL VERSUS LOCATIONAL DISADVANTAGE

If one is to consider the ways in which regional policy might be developed so as to become more effective, or even if the aim is simply to evaluate existing measures, the right starting point is to consider the underlying causes of the problem. Obviously above-average unemployment, high net emigration and low incomes could all be mitigated if there was a faster rate of economic growth. To that extent inadequate growth may be thought to be the problem. But why should growth be inadequate? Clearly, there may be a variety of reasons for this, each of which ought to be examined.

There are two alternative hypotheses which may be offered. According to the traditional view, as expressed in a variety of reports from Barlow to Toothill, the prime cause of the problem is that the regions have inherited an unfavourable economic structure, and that there is no reason why other industries should not be established in these regions to provide the necessary growth.[1] Policy has largely been based on this view, and the attempt to take work to the workers, wherever they may be, found its most extreme expression in the 1960 Local Employment Act. Alternatively, it could be suggested that the problem regions, because of some endemic disadvantage such as their peripheral situation as regards the centre of the British economy, do not provide a satisfactory environment for the modern growth industries, that this is why these industries did not establish themselves in these areas in the first place and why it requires so much effort to persuade them to go there now.

If the cause of the problem is mainly structural, one need not

[1] Report of the Royal Commission on the Distribution of Industrial Population, Cmnd. 6153, HMSO 1940.
Report of the Committee of Enquiry into the Scottish Economy, Scottish Council (Development and Industry) 1961.

worry too much about regional policy resulting in loss of efficiency. But if, on the other hand, the problem turns out to be largely due to locational disadvantages, the implications are more serious. It may be that industry's locational disadvantage would be outweighed by the cost to the community of allowing centripetal forces to continue unchecked. But the costs and benefits would need to be assessed, and policy should be directed to minimizing locational disadvantage so far as is possible by such measures as improved infrastructure and concentration on growth areas.

Unfortunately, it is extremely difficult to assess how much importance should be attached to each of these explanations. Regional data of this kind are for the most part poor, and as far as costs are concerned are almost entirely lacking. As a first step, however, some idea of the structural pattern of the regions may be obtained from Tables I and II. These show the contribution of different sectors to gross domestic product and manufacturing net output in 1958 and 1960.[1] It is at once clear that Northern Ireland has a heavy concentration of agriculture, ship-building and textiles, the Welsh economy is greatly dependent on coal and metal manufacture. Scotland has above-average representation of agriculture, forestry and fishing, mining, ship-building and textiles; but, at least according to these figures, her economy shows much more structural resemblance to that of the United Kingdom than any of the other regions.

Since coal, ship-building and textiles are heavily represented in the problem regions, and are either declining or slow-growing industries, the structural argument clearly has some validity. At first sight it might seem relatively straightforward to estimate the significance of this by calculating what aggregate rates of growth the regions would have achieved if their industrial composition had been the same as the United Kingdom's. This might be done by weighting the regional growth for each sector by the national industrial structure instead of their own. Lack of data makes it hard to do this for output, but it may be done for growth of employment.

Several attempts have been made to do this, the most recent being that of Professor Brown.[2] Taking the 1966 Development

---

[1] No official estimates of GDP for regions are published on a yearly basis and at the time of writing the last full census of production to be published was for 1958. It was therefore not possible to give figures for more recent years.

[2] A. J. Brown, The 'Green Paper on the Development Areas', *National Institute Economic Review*, May 1967, pp. 26–9.

Areas, Scotland, Wales, the Northern Region, Merseyside and the South-West, he analysed industrial structure by Order Groups and found substantial differences from the national pattern; primary and extractive industries being more strongly represented in these regions. For example, whereas mining in 1961 accounted for 3.1 per cent of the employees in Great Britain, the comparable figure for Wales was 13 per cent and for the Northern Region 11.7 per cent. Agriculture played a large part in the South-West, while manufacturing employed only 13.7 per cent of total employees compared with a national figure of 35.8 per cent. He estimated the consequences of these structural differences for regional growth by applying the National Plan target growth rates by sectors to the regions and comparing the figures thus aggregated with the national figure. As a result he was able to estimate that: 'By virtue of their structure alone, the growth prospects of these areas are thus shown to be only half those of the country as a whole.'[1]

However, he also showed that over the period 1953–63 individual industry groups performed less well in the Development Areas than elsewhere. The only major exceptions to this were manufacturing industry in Wales and the Northern regions, whose growth of employment over the period 1953–63 was actually faster than the rate for Great Britain. Scotland, on the other hand, suffered a drop in manufacturing employment between 1953–63, whereas if each Order Group had grown at the British rate she would have had an increase. Growth in services and construction fell below the national rate in all regions except for services in the South-West. He therefore suggests: 'It is possible that the generally poorer industry by industry performance of the Development Areas in comparison with the country as a whole reflects general locational disadvantages.'[2]

There are, however, several points on which Professor Brown's analysis can be faulted. In the first place, growth rates by sectors are not independent of each other. The growth or decline of one industrial group such as ship-building affects other groups related to it such as steel and engineering. Above all, the growth of service industries responds in large measure to growth of incomes and the expansion taking place in other sectors. A poor regional rate of growth in services and in construction, therefore, is much more likely to be a consequence of regional depression than of locational disadvantage.

[1] *Ibid.*, p. 26. [2] *Ibid.*, p. 29.

TABLE I

COMPOSITION OF GROSS DOMESTIC PRODUCT

Percentage Distribution 1960

	Scotland	Wales	Northern Ireland	United Kingdom
Agriculture, Forestry & Fishing	5.8	4.8	12.9	4.0
Mining & Quarrying	3.2	8.4	0.3	3.0
Manufacturing	36.1	35.0	33.5	36.1
Construction	6.4	7.9	7.4	6.0
Gas, Electricity & Water	2.5	2.5	2.3	2.7
Transport & Communication	9.2	7.6	3.8	8.6
Distribution	11.2	7.6	12.4	12.1
Insurance, Banking & Finance	2.2	2.8	2.2	2.9
Public Administration & Defence	6.2	5.1	5.4	5.7
Other Services	17.2	18.3	19.8	18.9
	100.0	100.0	100.0	100.0

Note: The Scottish figures are based on the 1948 Standard Industrial Classification. Compared with the other figures this slightly overstates the figure for manufacturing and understates distribution.

Sources: National Income and Expenditure, HMSO.

E. T. Nevin, A. R. Roe and J. I. Round, *The Structure of the Welsh Economy*, University of Wales Press 1966.

Gavin McCrone, *Scotland's Economic Progress 1951–1960*, George Allen & Unwin, 1965.

TABLE II

MANUFACTURING INDUSTRY

Percentage Distribution of Net Output 1958

	Scotland	Wales	Northern Ireland	United Kingdom
Food, Drink & Tobacco	16.8	5.5	24.2	11.7
Chemicals & Allied	7.7	11.7	*	9.4
Metal Manufacture	10.0	39.5		8.8
Engineering & Electrical	21.4	11.3		22.2
Shipbuilding & Marine Engineering	8.0 ⎱	5.3†	34.3	2.9
Vehicles	5.0 ⎰			10.4
Metal Goods	3.5	5.9		5.6
Textiles	9.9	7.7	22.8	7.8
Leather	0.4	0.5	*	0.6
Clothing & Footwear	2.2	1.9	8.4	3.9
Bricks, Pottery & Glass	3.0	3.4	2.6	3.8
Timber & Furniture	2.4	1.4	1.8	2.7
Paper, Printing & Publishing	7.7	2.6	3.3	7.4
Other Manufacturing	2.1	3.3	2.6*	2.9

Using 1958 Standard Industrial Classification.

* Chemicals and Leather included in other manufacturing industry.

† Non-disclosed trades, percentage figure obtained by subtraction from total.

Source: Census of Production, 1958.

172

But secondly, it is simply not adequate to analyse the effects of industrial structure merely on the basis of Order Groups. It is true that this does reveal some interesting differences, but it conceals as much as it reveals. A globel figure for agriculture, forestry and fishing, for instance, will not reveal that while Scotland accounts for about 11 per cent of British agricultural employment it constitutes around 30 per cent of employment in forestry and fishing. In manufacturing the problems are even worse since many different types of industry are grouped in one Order Group. Thus, vehicles, textiles, food, drink and tobacco each comprise one Order Group. Yet, within each of these groups important regional differences exist. Although vehicle production in Scotland in 1958 accounted for 5 per cent of manufacturing output compared with 10 per cent in the United Kingdom, the composition was entirely different. Scottish output was made up primarily of heavy goods vehicles, railway locomotives and aero engines; there was at that time no motor car production, yet this featured very large in United Kingdom output for this Order Group. Similarly, textiles in Wales are almost entirely synthetic; they are highly capital intensive and have a high rate of growth. In Northern Ireland, on the other hand, textiles are dominated by linen, which is labour intensive and declining. Food, drink and tobacco in Scotland includes the whisky industry which has no equivalent in any other region. Indeed, one is forced to conclude that there are probably as many structural differences within Order Groups as between them so far as the regions are concerned. This is particularly true of Scotland, which at the Order Group level has a structure apparently fairly similar to the United Kingdom.

Rather better results can be obtained if the analysis is taken down to the level of minimum-list headings, though even here the breakdown is still far from being sufficiently precise. The Toothill Committee analysed the structure of the Scottish economy on this basis and estimated that between 1950 and 1958, whereas Scottish employment in manufacturing fell by 5.8 per cent, it would have increased by 4.5 per cent if Scotland had had the same industrial structure as the United Kingdom.[1] The actual growth of employment in the United Kingdom during this period was 5.6 per cent, so that the structural factor accounted for by far the greater part of the difference between the United Kingdom's performance and Scotland's. Applying a similar type of analysis to the South-East

[1] Report of the Committee of Enquiry on the Scottish Economy, Scottish Council (Development and Industry) 1961, Appendix 2.

173

of England, Holmans found that structural factors accounted for over two-thirds of that region's above-average growth performance.[1]

The most detailed study, however, is that of Odber, who analysed at minimum list headings the effect of industrial structure on the growth of employment in Scotland, Wales and the Northern Region.[2] His results for the period 1952–61 are set out in Table III. According to these calculations the aggregate growth of employment for the three problem regions would have been considerably faster if they had had the same structural weighting as Great Britain, and the Northern Region's growth of employment would have exceeded the British rate. Taking primary and manufacturing industries only, all these problem regions actually suffered a fall in employment during the period, and this would have turned into a small increase if they had had the same industrial structure as Great Britain.

TABLE III

GROWTH OF EMPLOYMENT BY SECTORS 1952–61

	Scotland	Wales	Northern Region	Great Britain
All sectors:				
Actual Growth	102.1	104.6	105.6	108.6
Hypothetical Growth	103.6	107.6	109.5	—
Primary and Manufacturing only:				
Actual Growth	95.6	95.9	98.7	103.3
Hypothetical Growth	100.3	100.9	104.8	—

Source: A. J. Odber, op. cit., pp. 418–20.

Obviously the results one gets from this type of exercise depend to a considerable extent on the time period in question. What may be a favourable industrial structure at one time may become adverse later. Odber's figures do not cover the period in the 1960s, when regional policy was given greatly increased priority. It seemed worth while, therefore, to repeat the exercise for the period 1959–65 using data supplied by the Ministry of Labour. Growth rates were calculated by minimum list headings for Scot-

[1] A. E. Holmans, 'Restriction of Industrial Expansion in South-East England', Oxford Economic Papers, July 1964, Appendix A, pp. 259–60.
[2] A. J. Odber, 'Regional Policy in Great Britain', published in Area Redevelopment Policies in Britain and the Countries of the Common Market, us Dept. of Commerce and Area Redevelopment Administration 1965, pp. 410–21.

land, Wales and the North of England. Appropriately weighted by the 1965 minimum list composition in Great Britain it was possible to show hypothetical growth rates for Order Groups. These are the aggregate rates the regions would have achieved if their structure within Order Groups had been the same as Great Britain's. Reweighting the Order Groups in turn by the composition for Great Britain, hypothetical growth rates for manufacturing industry as a whole were obtained.

As Table IV shows, these results are remarkable. According to this Table all these regions would have had much faster rates of employment growth than Great Britain if they had enjoyed Britain's structural weighting. In general, this was because the growing sectors grew much faster in these regions between 1959 and 1966 than they did in Britain. This is particularly apparent in engineering and vehicles, but is also seen in chemicals in Scotland, metal goods in Scotland and Northern England, and bricks, pottery and glass in Wales.

One must, of course, interpret these results with caution. The calculations are entirely hypothetical, and in practice it is not possible to imagine that every region could have an industrial structure similar to the United Kingdom, nor that its sectoral growth rates would remain unaltered if it did. Some of the very high regional growth rates for individual sectors simply result from new industries setting up which were previously almost unrepresented in the region. Moreover, the calculations take no account of interdependencies; clearly the hypothetical growth rates calculated for some Order Groups, if they had been achieved in practice, would have greatly stimulated expansion in others. And, if manufacturing employment had expanded on the scale suggested by these figures, it would have stimulated considerable growth in the services sector.

Despite these qualifications, a number of interesting conclusions may be drawn from these calculations. First, in the period 1952–61 covered by Odber, the slow growth of employment in Scotland and Wales was due to a combination of structural disadvantage and a failure on the part of individual industries to grow as fast as in the country as a whole. This latter effect in Wales's case was small and might easily have been eliminated if it had been possible to take an even finer breakdown than minimum list headings. The Northern Region's performance appears to be entirely accounted for by structural factors. In the later period, Wales's actual growth of employment in manufacturing was above the British rate and

175

Scotland and Northern England were only slightly below. The slight lag of these two regions behind the British rate may be entirely accounted for by structural factors, since it is clear that individual industries in all three regions expanded much more rapidly than in Britain as a whole.

The light which this sheds on the operation of policy is interesting. The later period, 1959 to 1966, coincides approximately with the period covered by the Local Employment Act and the much greater emphasis which was given to regional policy. The figures show that this policy had considerable effect and that the industry by industry performance of the regions exceeded that of the United Kingdom where previously, in Scotland and Wales at least, it had lagged behind. Only in ship-building and leather was the performance of all three regions poorer than Britain's. This also provides evidence to support the view advanced earlier in this book that

TABLE IV

GROWTH OF EMPLOYMENT BY SECTORS 1959–65

Manufacturing Industry

| | Actual Growth | | | | Hypothetical Growth* | | |
	North	Scotland	Wales	Great Britain	North	Scotland	Wales
	Employment in 1965 as % of 1959						
Food, Drink & Tobacco	100.6	107.3	102.9	103.5	101.4	102.1	95.0
Chemicals	94.7	97.5	93.0	99.9	94.4	142.2	108.3
Metal Manufacturing	108.4	97.4	114.5	110.2	117.6	104.5	114.7
Engineering & Electrical	124.8	124.7	130.9	118.4	150.1	156.8	150.0
Shipbuilding & Marine Eng.	72.5	73.8	71.9	76.7	73.5	74.7	123.9
Vehicles	71.2	104.4	126.4	101.1	131.2	196.9	157.3
Metal Goods	121.4	103.0	114.9	116.4	120.7	124.3	114.9
Textiles	115.3	97.2	110.7	91.3	109.5	97.7	109.2
Leather	85.2	95.2	105.0	95.9	94.4	90.9	95.9
Clothing	115.2	104.2	126.5	97.2	121.6	93.5	131.9
Bricks, Pottery, etc.	121.6	112.8	123.9	109.5	109.5	115.0	142.0
Timber & Furniture	117.1	100.8	103.2	105.9	125.6	104.1	108.9
Paper, etc.	125.9	109.2	128.4	111.3	126.4	110.1	152.6
Other	125.5	102.9	143.1	119.4	114.8	176.9	142.9
	105.8	104.1	115.7	106.4	123.4	131.7	131.1

* Based on GB weighting by minimum list headings.

Source: Data on employees in employment supplied by the Ministry of Labour.

the economic structure of the regions was undergoing much more rapid change than that of the country as a whole.

But if structural factors are clearly important, it is much more difficult to assess the significance of locational disadvantage. It is unsatisfactory to suggest, as some authors have done, that since structural factors as calculated here do not account for the whole of Scotland's and Wales's lag in growth performance in the earlier period, the rest must be due to locational disadvantage. On this basis in the later period, when their industry by industry performance was better than Britain's, they might be thought to have a locational advantage. Growth in employment is the result partly of existing firms expanding and partly of new firms setting up. A poor growth rate, therefore, cannot be taken as evidence that the existing industry suffers from locational disadvantage in that particular region and that the firms are therefore unable to expand. It may well be that the firms already in the region are doing perfectly well but that there have been few newcomers. Similarly, high rates of growth may be due to a big influx of new firms rather than to any peculiarities in the performance of those already there.

In fact, this seems likely to be the main explanation of differing regional growth rates. The early period, during which Scotland's and Wales's industry by industry performance lagged behind Britain, covers the years in the 'fifties when regional policy was almost in abeyance and little effort was made to encourage firms to set up in the problem regions. By contrast the later period witnessed a much more determined effort to control development in the South-East and Midlands and to encourage it to go to the poorer regions. The figures bear witness to the effects of this policy. It may be thought that the inducements offered have simply been a means of overcoming the locational disadvantage of the problem regions. But, as a later chapter will show, these have not, at least until recently, been on a particularly large scale. They have been intended primarily to help firms with the cost of setting up and until the introduction of the Regional Employment Premium in 1967 offered no permanent subsidy to operating costs such as would be necessary to overcome a permanent locational disadvantage.

Such studies as have been carried out of the locational disadvantages of the problem regions by and large confirm the above conclusions. Luttrell, for example, drew the conclusion that most of British manufacturing industry could in the long run operate

177

equally successfully in any of the main industrial centres in the country, though the initial settling-in costs in a new location might well be high.[1] The Toothill Committee took much the same view, and a survey commissioned by them concluded that transport costs formed a more or less insignificant proportion of the total costs of Scottish firms and were in any event likely to be offset by lower costs for other factors.[2] Hart and MacBean, in a study of growth and profitability, came to the conclusion that there was no significant difference between the performance of Scottish firms and their counterparts elsewhere in the United Kingdom.[3] There was, therefore, no evidence of a locational disadvantage.

Before one concludes, however, that there are no important locational disadvantages in the British problem regions and that the location of economic activity is therefore either entirely random or determined by non-economic factors, it is important to note that in an important respect all the above three studies were biased. They were studying firms which were already in a problem region. A firm which found that a location in Scotland imposed costs of such a nature that it could not compete with its rivals elsewhere would not go to Scotland, or if it did, would fail. In neither case, therefore, would it come within the Toothill or Hart and MacBean samples. All that can safely be deduced from these studies, therefore, is that the type of industry established in Scotland operates perfectly satisfactorily there and has no serious locational disadvantages. It does not follow that any type of industry could be sent there and expect to prosper, or that the location of industry is devoid of economic significance.

A somewhat different picture emerges from a study of firms which after careful consideration rejected a location in one of the problem areas. This is a sample with the opposite bias. Cameron and Reid, who investigated such firms in relation to Scotland over the period 1958–63, found that locational economic disadvantages did play an important part, at any rate in the minds of the businessmen. They state:

'The major defect was clearly associated with Scotland's geographical position in relation to the location of main markets, or

[1] W. F. Luttrell, *Factory Location and Industrial Movement*, NIESR, 2 vols.
[2] Report of the Committee of Enquiry on the Scottish Economy, *op. cit.*, pp. 72–75.
[3] P. E. Hart and A. I. MacBean, 'Regional Differences in Productivity, Profitability and Growth', *Scottish Journal of Political Economy*, Vol. VIII No. 1, Feb. 1961, pp. 1–12.

to a lesser extent the facilities for the transport of goods, the expected quality of labour management relations and the availability of ready-built factories.'[1]

Of course, not all the firms which rejected Scotland as a location did so for geographical reasons; but it was clear that some firms, especially those wishing to establish branch factories, were concerned at the problems which distance would involve. This was not simply a matter of transport costs, though these did feature, especially as regards the transport of final goods to the market. Perhaps equally important were the managerial problems which distance would involve; executives from head office would be less able to watch over the affairs of the branch, and the branch would therefore have to have its own managerial personnel. Contacts with suppliers would be more difficult to maintain, and rush orders harder to get to the market on time.

It is not possible to tell to what extent these objections were the result of careful evaluation of the costs involved in operating at several different locations. Evidence suggests that many businessmen do not carry out a careful and critical evaluation of a variety of different sites. They look for something which seems to meet their requirements, and if on closer examination it does so, that is the end of the matter. Indeed, a study of Midland firms showed that many found greater advantages in their new location than had been anticipated before the move.[2] It could be, therefore, that some of the answers to the Cameron and Reid questionnaire were the expression of prejudice used to fob off the representatives of a disappointed region rather than the results of serious analysis. Nevertheless, it is impossible to dismiss all the replies in this way and one. must, therefore, conclude that locational disadvantage does play a part at any rate for certain types of industry.

What then is one to conclude on the structural versus locational issue? First, it is quite clear that the structural argument does go a long way towards explaining the problem. Regions with the type of industrial structure which the problem regions had must be expected to have an aggregate rate of growth which is lower than the national average. It follows from this that if the regions are

[1] G. C. Cameron and G. L. Reid, Scottish Economic Planning and the Attraction of Industry, University of Glasgow Social and Economic Studies Occasional Paper No. 6, Oliver and Boyd 1966, p. 17.
[2] B. J. Loasby, 'Making Location Policy Work', Lloyds Bank Review, Jan. 1967. See the discussion of this point in Chapter I, p. 31–2.

to achieve the same growth rate in employment as the nation as a whole, the growing sectors have to expand much more rapidly in the regions than in the nation as a whole to counteract the effect of an adverse structure.

But it would be a mistake to conclude from this that there is no such thing as locational disadvantage. Just because firms established in a region do as well as their counterparts elsewhere, it does not follow that any firm, of whatever industry, would do equally well if forced to go there. This may seem fairly obvious. But it is important to modify the view which is fairly widespread in some informed circles, and notably on the left in politics, that locational factors are of little consequence and that it should be the aim of policy to bring work to the workers in pretty well every circumstance, regardless of the location involved and regardless of the industry in question and its particular requirements.

The evidence suggests that while a large range of industry is potentially mobile without loss of efficiency in the long run, at least to the more developed industrial areas in the problem regions, there is another group where locational disadvantages may be serious. This group consists of (a) firms which derive important benefit from being near the centre of the national market; (b) branches of existing firms where the organizational difficulties of being separated by a long distance from the parent plant imposes additional costs, and (c) firms relying on external economies derived from close proximity to related industries and suppliers.

It follows that it must be one of the main aims of regional policy to reduce where possible the locational disadvantages of the problem regions. One cannot move the centre of the national market, at any rate in the short run, but the provision of better and more efficient transport facilities may reduce the handicap of a distant location. If loss of external economies makes it costly to move a firm which is closely linked to other industries and suppliers, then perhaps it would be more economic if an entire industrial complex of inter-related industries could be set up in the new location. If some parts of a region suffer more locational disadvantages than others, perhaps efforts should be concentrated on those parts which have the best chance of success. In both these latter situations the notion of growth poles or growth points may have a contribution to make, and this subject is discussed fully in a later chapter.

CHAPTER VIII

THE CHOICE OF POLICY MEASURES

Some attempt has been made in Chapters VI and VII to show that Britain's regional policy measures have had some effect, particularly since they were applied with greater determination after 1960. But this is the combined result of a package of measures including controls, grants and fiscal inducements of numerous kinds and public investment expenditure. Little is known about their effect individually; indeed, for all one knows, the achievements so far might even be due to one type of measure, in which case the others might be discarded without loss of results. If the effectiveness of policy is to be increased, therefore, it is necessary to evaluate the measures from two angles: first, to consider whether they are the right *type* to achieve the objectives of policy, and second, to see whether they are applied on the right *scale*. The purpose of this chapter is to consider these questions for each of the measures, controls, grants and inducements, and public investment in turn. This can only be done, however, if the general objectives that the various measures are designed to achieve are first clarified.

I. THE OBJECTIVES

Though there is general agreement that the purpose of regional policy measures is to promote the development of the less prosperous regions, there appears to be some difference of opinion as to how this is to be achieved. Three distinct approaches might be considered: (*a*) the promotion of sound, commercially viable, economic growth; (*b*) the promotion of economic growth having regard to the social costs borne by the community rather than purely manufacturer's private commercial costs; (*c*) the running of the economy so as to ensure the finest balance of macroeconomic aggregates by using Keynesian techniques of economic management at the regional as well as the national level. Clearly, these

181

three objectives cannot all be pursued simultaneously, and it is important, therefore, to decide which is being followed.

The most frequently quoted objective is 'sound economic growth'. Sometimes this is put forward in a protesting rather platitudinous manner to gain the sympathy, one suspects, of those in other regions. Its precise meaning is seldom clear. For a start it may be assumed that it means that no regional development should be assisted unless it is capable of being commercially profitable in the region, and that no development should be encouraged in a region unless it can be as profitable there as in any other location in the country.

If these are the objectives, it would seem that any element of permanent subsidy would be mistaken, and that assistance should mainly take the form of creating an environment favourable to growth by means of improvements in infrastructure and helping firms with the settling-in costs of operating in a new location. Transfer to almost any new location probably implies a low initial level of productivity until the labour force acquires the necessary skills, appropriate services are laid on and teething troubles are overcome. Very often these appear to be the main cost barriers to industrial movement.[1] According to this view, assistance could most appropriately take the form of special loans or grants to help the firm during the initial years of operation as well as special grants for labour training and training schemes. The BOTAC loans and grants, which are individually negotiated, might be construed as meeting these requirements; and, although training problems are far from solved, much more is now being done to tackle them.

Assistance of this type may be said to contribute towards excess costs which the firm would temporarily incur by moving to a new location. This cannot, however, be said of building grants, investment grants or the employment premium. All of these are related to either capital or labour costs, but there is no evidence that any of these are higher in the problem regions than elsewhere. Indeed, if anything, they are probably lower. It could be argued, therefore, that measures of this type artificially lower production costs and so enable firms to stay in existence which otherwise would not be economically viable.[2] This could become merely a form of protection for decayed and inefficient industry. In particular, this view might be taken of the Regional Employment Premium, which is

[1] This point is more fully discussed on p. 178.
[2] See for instance T. Wilson, 'Finance for Regional Industrial Development', *Three Banks Review*, Sept. 1967.

received by all manufacturing firms in Development Areas, efficient and inefficient, expanding or declining. The investment grants at least are only paid for expansion which is actually undertaken; but they too could be a form of protection for inefficient industry or for projects which would otherwise be uneconomic.

But if assistance were confined to settling-in costs in the interests of sound economic growth, it would take no account of the problem of externalities. It may be that individual developments by themselves would be uneconomic, but once sufficient growth had taken place in area, the economies of scale and external economies thus created would lower production costs and make it an economic location for development. This argument, which is not unlike the infant industry case for imposing tariffs in an under-developed country, may justify subsidies on capital or labour costs, but only if there is reason to suppose that once development has got under way it can continue without the support.

But the real trouble with the sound economic growth argument is that it glosses over what is meant by sound economic growth. It has already been argued in Chapter I that the commercial considerations on which manufacturers base their decisions may differ substantially from the costs, both social and economic, which the community has to bear as a result of them. Development in a congested area, for example, may seem cheap to an industrialist, even if it is not the optimum location as far as the community is concerned.

A second aim of regional policy measures might, therefore, be to make the pattern of manufacturer's private costs more clearly reflect these social considerations. Where a particularly important divergence occurred between manufacturer's private costs and social costs, a tax or a subsidy might be applied to bridge the difference. Manufacturers would then be more likely to take decisions which coincided with the community's interest. Thus some form of tax might be imposed in particularly congested areas, or a system of subsidies in regions where increased development would be specially advantageous. In some respects the present aids to regional development may be justified in this way, and so may the controls imposed on industrial and office building. But the trouble with this approach, as was emphasized in Chapter I, is that the available data is quite inadequate to apply this type of cost/benefit calculus. It may be that it should be applied, and that the nation's resources would be much more economically utilized if it were. As argued in a later chapter, such considerations might form the basis of a system of regional planning. For the moment, however, its application is not possible.

But these are not the only aims of regional policy nor the sole basis on which particular measures must be justified. It is a widely accepted doctrine that the nation should manage the level of aggregate demand in such a way as to maintain full employment while, as far as possible, avoiding inflation. Yet, one of the lessons of the last ten years is that these aggregates cannot be managed at the national level alone. Because the pressure on resources varies widely from one region to another, a level of national demand which will avoid inflation in the South-East, for example, may produce an intolerable level of unemployment in Scotland and the North; while an attempt to reduce the latter will produce excessive inflation in the South. This can only be overcome with a fiscal policy which is regionally more selective. Any national administration whose economy faced the kind of conditions which are prevalent in the British Development Areas would reduce taxes and seek by all means to encourage investment. Similar measures have to be adopted on a regional basis if the British economy is to make the best use of its labour resources and attain the maximum level of production. The notion that, by increasing the level of inducements in the Development Areas, the Government is subsidizing them at the expense of the rest of the country and protecting inefficient industry, seems to be a hangover from the idea that budgets should always be balanced. If the prosperous regions' resources are fully employed, the release in such regions of further purchasing power cannot benefit them at all and will only result in inflationary tendencies; its release in the depressed regions, on the other hand, can raise output and employment.

This Keynesian type of approach is not necessarily in conflict with the aim of promoting economic growth in accordance with the social cost considerations discussed above. The purpose of the Keynesian approach is, as far as possible, to bring idle resources into productive use; and, were it possible to prepare a proper cost-benefit calculus, this would show that the benefits to the community of employing idle labour resources, which would otherwise be a charge on public social security schemes, would be much greater than employing labour which was enticed away from other employment.

This approach does, however, conflict with the aim of 'sound economic growth' based on purely commercial criteria of profitability. It is the purpose of this approach to stimulate economic activity in an area where resources are available by discriminating in favour of it. To this extent, firms operating there are given a competitive advantage compared with firms elsewhere. This will be so whether the measures take the form of boosting demand through tax cuts or public spending or through subsidizing labour and capital costs.

But if a boost is to be given to regional economic activity, there are several ways in which it might be done. Were it possible to cut taxes in the Development Areas, this would increase spending and give a stimulus to regional production. But a region depends very heavily on trade flows and a large part of regional consumption is met by goods imported from other regions or abroad. A boost in regional spending will, therefore, only partly affect regional production; it will also stimulate imports from other regions and abroad, thereby aggravating inflationary tendencies in the more prosperous regions and increasing the strain on the national balance of payments.

An injection of public expenditure to a region can, however, provide a much greater stimulus if it is used to bring about a much larger injection of private investment. Thus, a relatively small sum provided in capital grants may be sufficient to bring to the region private capital investment several times as large. Sums spent on infrastructure improvements which enhance the region's attractiveness as an environment for growth may have a similar effect, though in a less direct manner. An employment subsidy may have a similar effect. Once the initial investment has taken place, the boost in regional incomes which it will bring about will raise consumption and so stimulate production in the way described above. Again owing to a high propensity to import this multiplier effect will be fairly small, but the total boost to regional economic activity will greatly exceed the original expenditure on capital grants.

This approximates to the effect which many of the British regional measures may have. This sort of approach, however, still entails a serious difficulty. While a boost has been given to the regional economy, owing to the high propensity to import and therefore the high foreign trade effect of the multiplier, the effects of the measures will spill over into other regions of the economy. An attempt, say, to boost the economies of Scotland and Northern England by these means will inevitably raise Scottish and Northern English imports from the rest of the United Kingdom and abroad without necessarily raising their exports to these areas. This will provoke increased inflationary pressure in the prosperous regions and worsen the balance of payments. Inevitably, therefore, such measures to stimulate the problem regions will have to be combined with stricter restraint in the prosperous regions. This is simply a consequence of the open nature of a region's economy and illustrates the difficulty of pursuing different types of economic policy within one nation.

If the problem regions were a separate nation with its own balance of payments account, it would find that measures of the kind described above would plunge it into balance of payments deficit. If it wished to boost its level of economic activity so as to secure full employment, it would, therefore, be obliged to alter the exchange rate of its currency or find some other way of stimulating exports.

Similarly, in order to minimize the undesirable spill-over effects of boosting the economy of a region, something must be done to stimulate regional exports. If the increased regional imports which result from higher regional income can be matched by a greater volume of exports to the prosperous regions and abroad, then the inflationary and balance of payments problems will be avoided and there will be no need to impose increased restraint.

It is important, therefore, to find measures which can promote regional exports. This may be done by reducing costs of production, so enabling some reduction in prices to be made and thereby enabling the competitive position of regional products to be improved *vis-à-vis* similar products produced in other areas. Various types of measure may have this effect. Public investment in transport, harbours and other forms of infrastructure may cut operating costs if it reduces locational disadvantage; the promotion of regional development in such a way as to maximize internal and external economies of scale is also important. The most obvious means, however, is by using fiscal measures which can directly cut the cost of production. Thus, the Regional Employment Premium, by cutting labour costs, should enable the prices of regional output to be more competitive, thereby bringing about a boost to regional economic activity while minimizing the undesirable spill-over effects.

Thus, in considering the various measures in the remainder of this chapter, two effects must be borne in mind: first, the extent to which a given public outlay can trigger off a much larger injection of private capital investment; and secondly, the extent to which regional exports may be promoted and the undesirable spill-over effects minimized.

II. THE CRITERIA FOR SCHEDULING ASSISTED AREAS

Before discussing the individual measures in detail it is important to consider the areas to which they are to apply. As was shown in Part II of this book the Development Areas and Development Districts have varied substantially in geographical coverage during the time that regional policy has been in operation. The criteria for scheduling Development Districts were subjected to considerable criticism and the geographical extent of the areas covered has increased steadily since 1961, culminating in the new Development Areas introduced in the 1966 Act.

As at present operated the legislation appears to divide Britain into two types of area, Development Areas and the rest. Inducements are used to encourage expansion in the former and controls to restrain it in the latter. With the exception of the new Special Development Areas, within each group there would appear to be no discrimination or scale of priority. But this is not quite correct. The standard grants certainly apply in a uniform manner throughout the Development Areas; but the specially negotiated grants and loans from BOTAC give scope for discrimination and it would seem that this has been used, at any rate in the early 1960s, to provide assistance on more generous terms for some especially hard-hit locations.[1] Moreover, Northern Ireland with its own legislation is able to offer more generous assistance than any of the Development Areas. It has something of the position, therefore, of a specially favoured problem region. Within the rest of the country, too, there is an element of discrimination. The IDC and Office Development Permits may be applied with greater or less stringency depending on the area in question. Generally speaking, a much stricter control is likely to be exercised in London and the South-East than elsewhere.

The present system has been criticized from two quite separate and opposing viewpoints. The first suggests that inducements should be in some way related to the gravity of the problem, so that the more acute the distress of a problem area, the higher the inducements offered. Thus, Colin Clark's proposals for a regionally differentiated payroll tax involved varying rates which, at one extreme, penalized most heavily locations in London and, at the other, gave enormous benefit to firms operating in the Hebrides.[2]

[1] Seventh Report from the Estimates Committee, Session 1962/3, Administration of the Local Employment Act, HMSO, p. 56 ff.

[2] Colin Clark, 'Industrial Location and Economic Potential', *Lloyds Bank Review*, Sept. 1966.

The other suggestion is almost the reverse: that discrimination should be given in favour of growth areas, or those parts of the problem regions which have the greatest growth potential.[1]

Clearly, these two approaches are incompatible with each other and the present legislation occupies something of a mid-point between them. The first approach would be open to all the objections of the original Development District legislation, already discussed in Chapter V. It will be recalled that the 1960 Act based the scheduling of areas on the unemployment criterion; inducements were only provided through BOTAC and these tended to be given on a more generous scale for developments in those Development Districts where the problems were especially severe. Distress is no guide to an area's potential for economic development, and if very strong attempts are exerted to push new industries to such locations, they will either not be successful or, if they are, risk the danger of producing a very inefficient locational pattern for economic activity.

It was partly as a reaction to this type of approach that the growth area philosophy developed. As will be shown in a later chapter, however, it has never been very clear how a growth area should be selected or by what means it should be developed. Politically it may be impossible to cut off inducements for all other problem areas; even economically this would seem to be going rather far. The firms that would benefit from being in a growth area would tend to go naturally to them; and if there are other types of firms who feel they can operate in parts of the problem regions which are not growth areas, surely they should be given this opportunity. An economic administrator would have to be pretty sure of his facts and his judgments both in selecting growth areas and in the factors which determine industrial location to do otherwise. This is not to deny that growth areas should be set up or that they should be given priority; but this should be done through the discrimination possible in the terms of BOTAC assistance and in the provision of public investment and infrastructure rather than through an attempt to define the assisted areas in a particular way.

There is, therefore, much to be said for large Development Areas permitting considerable flexibility. Only if large coherent areas are scheduled can regional planning be conducted in a satisfactory manner, and only if the definition lasts for some time can

[1] P. A. Bird and A. P. Thirlwall, 'The Incentive to Invest in the New Development Areas', *District Bank Review*, June 1967.

a long view be taken of an area's future. It is important that the scheduled area should include a region's natural growth points since any attempt to promote growth elsewhere is likely to be less successful and will provide less employment for the population of the region as a whole. For this reason it would seem right to review the position of Cardiff and Plymouth with a view to including them in the Welsh or South-West Development Areas. Even if the position of these towns is not itself critical, their development would probably do more to provide the population of their surrounding region with employment than any other measure.

A rather different problem arises with what have come to be known as the 'grey areas'. Much of Yorkshire and Lancashire, other than Merseyside, although at present suffering no serious unemployment, could be regarded as potential distressed areas. Economic growth is poor and the expected decline in coal and textiles may yet lead to serious unemployment. The scheduling of the new Development Areas and the increased grants available for them have aggravated the problem of the grey areas because much of the development which might otherwise have gone to them is now attracted further North by the grants. The result may simply be to ensure that these areas become the problem areas of the future.

The Hunt Committee has been set up to consider this problem. Obviously it must be one of the functions of regional policy to prevent problem areas arising by taking remedial action in time. Moreover, it is a characteristic that where inducements are offered on a clearly defined geographical basis, the area bordering the scheduled regions becomes denuded of development. There is, therefore, a strong case for providing some limited form of assistance for the grey areas.

III. THE USE OF CONTROLS

Traditionally the Board of Trade have regarded their power to withhold Industrial Development Certificates as their strongest weapon in influencing the location of new industrial development in favour of the problem regions. The great importance of this instrument was emphasized in the report of the Estimates Committee and, precisely because of its value, various authors had suggested that controls should be extended to commercial and office development.[1] As has been seen, this was eventually done in 1964.

[1] Estimates Committee, *op. cit.*, pp. xv and 42 f. See Chapter VI, pp. 129–30.

189

No other country in Western Europe has a control on development so rigorous as the British Industrial Development Certificate. The French attempt to restrict development in the Paris region, but this' is inclined to lead to a ring of new development in the area immediately outside instead of in the problem regions. The Industrial Development Certificate, on the other hand, is required for new development in any part of Great Britain. Control is effected by granting these certificates more or less automatically in the Development Areas but only under exceptional conditions elsewhere. Considerable flexibility can be applied to the use of this control. For instance, the Board of Trade have tended to apply it with particular stringency to the Midlands, the London conurbation and the South of England. But even in the rest of the country it has been used to favour particularly hart-hit areas. During the time that the Development District system applied, for instance, the Board tried to influence the location of new development within, say, South Wales or Central Scotland in favour of those black-spots which were scheduled as Development Districts. It could use its reluctance to give IDCs for other Scottish or Welsh locations as a means of doing this. With the adoption of the much larger Development Areas in 1966, such a fine degree of control over location is not attempted, but control over other parts of the country is applied with even greater stringency.

One obvious advantage of this type of measure, which commended itself to the Estimates Committee, is that it does not involve huge sums of public money. But although its use is obviously desirable and, indeed, indispensable, there are limits to the extent to which this negative type of power should be pushed. There is no guarantee that firms which are refused permission to set up in one part of the country will go to a problem region. If such a location is unattractive to them, the effect of too rigorous a use of the control will make them either (a) cancel their plans for growth altogether, or (b) decide to expand abroad instead, or (c) set up in a problem region but with considerable loss of efficiency. In none of these cases would the interests of the nation be well served. Thus, though the financial costs to the public purse of the IDC system may be negligible, the economic costs to the nation of pushing it too far may be great. Its use requires an immense amount of skill in evaluating each case on its merits. For this reason it would seem that this type of measure is now playing as large a part as can be expected of it in regional development.

IV. THE RANGE OF INCENTIVES AND INDUCEMENTS

The range of possible incentives and inducements to encourage regional development is extremely wide. All sorts of taxation allowances, grants or loans may be given and these may be related to either labour or capital costs or be made to vary geographically in a number of different ways. As Part II of this book has shown, Britain now has a long experience of such measures and many different combinations have been tried.

The development of British policy already described showed certain clear trends in the way these measures were coming to be used. First, the scale and scope of the incentives was greatly increased in the 1960s. Second, to meet the requirements of simplicity, there was an increase in the use of standard benefits compared with individually negotiated assistance. Thirdly, there was an increased use of grants in relation to expenditure on loans and factory building on industrial estates. The non-returnable element in the assistance given has therefore increased. Fourthly, there was some relaxation in the employment criterion. While BOTAC has always had to have regard to potential employment in giving assistance, the new investment grants are independent of employment created. Yet, on the other hand, the new Regional Employment Premium was the first inducement to be directly related to employment and, therefore, to give especial encouragement to labour-intensive types of industry.

If it is accepted that one of the main aims of regional policy is to apply Keynesian techniques of economic management at the regional level so as to achieve a better balance between aggregate demand and resources available, then most of the present incentives may be justified. The purpose of the inducements is to attract development to locations where resources are available and this can best be achieved by influencing the costs of operating in those locations.

Before the introduction of the Regional Employment Premium by far the greatest part of the grants and tax allowances were related to capital investment. They were thus used, as described earlier in this chapter, to trigger off an investment in the problem regions which was much larger than the outlay of public money. Indeed, the inducements were only received by those who actually undertook development. On the other hand, they had the theoretical disadvantage that they subsidized capital costs and thereby, it may be supposed, encouraged capital-intensive forms of production

191

when it was not capital but labour which was the resource in excess supply. More importantly the spread effects of such development in the form of inflationary pressure on other regions may be quite large.

The Regional Employment Premium was introduced, as explained in the original outline proposals, to cut regional production costs and thereby have some of the effects of a regional devaluation. It is paid to all firms in manufacturing industry and is, therefore, not directly related to expansion which is undertaken. On the other hand, it is expected that it will provide a substantial incentive for expansion. It was suggested that, provided the £100 million premium is not absorbed by higher wage levels, it would reduce labour costs by $7\frac{1}{2}$ per cent.[1] If this is passed on in lower prices, it will boost regional aggregate demand by enabling more regional production to be sold in competition with the output of other areas and countries both inside the region and elsewhere. Output should, therefore, be able to expand without producing either inflationary or balance of payments pressure.

It is clearly too soon to assess the effect of this measure. In the outline proposals it was officially suggested that it might ultimately lead to an increase in employment of about 100,000 in the Development Areas, provided that the Premium was not simply absorbed by higher wages or profits but led to a genuine reduction in prices. It is perhaps unrealistic to suppose that the full effect of the Premium would be passed on in this way. Total wage and salary earnings may increase, not simply because labour succeeds in bargaining for higher rates, but because, with lower labour costs, firms can afford to employ more labour without the same effort to raise productivity. Profits may also absorb a substantial proportion of the Premium, since many firms, especially those producing mainly for the home market and facing little competition, may not reduce their prices in line with costs.

A detailed analysis of these possible effects has been carried out by Professor Brown.[2] According to his study, if the whole of the £100 million were to be absorbed in increased wages or salaries, this would lead via the regional multiplier which he estimates at 1.28 to an increase in employment of 25,000 to 30,000 in the

[1] The SET premium, available only in the Development Areas since devaluation, adds a further £25 million and would bring the reduction in labour costs to $8\frac{1}{4}$ per cent. See p. 137.
[2] A. J. Brown, 'The Green Paper on the Development Areas', *National Institute Economic Review*, May 1967.

Development Areas. In this case, however, there would also be a leakage to other regions via the foreign trade multiplier. Higher incomes in the Development Areas would lead to higher demand in the Areas for all goods, including those produced in other parts of the United Kingdom. The effect of this Brown estimates as an increase in employment outside the Areas of 15,000 to 20,000.

Alternatively, if the Premium is all absorbed in higher profits, this would lead to increased investment on the part of firms already in the Areas and the diversion of other firms to the Areas. Professor Brown estimates the consequence of this to be an increase of employment in the first year of 25,000 to 35,000, rising over three to five years to perhaps 60,000 to 80,000. Again there would be a leakage, this time in the form of increased demand for investment goods imported from outside the Areas, but it is suggested that the stimulus thus provided to the rest of the economy would be more or less offset by the diversion of development from the rest of the economy to the Areas which the increased profitability would cause.

There is thus a range of possibilities any one of which will give a substantial boost to the Areas. But it is obviously most desirable that the main effect of the Premium should go in price reductions and in the expansion of production. Only in this way will the maximum employment effect in the Areas be obtained, the spill-over effects to the rest of the economy be minimized and the balance of payments be assisted rather than worsened. The chances of it having this effect, however, depend not only on an enlightened attitude on the part of trade unions and employers, but on the removal of obstacles to expansion the availability not simply of labour, but labour appropriately trained; and the provision of public services and infrastructure.

The Premium has not always been welcomed in the regions with the enthusiasm which might be expected. The Scottish Council, for instance, expressed the view that if £100 million was available for the regions it would be better spent in other ways, notably the improvement of communications and infrastructure. This, however, misses the point, since such measures, while giving a welcome boost to the regions, would have spill-over and balance of payments effects which it is the virtue claimed of the Regional Employment Premium to avoid. A more important objection comes from the limitation of the scheme to manufacturing industry. Thus, the South-West Regional Planning Council were opposed to the scheme, because the only part of their region which was a Develop-

193

ment Area was North Devon and Cornwall, and manufacturing industry played only a very small part in the economy of that area.

Probably the main reason that the scheme is limited to manufacturing is that it is linked to Selective Employment Tax, which is itself designed to favour manufacturing while penalizing services. In view of the analysis in the first part of this chapter, however, there is good reason to limit REP to the exporting sector of the regional economy. Only in this way will the devaluation effect be maximized and the spread effects to other regions minimized. If REP had been paid on all activities in the Development Areas, then the £100 million would have given a subsidy per man only half as great as it is when confined to manufacturing industry.

The problem arises in that manufacturing, while roughly corresponding with the exporting sector of the economy, is by no means the same thing. Some manufacturing industries do not export at all, nor may their production be substituted for imports. On the other hand, some services, notably hotels and catering, are the equivalent of major exporting industries.

This has led to a very unsatisfactory situation in the regions, which badly needs to be rectified. Extensive parts of the problem regions, the Highlands of Scotland, the Lake District, North Wales and Cornwall, benefit very little from REP and are heavily penalized by SET. It is essential that the tourist business, which plays such an important role in their economies, be encouraged instead of handicapped. This is not only vital for the welfare of the regions concerned, but would be greatly to the advantage of the British balance of payments.

As regards the future development of incentives, clearly it is important to find a satisfactory balance between the different measures. In large part this is a question of trial and error. But attempts should be made by Government to discover the effectiveness of different measures, and in particular the consequences of the REP need to be carefully watched. A critical matter, however, is the balance between development taking place and retraining facilities for labour. For too long this aspect tended to be neglected and, despite above-average unemployment percentages, firms had difficulty in finding the skilled labour they needed. The recent measures should greatly improve this situation, but it is important, if possible, to avoid its recurrence. Economies of regions and nations are always going to be undergoing changes in their economic structure and the labour force must therefore have a greater degree of flexibility than in the past. Long apprenticeship schemes and the jealous traditions of craft unions have imposed an excessive rigidity on the labour force which it should now be the object of policy to reduce. It may be that an official committee to study this question is now required.

As regards the form· of the inducements offered, it is clear that there are advantages in simplicity so that firms thinking of moving and foreign firms interested in establishing in an area can see at a glance what the benefits are. This is an argument in favour of standard grants rather than specially negotiated assistance. The latter undoubtedly have a part to play, but it is a serious drawback that a firm may have to wait a very long time before it hears what assistance it may expect. Simplicity is by no means achieved under the present system whereby the activities of the tax collector greatly reduce the value of the assistance given, as will·be explained below. This situation needs to be clarified.

Secondly, a case can be made out for preferring tax remissions to grants. The main advantage of the latter was always supposed to be that they gave more help to the small enterprising firm which was not yet in a position to earn large profits. On the other hand, the tax remission provides an incentive to efficiency which is absent with the grant. If taxes are remitted on profits, then a firm has to prove itself sufficiently efficient to make a profit before it obtains any advantage. Moreover, the more profitable it is, the greater the advantage it receives. The present investment grants are paid to all firms alike, quite regardless of the commercial soundness of their ventures or the efficiency with which they are run. From their own reaction it appears that firms themselves prefer tax remissions to grants. This is partly because many systems of grants, and certainly the present investment grants, involve a considerable time lag before payment is made. But there is probably also a psychological reason. To receive subsidies or grants sometimes seems slightly demeaning, a slur on industrial efficiency and an indication that a particular area or firm in some vague sense is unable to pay its way. No doubt such feelings are illogical, but they exist. The same objections do not apply to tax remissions, which entitle a firm to retain a larger proportion of profits which it itself has earned.

It seems clear that the possibilities of using a regionally differentiated tax system require further investigation. The relative freedom to determine its own fiscal policy is perhaps the greatest advantage the Irish Republic has when compared with the British problem regions in attracting industry and stimulating growth. It is not

195

simply a matter of adjusting the composition of taxes so that they suit the requirements of particular areas, though this may confer substantial benefit. A tax designed to move employees from services to manufacturing is of little value where there is little or no manufacturing industry, just as measures to divert traffic from road to rail is of no relevance in the Hebrides. What is more important is that the problem regions should not be made to feel the lash of restrictive fiscal policies imposed to meet conditions in the greater part of the country but which may not apply to them. For example, throughout most of the post-war period inflation and labour shortage have predominated in the British economy. Restrictive monetary and fiscal policies have therefore been applied, and from time to time Governments have budgeted for large revenue surpluses. Yet these measures have not been appropriate to the problem regions whose need was for growth and investment. Were they economically independent, they would use fiscal policy as an instrument to encourage this, running occasionally a budget deficit. In practice the present system has had something of this effect: public expenditure per head has often been higher in the problem regions than in the country as a whole, while owing to their lower incomes, tax revenue per head has been lower. The revenue surplus per head in Wales, Scotland and Northern England has, therefore, probably been below the average for the British economy. But as Professor Nevin shows for Wales, there has nevertheless been a surplus, even at a time when it seemed hardly appropriate for regional economic conditions.[1]

The regionalization of fiscal policy, therefore, offers one way in which regional policy might be developed. Indeed, this may be the biggest advance that could be made and the one most likely to yield results. Policy has, of course, been tending in this direction already during the last four years. Regional tax discrimination was first used in post-war policy when the 1963 budget introduced accelerated depreciation. But differential tax rates have always been regarded as administratively impossible until the introduction of the Regional Employment Premium achieved a major breakthrough in this respect. This, however, does depend on the Selective Employment Tax mechanism, a tax which is both cumbersome and, so far, not particularly effective in achieving what was expected of it. If it were ever decided to abolish or drastically alter SET this could gravely prejudice the continuation of REP.

[1] E. T. Nevin, A. R. Roe and J. I. Round, *The Structure of the Welsh Economy*, University of Wales Press, 1966.

It is important, therefore, to think of other ways in which taxation could be regionally differentiated. Clearly, many taxes must be uniform throughout the country if absurd distortions or administrative difficulties are to be avoided. There may, however, be scope for differential rates in company taxation. The difficulty here is that many companies operate throughout the United Kingdom with branches in many regions and perhaps a head office in London. In what region, therefore, would they be considered to be operating for tax purposes? This is perhaps not so difficult as it sounds. Firms are at present required to estimate the 'net output' of each of their establishments for the regional figures in the Census of Production. Net output as defined for census purposes is a concept not very different from value added. It might, therefore, be possible to operate some type of value added tax with regional variations. This deserves serious consideration, especially as a value added tax is now to become the basis of Common Market company taxation. It is clear that if Britain were ever to join EEC she would have to adopt this tax as a replacement for much of the existing company taxation. Moreover, since this type of tax can give a powerful incentive to exports, it may become desirable to adopt it anyway, if only to preserve Britain's competitive position with other countries.

V. THE SCALE OF INDUCEMENTS

Up to the 1960s the cost to the Exchequer of its regional policy was extremely small by almost any standards. As was shown in Chapter IV the total annual expenditure of the Board of Trade and the Treasury combined fell from a peak of £12.8 million in the year 1947–8 to £2.8 million in 1957–8 and rose again to £8.6 million in 1959–60. Moreover, the bulk of this expenditure produced a financial return to the Government in the form of rents on factories let or interest payments on loans. The non-returnable cost was very small indeed.

Since 1960, however, much greater sums have been spent. Though the annual cost of loans, grants and factory building has fluctuated between £16 million and £50 million, there has been a steady upward trend since 1962–3 (see Chapter V, Table I). Moreover, the proportion of total expenditure which was given in grants (i.e. non-returnable) rose from 12 per cent in 1960–1 to 50 per cent in 1966–7. These figures do not include tax incentives, among which the accelerated depreciation introduced in

1963 was an important regional measure. The replacement of this measure by the new investment grants will, of course, lead to an apparent large increase in expenditure on grants without the firms concerned necessarily being much better off. The cost of the investment grants in the Development Areas over and above the rate prevailing in the rest of the country was expected to amount to around £40 million, but now appears nearer £65 million.[1]

The Regional Employment Premium, as already explained, involves a major increase in Government expenditure on regional policy. REP itself is expected to cost £100 million and the SET premium which the Development Areas retain will cost a further £25 million. The total gross expenditure by the Government on regional policy in the Development Areas is therefore now running at approximately £240 million per annum, excluding sums spent by the Northern Ireland Ministry of Commerce. This, however, is only the gross cost, the net cost may be much lower, since it is the purpose of most of these aids to raise firm's profits and, insofar as they do so, they operate to the advantage of the Inland Revenue as well as of the firm, as will shortly be shown.

Despite these huge increases in expenditure on regional incentives, the total sum is still not particularly large when seen in the perspective of other comparable forms of Government assistance. Subsidies to agriculture, for instance, have varied between £250 and £350 million a year during the 1960s. Yet the agricultural population is only 3½ per cent of the national total, compared with 15 to 20 per cent for the population of the Development Areas. There is little evidence that their potential contribution to the balance of payments is any greater. Subsidies to the British Transport Commission have likewise been well in excess of expenditure on regional policy incentives until recent years. These are obviously crude standards of comparison, but they show that expenditure on regional development even now certainly cannot be judged excessive.

It is by no means a simple matter to estimate the significance of these measures to the firm but a number of studies are now in existence.[2] The importance of accelerated depreciation was that it

[1] See Chapter 5. £40 million was the estimate in *Development Areas: a Proposal for a Regional Employment Premium*, but the figures for expenditure in the Board of Trade *Journal*, March 1968, pp. 961–4, suggest that £60–65 million was spent in 1967–8.
[2] T. Wilson, 'Finance for Regional Industrial Development', *Three Banks Review*, September 1967; P. A. Bird and A. P. Thirlwall, 'The Incentive to Invest in the New Development Areas', *District Bank Review*, June 1967; W. Black, N. Cuthbert and

allowed investment to be written off more quickly than normal for tax purposes. A firm's liquidity was greatly increased in the early years and its tax payments reduced. In later years tax payments would be correspondingly higher so that there would be no difference in total tax payments, only in the date by which they had to be made. The effect was, therefore, exactly similar to an interest-free loan from the tax authorities. The main disadvantages of this scheme were that it was of little help to the newly established firm which could expect to make very little profit in the early years even if it hoped to do well later. Such a firm would be unable to write off its equipment at an accelerated rate even if it wanted to. The scheme was also criticized for its complexity and it was thought that a simpler system might have more impact.

The new system was probably intended partly to meet these criticisms. At first sight it also appears very generous; but it is neither as simple nor as generous as it seems. In the first place it must be remembered that while the Government is giving firms assistance with one hand, it is taxing their profits with the other. Although it pays for 45 per cent of a firm's investment under the new Act, it takes away 40 per cent of its profits in Corporation Tax. The purpose of an investment grant is to induce more investment by making it more profitable than it would otherwise be, but the firm only retains 60 per cent of these additional profits, the remainder going in tax. This is equivalent to a very much lower rate of grant tax free.

Another feature of the system is that the share of investment financed by grant cannot be depreciated against income for tax purposes. This may seem fair enough, since the firm did not pay for that part of the investment in the first place; but in the long run it will nonetheless wear out and have to be replaced. If the firm is able to count on the present legislation continuing for the life of the plant, well and good. It will then still be in a Development Area and still entitled to investment grants when the plant falls due for replacement. It will have been able to amortize its share of the original cost against taxation and can obtain a new grant for the remainder. But no firm would be wise to count on these assumptions, for no one knows what changes in the legislation there might be. The alternative policy would be for the

J. V. Simpson, 'Investment Incentives and the 1965 Finance Act: Regional Implications', Scottish Journal of Political Economy, February 1967; A. M. Alfred, 'Investment in the Development Districts of the United Kingdom: Tax and Discounted Cash Flow', Journal of Accounting Research, Autumn 1964.

firm to reckon to meet the whole cost of investment itself when the plant is replaced; but if it does this, it is in a difficulty. Since it received a grant in the first place, it can only amortize against taxation the cost of the plant minus the grant; and to meet the whole cost of replacement it must finance the remainder from post-tax profits. If, on the other hand, it financed the whole cost itself originally, it could write off the whole cost of the investment against taxation. Thus, in this respect also, the value of the grant is diminished by the effects of the tax system. This situation is, of course, not new; it applied with the grants introduced in 1963 as well as with the present system. But it means that the real value of the grants is very much less than it appears. According to Professor Wilson's calculation the 10 per cent machinery grant introduced in 1963 was really only worth about 3 per cent in real terms.[1]

The effect of the 1966 measures on the cost of an investment project have been calculated both by Wilson and by Bird and Thirlwall who obtained almost identical results.[2] The overall effect for an individual firm naturally depends on the relative proportions of its investment which it devotes to buildings and plant and machinery. Using Professor Wilson's figures, the final gross cost of plant and equipment would be reduced by 13 per cent, buildings by 19 per cent and a weighted average of the two by 15 per cent. These figures he finds to be slightly more generous than those obtaining under the 1963 system which were 10 per cent, 14 per cent and 12 per cent respectively, but the 1963 system gave a greater part of the advantage in the early years of a plant's life.

The cost of investment is, of course, only a part of the cost which a firm has to bear in manufacturing a product. The main disadvantages which firms suffer in setting up in a new area are all the teething problems which a new venture has to face, in particular the low productivity of the labour force until the new skills are properly acquired, a new routine established and appropriate services made available. Luttrell's study, for example, shows that for thirty-six cases studied, the cost per unit in a new branch in the first year was on average twice the cost per unit in the

[1] T. Wilson, op. cit., p. 14.
[2] Op. cit. I am much indebted to Mr P. A. Bird for recalculating the figures used by Mr Thirlwall and himself on the same basis as Professor Wilson's figures to show that the results were virtually identical. In their respective articles Professor Wilson expresses the value of assistance in relation to the gross cost of the investment while Messrs Bird and Thirlwall express it as a percentage of net cost to the firm.

parent factory.[1] This was far from implying that the venture was unprofitable, because the disparity was reduced sharply in subsequent years. But he summarizes the importance of this by saying: 'It was fairly typical in the range of industries we covered, for the extra operating costs in the early years to vary between a half and the whole of the capital cost of construction of the new factory.'[2]

Thus, the Government investment grants may give an advantage of 15 per cent on the capital cost of a project, assuming investment costs to be similar from one region to another. But the main barrier to movement is settling-in costs, and though these will no doubt be helped by training schemes, there is every indication that in many cases these costs exceed the inducements that have up to now been provided.

To this must be added the effect of the Regional Employment Premium. At the rate of 30s per man per week, this is estimated at approximately 7½ per cent of the wage bill.[3] If the SET premium is added, the two combined may come to about 8½ per cent of the wage bill. Again, insofar as this gives any increase in profits, 40 per cent of that increase will go in taxation payments. The real advantage of the premium is, therefore, somewhat less than it appears at first sight.

The effect of these various forms of assistance both to capital and to labour on the total operating costs of a company will vary from firm to firm depending on the structure of their costs. Before the introduction of the Regional Employment Premium, the inducements were certainly more advantageous for a capital intensive than a labour intensive industry except insofar as BOTAC loans and grants are geared to the provision of employment. The balance in this respect has now been somewhat redressed. According to Wilson's estimate the investment grants, approximating to 15 per cent of the cost of a project, may come to around 2½ to 3 per cent of total annual operating costs. The Regional Employment Premium, at 7 per cent of the wages bill, he estimated after tax to be worth approximately 1½ per cent of operating costs. He concludes: 'At a rough guess, therefore, the combined effect of the capital grants, BOTAC assistance and the employment premium may be

[1] W. F. Luttrell, *Factory Location and Industrial Movement*, National Institute of Economic and Social Research, London 1962.
[2] *Op. cit*, p. 300.
[3] *The Development Areas: A Proposal for a Regional Employment Premium*, HMSO 1967. See also T. Wilson, *op. cit*.

put at 5 per cent of the total costs of a profitable firm which has been following an active investment policy.'[1]

Such a level of inducement is not particularly generous, especially when one remembers that the problem of a depressed region attracting new industry is in some ways analogous to an under-developed country trying to industrialize. In both cases settling-in costs have to be overcome and external economies built up. An independent country in these circumstances might well enjoy a tariff barrier of 15 to 25 per cent on imports, which it would justify with reference to the 'infant industry' argument. Seen against this background, inducements which amount to around 5 per cent of total annual operating costs are not particularly large.

If regional policy is to be made more effective, therefore, there may be some case for increasing the level of inducements. The easiest way to do this would be by preventing the Inland Revenue from taking away what the Exchequer gives out. The nominal rates could even be reduced if the grants for capital investment or the Regional Employment Premium were tax free. For if their value could be deducted from profits before assessment for tax, their effect would be tremendously increased and the impact on regional development would no doubt be considerable.

VI. THE ROLE OF THE PUBLIC SECTOR

It is the role of the public sector to provide the environment in which regional economic growth can prosper. Often the disadvantages of a particular location from an industrial point of view are due to absence of suitable communications, access to ports, and housing in places capable of industrial expansion rather than to something endemic in the particular site. Much of this can therefore be rectified, if modernization of docks and railways, the building of roads and airports, the setting up of new towns and programmes of urban renewal are carefully planned with their economic impact in mind. Thus, the Italians in the earlier stages of their regional policy devoted huge sums to the building of the *Autostrada del Sole* and other motorways which would provide easy access to the South. Money was spent on the improvement of public services and the provision of power supplies. Many Belgians similarly attach great importance to the building of the *Autoroute de la Wallonie* running from Germany to Calais and the *Autoroute Paris-Bruxelles*, since it is thought that these would

[1] T. Wilson, *op. cit.*, p. 16.

transform the stagnant Walloon region from the backwater which it is at present into the crossroads of Europe which it ought to be.

It is quite clear that it is of little use offering aids and inducements and trying to operate controls, if nothing is done by means of public investment to create the conditions in which growth can succeed. But unfortunately the economic impact of public investment seems rarely to be analysed properly and decisions are too often taken purely in response to political or social pressure. Britain is no exception to this and, indeed, many major items of public investment have been undertaken with little thought of the economic consequences.

The building of new towns provides a good example. This was at first regarded primarily from social or physical planning point of view and the economic impact of neither their size nor their siting was sufficiently considered. When experience showed the success of such towns in attracting industry and their economic impact was realized, a number of much larger new towns were planned and their economic potential more carefully considered. Similar considerations are also relevant to the modernization of existing urban structures. So far, this is determined mainly by social considerations. and although this must largely remain so, there may be a case for giving some priority to places whose development is essential to the success of a growth area.

In transport planning there are many similar examples. For instance, the location of airports provides a striking case where the consequences for regional economic development have been inadequately taken into consideration. Thus, at one extreme, despite much agitation, Plymouth remains without a satisfactory airport, although it is essential to good personal communications and its case is at least as good as that of many towns who have had airports for years. Scotland, on the other hand, has numerous airports, no less than three major ones being within fifty miles of each other in the Central Belt. The North-West has one at Manchester and one at Liverpool. At the very least it is open to question whether this is a satisfactory arrangement. Apart from possible waste of public investment, too many airports pose the same problems as too many railway stations, one of the big mistakes of nineteenth-century development. If flights are distributed between several airports in a region, at any one they must be less often and connect with fewer areas than if all services were concentrated. The existence of competitors prevents any of the airports from achieving the scale of domestic link services which would ensure that it could also be a first-class international airport. It therefore remains necessary to go to London for most international connections; yet it is quite probable that, if services had been concentrated, either the North of England or Scotland could have supported an airport with international connections at least on the scale of Brussels or Amsterdam. This would almost certainly have been a major economic advantage for the regions and would have assisted their growth. But it would have required some of the money which was spent on city airports to go instead into the development of rapid ground transport systems.

The importance of public investment is particularly great if it is intended to develop major new growth areas. This question will be discussed in more detail in Chapter IX. Because these schemes envisage development on a colossal scale they may well be turned down. Yet the costs of further development in already congested areas may easily turn out to be greater in the long run. Here is a case where an economic appraisal is badly needed. And there can be no doubt that the regional economic impact of public investment on the scale that would be required for these schemes would be enormous.

All these aspects of public investment it will now be the function of the Regional Planning Councils to investigate. They should, therefore, receive more attention in future. Not only have the merits of particular schemes to be considered, but a balance must be obtained between the needs of different regions and between public investment and other measures to promote regional development. These are tasks requiring research and a level of expertise which it is not yet easy to find.

A quite different way in which public authorities may directly intervene to promote regional development is by the use of public companies. Whereas private industry has to be induced and cajoled into locating in the areas where the Government wants it to go by all the complicated machinery of controls and incentives already described, no such problems need arise with nationalized industry, at least in theory. In practice, nationalized industries in Britain have shown themselves to be almost as independent in spirit as private industry. There has been little attempt to use them as an instrument of regional policy: indeed, because of the nature of the products and services they produce, this has scarcely been possible beyond requiring them to operate particular services, notably in transport, which have not been commercially profitable.

Nationalized industry could, however, play an important role in starting new enterprises in the problem regions. This is particularly useful if the needs of regional policy require a certain industry to be started in a particular place. This may be done either as the foundation of a new growth centre, or because an important gap needs to be filled in the structure of the regional economy without which the location is not attractive to other enterprises, or their future profitability is in doubt.

This type of policy has been pursued in Italy where it is one of the main instruments open to the Government in tackling the regional problem. The two state holding companies, IRI (Istituto per la Riconstruzione Industriale) and ENI (Ente Nazionale Idrocarburi), have each been required to devote a high proportion of their investment to the South. Among numerous projects which it has undertaken, IRI, through its subsidiary Italsider, has been responsible for building the huge integrated steelworks at Taranto, and is now considering putting a large Alfa-Romeo motor car works in Campania. IRI owns a very large proportion of Italian industry as a result of its activities in the 1930s, when it was founded to take over industries which were being forced to close down. It has used this control to favour southern industry. It has also been responsible for the construction of much of the southern motorway network. ENI's activities are more limited; but it has been responsible for exploiting natural gas and oil resources, the development of the latter in Sicily leading to the establishment of the petrochemical complex in the Catania-Syracuse area.

The British Government have never used nationalized industry in this way. The relocation of the steel and motor car industries, which were perhaps the biggest operations of their kind, were achieved by influencing private industry and making large loans of public money. The results certainly leave something to be desired. As pointed out in an earlier chapter, the steel project, which was split between Wales and Scotland, produced two mills of sub-optimal size and probably poorly located. Both the motor plants in Scotland have had their teething troubles. No doubt these problems have been due to faulty execution rather than the form of ownership which controlled the enterprises. At the same time, there is no reason why state holding companies should not perform a useful role in this field in Britain. The fulfilment of regional plans and the establishment of growth areas might be achieved more readily if key enterprises could be started in this way instead of always having to rely on the rather roundabout techniques for inducing private enterprise. That this approach has not been used up to now is largely because of the Conservatives' aversion to all forms of nationalization and the Labour Party's preoccupation with a rather old-fashioned view of nationalized industry. The Government's purchase of Fairfield's shipyard on the Clyde, however, and the proposed purchase of a large share of the aircraft industry[1] open up the possibilities of some regional action of the kind envisaged above. It is also possible that the IRC (Industrial Reorganization Corporation) may use its influence to give some priority to regional development. This is a field which the Government would do well to examine more closely.

VII

Thus, the range of possible policy measures for regional development covers controls on development, inducements, including grants, loans and tax relief, labour training, the planning of public investment and the use of public enterprise. All of these, except the last, have been used in Britain in one form or another. The roles of growth areas and regional planning are discussed in later chapters. It is hardly possible to envisage any other types of measures, at least in a free enterprise economy, and the success of policy is therefore dependent on increasing the effectiveness of these weapons. Some political circles undoubtedly underestimate the difficulty of tackling the regional problem and on the left reference is sometimes made to 'direction of industry' as if that would cure all the problems almost by magic. But private enterprise cannot be 'directed' to operate in particular places or under particular conditions. If the directors of a company were to refuse to be 'directed' what sanction could be employed against them? Success can only be achieved by creating an environment suitable for growth, by offering incentives, by ensuring that labour is appropriately trained and by providing public investment. If the conditions for expansion are appropriate, private enterprise can be induced to take advantage of them; but, if they are not, no amount of 'direction' or administrative red tape will succeed.

The task is, therefore, to make the existing weapons more effective. The IDC control has probably gone as far as it can go. But further thought needs to be given to the use of incentives. Too little is known about the effectiveness of different types of measure and the further development of a regionally differentiated

[1] As recommended in the Report of the Committee of Inquiry into the Aircraft Industry, Cmnd. 2853, HMSO, London 1965.

fiscal policy needs to be encouraged. The control of the regional economies needs to be thought of more in Keynesian terms and less from the old-fashioned view of one region subsidizing another. The control over the economy in the past has depended too much on general measures which were appropriate for conditions in some parts of the country but not in others. Further attempts should be made to replace the management of macro-economic aggregates at national level by their management at regional level. This involves regionally selective measures and, of course, a great improvement in regional statistical data so that the true economic condition of the various regions can be established. The scale of the present inducements, while much greater than previously, is by no means as large as it appears at first sight to be. There appeared to be a case for giving somewhat smaller inducements which would escape tax liability rather than going through the strange procedure of handing out huge, and apparently very generous, sums only to collect a high proportion of them back again as tax revenue.

Labour training clearly received insufficient attention in the past. More is being done now, but the whole question of ensuring a flexibly trained labour supply in an economy undergoing rapid structural change needs further investigation. Public investment has been undertaken with insufficient regard for its economic impact. Perhaps the main impediment to a solution of the regional problem is the lack of external economies and the existence of costly teething troubles when a new activity moves to a different location. All this is temporary and the enterprise, once established, may well be profitable in the long run. This is where state enterprise on the Italian model might perhaps play a useful part, since it could afford to take a longer view. The obstacles can also be reduced by intelligent use of public investment, by the use of a growth areas and regional planning. If the potential effectiveness of all these measures is realized they should have a major impact on the regional problem.

CHAPTER IX

GROWTH AREAS: THE CASE FOR CONCENTRATION

'Quelque confusion règne dans notre politique "regionaliste":
on y distinque mal encore entre une politique localiste
d'assistance à toutes les régions qui contradit la spécialisation
et l'abaissement des couts en longue période, et une politique
fonctionelle de concentration des moyens sur des centres de
développement, convenablement choisis.'

Francois Perroux

In Britain, as in other European countries, it has been suggested that regional development policy would be more effective if it was based on 'growth areas'. The assumptions underlying this idea are: first, that the cost in terms of public outlay would be less for a policy based on concentration; second, that owing to the external economies which would be generated, concentrated economic activity would be more efficient and, therefore, more likely to grow; and third, because of the above factors, a policy based on growth areas would be more likely to be successful in raising regional growth rates and, in the long run, in curing unemployment than a policy of diversification and dispersion.

I. GROWTH AREAS IN BRITAIN

The growth area idea is not new in Britain. Even in pre-war days the Barlow Commission, at any rate those Commissioners responsible for the Minority report, showed themselves aware of the concept.

'Where it may not be possible to start new industries, the key to the problem is that long-distance mobility of labour is difficult to stimulate, but short-distance mobility is easy to stimulate. . . . Industry would be located in existing key points, as near as possible to the distressed areas or other areas of high unemployment, where there is now some prosperity.'[1]

[1] Report of the Royal Commission on the Distribution of Industrial Population, Cmnd. 6153, HMSO 1940, p. 223.

208

Post-war legislation also shows evidence of thought along these lines as has been shown in an earlier chapter.[1] In particular, when the Highlands and Islands of Scotland was scheduled as a Development Area, it was decided to concentrate on: 'a district chosen because of its suitability as a focal centre of industrial development for the Highlands as a whole and not merely because of its local unemployment'.[2] Little was done, however, to develop the idea further, and subsequent legislation, particularly the 1960 Local Employment Act, abandoned this approach completely in tying regional policy measures rigidly to areas with high unemployment percentages regardless of their growth possibilities.

If the earlier legislation made a favourable reference to growth areas, however, it did so without establishing them as a specific instrument of policy. The development of the idea owes its origin to the Cairncross and Toothill Reports of the Scottish Council and to the work of Odber and others on the North-East of England.[3] The idea common to all these studies is that attempts to develop a region should be concentrated on those parts within the region which have the best growth possibilities. This was very often impossible under the legislation, especially after Development Districts were introduced in 1960. Places within the region which had good growth prospects were unlikely to have very high unemployment percentages and were, therefore, probably not scheduled as Development Districts. Yet they might be even within travel to work distance of unemployment black-spots which stood to gain substantially from their further development. The 1960 Act was a policy of taking the work to the workers in its most extreme form. Critics of the policy emphasized that this was likely to be both economically costly, in that many of the Districts, especially in mining areas, were quite unsuitable for industrialization, and also a failure in that the amount of growth which would result would be insufficient to narrow the gap between the regional and national unemployment rates. The alternative was to go all out for a regional growth policy. While large-scale inter-regional

[1] *Employment Policy*, Cmnd. 6527, HMSO 1944. See also Chapter 4, pp. 107–9.
[2] *The Distribution of Industry*. Cmnd. 7540, London 1948.
[3] Report of the Committee on Local Development in Scotland, Scottish Council (Development and Industry), 1952; Report of the Committee of Inquiry on the Scottish Economy, Scottish Council, 1961; E. Allen, A. J. Odber & P. J. Bowden, *Development Area Policy in the North-East of England*, NEIDA May 1957; and A. J. Odber, 'Regional Policy in Great Britain' in *Area Redevelopment Policies in Britain and the Countries of the Common Market*, US Department of Commerce & Area Redevelopment Association 1965.

migration was held to be undesirable, short-distance migration within a region was more likely to be acceptable and certainly an inevitable accompaniment of sound economic growth. Thus, this approach implies first taking a broad view of a region's growth performance as a whole instead of simply the difficulties of its problem areas, and secondly identifying the points in the region with the best prospects of growth and extending to them all the benefits of the regional policy measures. Some people pressed the point further and favoured giving additional advantages to the growth areas or possibly even limiting assistance exclusively to them. In any case, the assumption underlying the growth point philosophy was that the main task was to promote a more rapid rate of regional economic growth. If there was sufficient growth this would in time lead to the solution of unemployment, but this could only happen if development was promoted on a sound economic basis in the most favourable locations in the region.

The first step towards the adoption of this type of policy at the official level came in the White Papers on Central Scotland and North-East England in 1963.[1] The policy was expressed as follows:

'This programme represents a more positive approach to regional economic development than any Government in this country has yet attempted. It incorporates the conception of growth areas, chosen as potentially the best locations for industrial expansion. The development of these areas will be fostered by providing for them, in accordance with a coherent plan, all the "infrastructure" services, e.g. communications, water supplies, housing—that industry needs; and also by maintaining in them, as long as the economy of Central Scotland as a whole requires, the inducements available for industry in Development Districts.'[2]

The political difficulties of this type of policy were immediately apparent, however, in that within the narrow confines of Central Scotland no less than eight 'growth areas' were selected. In the North-East there was a large 'growth zone' covering the greater part of the area. Obviously, to concentrate on a smaller number of areas would have invited a storm both from Members of Parliament and their constituents.

The attempt to implement this policy also revealed several

[1] *Central Scotland: A Programme for Development and Growth*, Cmnd. 2188, 1963; *The North-East: A Programme for Development and Growth*, Cmnd. 2206, 1963.
[2] Cmnd. 2188, para 3.

weaknesses. Though the case for a growth area policy was quite well argued in the White Papers, the criteria for selecting such areas were at best extremely hazy. Centres had to be built up to receive overspill from Glasgow, whose rebuilding programme required the housing of a substantial proportion of the city's population elsewhere. Space suitable for urban development was limited in Central Scotland and the constraints imposed by physical planning therefore severe. To these factors were added the demands of political expediency tempered by little more than hunch as far as the economic criteria were concerned. Some of the areas, it is true, had shown a tendency to grow well in the past; this applied to the new towns in Scotland and to some of the other areas chosen. But some of the other 'growth points' selected, such as the Vale of Leven in Dunbartonshire, were simply depressed areas and it was not clear how their designation as growth areas was intended to make much difference to them. Presumably the fact that they were supposed to be growth areas would be taken into account in planning major items of public investment; if properly planned this could be important, but otherwise it was unlikely they would be much affected. Certainly such areas might have a capacity for development, but their conversion into growth areas in any meaningful sense would require an attempt to identify their particular strength and weaknesses followed by some definite step to develop them. Only for two of the areas was this type of approach followed. These were the new town of Livingston and surrounding area including the BMC factory at Bathgate and the Falkirk/Grangemouth growth area. Both of these areas clearly had good growth prospects, and studies were commissioned from independent consultants to outline what form this development should take.[1]

A similar approach is being followed in Northern Ireland as a result of the recommendations of the Wilson Report on the Northern Ireland economy and of the report of the consultants for the Belfast Region.[2] In the North-East the growth zone had the effect of extending the area covered by the regional policy legislation to some more attractive locations, but otherwise there appears to have been little follow-up to give it much meaning.

[1] The Lothians Regional Survey and Plan, vol. I & II, Edinburgh, HMSO 1966.
[2] Economic Development in Northern Ireland, Cmnd. 479, Belfast 1965; Belfast Regional Survey and Plan, Cmnd. 451, HMSO Belfast. These reports specified a number of growth centres and in particular recommended the establishment of a major new regional centre at Lurgan-Portadown, now named Craigavon.

These measures were implemented under the Conservative Government. And while they continue to be developed by the Northern Ireland Government, in Great Britain, since Labour came to power it appears that the growth area policy has been largely abandoned. The Scottish Plan made not a single reference to the growth areas in Central Scotland and new advance factories have been set up in a number of places without reference to the growth areas.[1] For the rest of Scotland, however, the concept is by no means dead. The new Highlands and Islands Development Board are following a clearly defined growth area policy in seeking to establish nuclei of industrial growth in the Moray Firth area and at Thurso and Wick.[2] In Southern Scotland, too, the proposals in the Scottish plan for the towns in the Borders likewise amounted to a sort of growth point concept.[3]

But the scheduling of the new Development Areas in 1966 to replace the old Development Districts has altered the case for growth areas in an important respect. The regional policy measures now no longer apply to small districts defined by their unemployment percentage, but are available on a wide regional basis. In most cases, therefore, the natural growth points in all the problem regions are included. They are not, of course, singled out for any special treatment, but industrial development is now free to go to the locations within a region which it finds most attractive. There are two main exceptions to this: Cardiff is not included in the Welsh Development Area, neither is Plymouth in the South-West. Yet both of these towns would appear to be the most natural growth points for the region that surrounds them and there is little indication that either of them are yet large enough to pose serious congestion problems. Their exclusion from their respective Development Areas, therefore, appears to be absurd.[4] The same might be said of the exclusion of Edinburgh from the Scottish Development Area. But with a population of approximately half a million, Edinburgh is much larger than either of the other two cities and, therefore, more congested. Its economy is prospering even without regional development assistance and there are, of course, many sites suitable for industrial development in the

[1] *The Scottish Economy 1965–70*, Cmnd. 2864, HMSO Edinburgh, 1966.
[2] *First Report of the Highlands and Islands Development Board*, Inverness 1967.
[3] Cmnd. 2864, pp. 44–56.
[4] Plymouth was for a time a Development District. Its inclusion in the South-West Development Area is strongly argued by the South-West Economic Planning Council (see *Region with a Future*, HMSO 1967).

Development Area immediately outside the city. For these reasons the case for its inclusion is less strong than that of Cardiff or Plymouth, but the position needs to be carefully watched.

II. THE CASE FOR GROWTH AREAS

Given these changes, it is important to consider what part the growth area concept might play in policy if it were reactivated. The case for it now rests on two grounds:

   (i) That public expenditure to promote development, particularly on infrastructure, will be more effective if concentrated in certain clearly defined areas.

  (ii) That new industrial development is more likely to be successful and become self-generating if external economies are built up and related industrial processes established together. This involves some sort of geographical concentration.

(a) *Public Expenditure*

It is clear that the public expenditure involved in stimulating and providing the necessary facilities for development will vary substantially, depending on whether the development is dispersed or concentrated, remote or accessible. Even an industrial estate provides quite a lot of benefits of concentration. It is cheaper to level a site and lay on public services for a number of firms occupying factories on the same site than it would be for each of them individually on separate sites. It is also more costly to provide industrial estates in a remote location.[1] But the location of industry involves much more public investment than this. Areas that are expanding economically require houses, schools, roads, airports, etc., and an adequate provision of these may be much more expensive in some areas than others. At one extreme are the large congested cities where it seems that public expenditure is likely to rise disproportionately with population increase; at the other are the small towns or villages too small to provide the necessary scale economies. Though the evidence is extremely fragmentary and the optimum size of urban unit greatly depends on the way it is constructed and the physical constraints of terrain, it seems to be increasingly accepted that 150,000 to 500,000 represents the sort of scale which should be aimed at.[2] In line with this, the

[1] Seventh Report of the Select Committee on Estimates, the Local Employment Act, Session 1962/3.
[2] See Chapter I.

213

most recently designated new towns are mostly on a much larger scale than those which were planned immediately after the war.

But apart from the cost of providing public services, there are certain types of public investment which cannot be provided at all except in large urban concentrations. Small units of 30,000 or so can scarcely justify frequent rail services or technical colleges, let alone airports or universities. Yet the existence of these facilities may be an important factor in making the location attractive for certain types of science-based industry. Up to a certain size, therefore, an urban area can offer an increasing range of services and facilities, and the more of these exist the wider its appeal as a suitable location for all sorts of economic activity. Thus, concentration of public investment around growth areas is likely to be not only cheaper but more effective in promoting the growth of economic activity.

In the past major items of public expenditure have often failed to make as much impact as they might because they were conceived in a local rather than a regional framework. Or as Chapter VIII suggests, because they have been planned as a result of social or political pressure without their economic impact on the surrounding region being properly assessed. This is particularly important in transport planning, in choosing sites for new towns and in planning the scale of their growth and that of older urban areas.

The lesson is that major items of public investment need to be viewed on a regional rather than a local basis if the maximum impact is to be realized. It may be cheaper to develop new large urban units than to plan for the expansion of existing cities or to spread development all over the region. Certain types of investment such as air services may only be practical at the regional level, and while large towns may have links to ensure that they are adequately served, the same cannot apply to small towns. From a public investment point of view, therefore, it may well be the best policy to concentrate the effort of regional development on building up towns of 100,000 or so. The proposed developments of new cities on Humberside, at Solway on Tayside, etc., therefore, merit careful consideration because they seem to meet these requirements. If, after examination, the promotion of these new cities turned out to be justified, they would certainly bring the growth area concept to reality.

(b) *Inter-Industry Linkages*
The other argument in favour of concentrating development is

214

that only by so doing will industry benefit from the advantages of external economies and inter-industry linkages. This notion originates from the work of Professor Francois Perroux and forms the basis of the pole of growth concept as developed on the Continent.[1] As we have seen, it has not so far played a large part in the British idea of growth areas, and there is therefore a distinction between British and Continental approaches to this subject.

The basic idea is quite simple. The production of goods is essentially a joint process between a variety of firms and industries, the output of one being the input of another. The ability of any one firm to face competition from competitors in other areas is, therefore, not simply a matter of its own efficiency, but of the efficiency of the complex of related industries to which it belongs. Past development has taken the form of concentration precisely because of these inter-industry linkages. Some basic industry such as power, or steel, would start up in a particular area, either because natural resources existed or possibly by pure accident; and a complex of related industries would in time be built up around it to benefit from the external economies to which such association gave rise. Such economies of association might take many forms. Apart from ease of personal communications at managerial level, there is the benefit to be derived from a labour force trained in an appropriate range of skills, the minimization of transport costs on semi-finished products and the sharing of specialist services of all kinds.

This idea runs directly counter to the traditional Board of Trade view favouring the *diversification* of industry as an insurance against mass unemployment. The conclusions suggested for regional policy by the pole of growth idea are: first, that self-sustained regional growth is more likely to be achieved if a complex of related industries can be set up in the area; second, that whereas one firm or industry may be hopelessly uneconomic in isolation in a particular location, if the whole complex of which it formed a part were set up in the region, the development might well prove viable; thirdly, that it is of no benefit to regional development to bolster up an inefficient power industry or to encourage the development of an uneconomic steel plant if this results in other firms in the area having to meet higher costs than their competitors elsewhere.

But obviously not every type of firm needs to be closely associated geographically with related industries. Probably this asso-

[1] F. Perroux, *Note sur la notion de pole de croissance*, Economie Appliquée, 1955.

215

ciation is more important with the older industries such as textiles, where cotton was concentrated in the North-West and wool in Yorkshire, the steel industries of Sheffield, shipbuilding, etc. Modern industries with products which are costly in relation to bulk are, in an age of a highly-developed transport system and universal electric power, much less tied down in this way. Nevertheless, it is clear that it is important in some cases. Some firms which have moved to the regions and regard their new locations as suboptimal do so because the inter-industry linkages which existed at their old locations are absent in the new one.[1] Moreover, it was widely believed in official circles that the setting up of the new strip mills in Scotland and in Wales would induce a substantial amount of secondary development. The same hopes were held out when the motor industry was induced to set up in Scotland and at Merseyside. In large measure the results have been disappointing, but this may be due to poor execution rather than a false theory. Because the steel project was split between Scotland and Wales, neither mill was large enough to obtain the maximum economies of scale. Both were substantially smaller than the new continental mills at Taranto, Dunkerque and Europort. The Scottish mill, in particular, seems likely to be uneconomic. The motor developments were also split between different regions. The largest share went to Merseyside and it has been relatively more successful in attracting component suppliers to follow it. Virtually no secondary development followed Rootes or BMC to Scotland, presumably because their scale of production is not large enough to make it worthwhile. When the industry was relocated no studies were undertaken to determine the scale of development which would be necessary to induce secondary development in related industries to start. It would be worth considering whether more success would have been attained if efforts could have been made to concentrate the development of the new motor plants in one region. A growth pole approach simply implies that developments of this kind should be properly planned on a regional basis so as to maximize the secondary effects and ensure that development is soundly based economically.

It follows, however, that a growth pole conceived as an interrelated industrial complex is quite different in geographical extent from the eight growth areas of the Central Scotland White Paper.

[1] G. C. Cameron and G. L. Reid, 'Scottish Economic Planning and the Attraction of Industry', University of Glasgow Social and Economic Studies, Occasional Paper No. 6, Oliver & Boyd 1966.

Industries need not necessarily operate in each other's backyards to enjoy the benefits of association. Some types of industrial complex, such as petrochemicals, admittedly do have to be close together, but others may be spread over a wide area. It follows that the geographical extent over which a growth pole may be said to operate will vary greatly, depending on the type of industry in question. For many types of industry an area such as Central Scotland, South Wales, the North-West Region or the North-East Coast is not too large to give rise to external economies for firms in related activities located within it.

Up till now no attempt has been made in Britain to steer particular types of industry to an area. The emphasis has always been on getting as much new development as possible, and virtually any firm which came was welcome. It would hardly be desirable to exclude any particular type of development as not being the type for which the planners thought the region was suitable. After all, the fallibility of the planners is likely to be at least as great as that of the industrialists. But it might nonetheless be valuable for each region to have a view on the type of development for which it thought it was best suited. This would enable industries to be canvassed on a selective basis and accordingly more pressure brought to bear. It would also enable the infrastructure to be planned with a particular type of industrial structure in mind, thus perhaps saving public expenditure and being of more benefit to industry.

If this type of development is to be properly planned, however, it would involve much research to determine the type of industrial growth that any given area is best suited for. The techniques for this type of analysis are still in their infancy and are far short of satisfactory. The task is, however, easier in some cases than in others. In an underdeveloped region, for example, where little or no industry exists and other industrial centres are some considerable distance away, the choice is bound to be limited. Many types of industry can probably be ruled out from the start, and pointers to the type of development which would be suitable may be obtained by assessing the area's natural resources, its labour supply, the cost of fuel, etc. Thus, the Highlands and Islands Development Board, in attempting to assess the industrial prospects of the Moray Firth area, starts from the areas' natural advantages which are its unequalled deepwater harbour facilities in the Cromarty Firth, the access that this affords to ships of all sizes and the possibilities of cheap imported fuel. To specify the type of development suitable for Central Scotland, on the other hand, is much more complex, simply because neither the advantages nor the disadvantages of the region are so clear-cut. The possible 'range of industry is much wider, a complex industrial structure already exists and the particular assets of the region are harder to identify.

Attempts have been made at selection of industry for depressed areas in other countries. The study of Davin, Degeer and Paelinck attempts to identify the sort of industry suitable for development in Liège.[1] This was an industrialized region suffering from decline and stagnation in the coal and steel industries. The task is to find new activities which would be suited to the particular characteristics and skills of the labour force, and would, if possible, be able to dovetail with existing industry to establish inter-industry linkages and would have growth prospects both in Belgium and EEC. These requirements may be used to limit the possible range, and the main suggestions for development were, therefore, in the metal manufacture, engineering and chemical industries. A study with a similar purpose was commissioned from Italian consultants by the EEC Commission to indicate how a development pole might be established in the heel of Italy.[2] This was a quite different situation, since the area was suffering from underdevelopment rather than the decline of existing industries. It was also, like the Moray Firth, remote from the main centres of industry in the country. There was, however, a starting point: the vast Italsider steelworks at Taranto had already been established and there existed a certain amount of engineering industry at Bari. The question was what other pieces of the jig-saw could be fitted to these. It was thought that the location ruled out a great number of activities which required either proximity to a large market, particular types of labour-skill or natural resources. Engineering was chosen as the most promising sector and a variant of input/output analysis applied to give a possible industrial structure. Such a technique may show the inter-industry linkages and consequently the group of activities which may go together to form an industrial complex. It may also give some indication of the scale necessary for each of the various links in the chain to be filled in. For example, what

[1] L. E. Davin, L. Degeer and J. Paelinck, *Dynamique Economique de la Région Lirègoise*, Edition de L'ASBL 1959; L. E. Davin and J. Le Pas, *Industries d'Avenir Marché Commun et Province de Liège*, Thome, Liège 1962.
[2] EEC *Studio per la creazione di un polo industriale de Sviluppo in Italia Meridionale*, Serie economia e finanza No. 5, Brussels 1966.

output of motor cars is necessary to justify the establishment in an area of firms making batteries, carburettors or tyres? The trouble with this type of approach is that the data for such complicated input/output techniques is far from adequate in most countries and is open to various interpretations. Moreover, though sophisticated techniques may be used to give inter-industry linkages once a particular sector is chosen for development, the choice of that sector in the first place may have to be done in a rough and ready manner.

This type of approach is similar in many ways to the industrial complex analysis used by Isard and others to plan a proposed industrial structure for Puerto Rico.[1] A summary of possible approaches to this type of problem are given in a recent book by Klaasen.[2] He distinguishes various methods, of which three may be mentioned: (i) the comparative cost approach, whereby a hypothetical plant of given size is assumed to set up in a variety of different locations to determine the lowest combination of transport and production costs; (ii) the access method which is mainly a system for considering the accessibility of inputs and markets, and (iii) a system of weighted inter-industry relations which is a refinement of the access method but designed to take into account the relative importance of communications both with supplies and with the market.

Obviously, neither the techniques nor the data are at the point where much guidance can be obtained on the selection of industry for British problem regions. Everything comes back to the shortage of data on the case for a regional policy already discussed in Chapter I. Further information on the costs of congestion and the effect on industrial costs of being obliged to operate in different locations would throw much light on the range of activities which could be expected to operate satisfactorily in certain areas. It should be possible by degrees to discover the cost characteristics of different regions and locations; and by comparing these with the cost patterns of various industries, gradually to identify the activities best suited to operate in particular areas. This would give the industrial planning of growth areas some meaning and enable regional planners to form a view of the structure of economic activity which might be promoted in their region.

[1] W. Isard, E. W. Schooler, and T. Vietorisz, *Industrial Complex Analysis and Regional Development*, MIJ 1959.
[2] L. H. Klaasen, *Methods of Selecting Industries for Depressed Areas: an Introduction to Feasibility Studies*, OECD, Paris 1967.

The French notion of the *pôle de croissance* does, however, throw one problem into perspective. It is often wrong to think of the disadvantages of a particular location as something endemic or immútable. Absence of external economies or inter-industry linkages rather than location as such may be the crucial factor. If this is so, while the establishment of one firm in isolation may be hopelessly uneconomic, the setting up of a complex of related activities, if it can be done, may offer every prospect of success.

III. CONCLUSION

It will be seen from this chapter that up to the present time the case for a growth area policy in Britain has rested mainly on the view that regional development is more likely to succeed if the locations most suitable for growth are identified and promoted. To a lesser extent it has been seen as a way of making better use of public investment. Little attention has been paid to the importance of inter-industry linkages and the development of external economies. In this there is a radical difference between the British and Continental conceptions of growth areas. The latter is based primarily on the external economies argument and this forms the basis of the *metropôle d'equilibre* in France and the development of particular types of industrial complex in Italy.

In reality these are quite different conceptions. The size of area, which it would be appropriate to designate as a growth point from a public investment point of view, would be relatively small and circumscribed. But for the purpose of inter-industry linkages it is more appropriate to think of a region or at least a sub-region as the relevant area. It is important that these two quite separate conceptions should not be confused. It is right that the planning authorities, in seeking the maximum input from public investment, should seek to identify and expand the places within, say, Central Scotland or South Wales which are most suitable for expansion; but when it comes to the external economies which a particular industrial structure provides, it is South Wales as a whole or Central Scotland which are the appropriate geographical units.

The case for growth areas, of whatever type, as an instrument of policy is rather different in underdeveloped agricultural regions from the depressed industrial areas which typify Britain. In many ways it is stronger in underdeveloped areas. Some concentration of population is essential to provide both a market and a labour force and to make possible the provision of all sorts of public services. A sparse population makes industrial development particularly hard to achieve. These problems are typical of the South and West of France and they also predominate in the Highlands of Scotland and the Irish Republic. Even where percentage unemployment rates are quite high, the actual amount of labour which can be recruited at one point is so small as to be inadequate for most firms seeking a site for development. In such conditions clearly a policy of concentration offers the only chance of success.

In a depressed industrial area, the population is usually concentrated already and public services such as education and transport exist. Growth area policy may therefore seem less applicable. Indeed, it may well be that the right policy is simply to build further on the centres of growth which already exist from the past. But if this policy is followed, adapting the existing centres to receive further growth may still be a considerable task: the physical conditions of many nineteenth-century cities are poor and a vast amount of urban renewal may be required as well as a much improved infrastructure. Alternatively it may be thought that the main nineteenth-century centres of growth have just about reached capacity, or that further expansion would be unreasonably expensive. This seems certainly to be the view which is taken of Glasgow, a city which is already extremely congested and which can only rehouse its existing population in conditions appropriate to the twentieth century by building high at great cost and by overspilling part of its population to other centres. In these conditions, it is clear that new centres must be developed to take the new growth. Whether it is an underdeveloped region or a depressed industrial area, therefore, the task of the planning authority is basically the same. It must decide at what places in the region further expansion can best be accommodated, where it will be most economic and most likely to be successful. The places chosen then have to be developed so that they are capable of receiving the expansion and can offer the appropriate conditions for incoming industry.

As regards industry selection there are also some important differences between underdeveloped areas and depressed industrial regions. In the former there is commonly little industrial activity already and the factors which have to be taken into account are the natural advantages and resources of the area, the availability of labour, its skills and cost, and the accessibility of supplies and markets. On the type of activity which it is desired to promote may depend the size of the proposed growth pole and the priorities

221

for public investment. In a depressed industrial area, the common feature is usually the decline of some key industry to which the fortunes of many other industries and activities may be linked. It would, of course, be ideal if a new growing key industry could be induced which was able to utilize the existing range of skills and could supply the necessary dynamic to the existing range of secondary industries. This may well be impossible, but there is no doubt that a development which can act as a stimulus to the existing industrial structure will be much more successful in promoting regional development, than one which does not. Thus, to take an example, if shipbuilding is declining, the introduction of some new activity which will provide a new stimulus to the engineering industry and rescue it from its former dependence on shipbuilding, might be sought. This kind of new heart operation may well prove impossible, but it is at least worth serious consideration.

Obviously both the industrial and public investment aspects of development poles or growth areas are among the most important tasks of regional planning. The two aspects interact to some extent, since the nature of the industrial structure will to some degree determine its location and its public investment needs. But the more clearly these factors can be assessed the better able will the regional planners be to chart the regions' possibilities for expansion.

CHAPTER X

REGIONAL PLANNING

'A belated awareness is creeping over the policy makers
that regional planning machinery will remain little more
than ornamental until the analytical tools necessary for its
effective use are in existence.'

Edward Nevin, A. R. Roe and J. I. Round

I. THE ORIGINS OF REGIONAL PLANNING IN BRITAIN

The development of British regional planning owes its origin to
two quite separate conceptions. The first is predominantly physical
and is concerned mainly with creating a better environment,
usually for the population of a large urban area. In this type of
plan the economic content was often small and there was little
attempt to fit it in with the economic capabilities of the nation as
a whole. The second type, which has really only emerged in the
1960s, arose out of a concern with the inadequate growth of
regions suffering from unemployment. It was concerned, therefore,
with fostering economic growth and with examining the prospects
for the region's economy within the nation as a whole.

Examples of the first type may be found in the regional plans
for London and the Clyde Valley, prepared by Professor Sir
Patrick Abercrombie and others.[1] The plans were advisory in
character, and there was therefore no official commitment to carry
them out. They were documents of considerable vision and undoubtedly they proved of great benefit to local authorities in
preparing schemes for urban development. Yet in a period during
which Britain suffered from constant inflationary pressure and
shortage of resources, many of their proposals, admirable though
they were, remained unimplemented.

Planning might have developed further from this beginning had
it not been for the change of Government in 1951. The Conservative Party, which tended to identify planning with controls and

[1] *The Clyde Valley Regional Plan*, Glasgow 1946, *The Greater London Plan*, HMSO,
London 1946.

223

restriction, were in general opposed to it; and it was only in the
early 1960s that they began to move in favour of both national
and regional economic planning. Several factors were responsible
for this change. First of all, recurrent economic crises, which were
showing a disturbing tendency to deepen with every turn of the
trade cycle, seemed to indicate that the existing methods of controlling the economy were inadequate. Secondly, from 1958 onwards the regional problem had suddenly become more acute
despite increased policy measures to tackle it. And finally, there
was much interest in the economic success of France, where a
sophisticated form of economic planning had been developed
totally different from the controls-type planning of war and post-
war Britain, different too from planning as conceived in Eastern
Europe.

This led to the creation of the National Economic Development
Council. NEDC was concerned with economic planning at the
national level, but in seeking ways to achieve a higher national
growth rate, they found themselves necessarily involved with the
regional problem. NEDC was convinced that fuller utilization of
labour in the problem regions could make an important contribution to national growth and that 'a successful regional development programme would make it easier to achieve a national
growth programme'.[1] The importance of this has already been
discussed in Chapter I. Underutilized resources would thus be
brought into productive use and at the same time the problems
of controlling the economy by fiscal means would be considerably
eased. Moreover, during these years the deteriorating situation in
Scotland and North-East England itself necessitated some special
action. Unemployment in these areas had risen to 4.8 per cent and
5 per cent during the 1962–63 recession. As a result the two White
Papers already referred to in the last chapter were published, one
for Central Scotland and the other for North-East England.[2] Each
was described as 'A Programme for Development and Growth'.
These documents were derided by the Left for not being proper
regional plans. This they certainly did not claim to be; but there
is no doubt that they were the first large steps towards regional
economic planning in Britain.

The main purpose of both documents was to create an economic

[1] NEDC, *Conditions Favourable to Faster Growth*, HMSO 1963, p. 29.
[2] *Central Scotland: A Programme for Development and Growth*, Cmnd. 2188, HMSO
1963. *The North-East: A Programme for Development and Growth*, Cmnd. 2206,
HMSO 1963.

224

environment conducive to growth in each of their problem areas. To this end the programmes promised to co-ordinate and increase public investment expenditures in their areas. Growth areas were selected, as explained in the last chapter, and these would be especially favoured by this expenditure on infrastructure and services. These, it was thought, offered the best locations for sound economic expansion in their respective areas; sometimes a new town was to form the nucleus of such an area, sometimes a rehabilitated and expanded old one. The programmes gave no targets of proposed industrial expansion, and in this they differed from some people's conception of a plan; but they assessed the scale of the problem in terms of the employment which had to be provided, and they made a commitment of public investment expenditure, 11 per cent of the national total for Central Scotland, 7 per cent for North-East England, compared with population ratios of $7\frac{1}{2}$ and $5\frac{1}{2}$ per cent.

It is a rather fruitless exercise to debate what constitutes a 'Plan' and what does not. At one extreme, obviously, there is the report or survey which analyses the problems of an area and may make recommendations without there necessarily being any official Government commitment to implement them. Examples of this are the Toothill and Hall Reports on Scotland and Northern Ireland.[1] At the other end of the scale is a document setting out a programmed development of the economy complete with target figures for industrial output and public expenditure to which the Government commits itself. Even such a commitment may mean little, as the National Plan has shown, but this is usually thought of as a Plan. In between one may find a range of documents which are part plan and part survey, and it was within this range that the White Papers fell. They can be regarded as an attempt to co-ordinate and plan public expenditure, itself an important exercise, but they do not contain sufficient detail to be plans of the whole regional economy.

Nonetheless, the White Papers raised some important questions for the future of regional planning in Britain.[2] First, both areas covered were small geographically, being only a part of their

[1] Report of the Committee of Inquiry into the Scottish Economy, Scottish Council 1961; Report of the Joint Working Party on the Economy of Northern Ireland, HMSO London, Cmnd. 1835.
[2] These were discussed in more detail in my article 'Next Steps in Regional Planning'. Papers on Regional Development, a supplement to the *Journal of Industrial Economics*, edited by Thomas Wilson, Blackwell 1965.

225

respective regions. They were defined more by the nature of their problem than by any other means. It is true they formed the main industrial area of each of their regions and held the greatest concentration of population; but, in making proposals for their development, no attempt had been made to study the problems of the rest of the region, or to see in what way they would be affected by the proposals put forward. In some cases, indeed, it appeared that the effect on the rest of the region might be adverse.

Secondly, the decision to devote a generous proportion of public investment expenditure to these two areas was taken without any consideration of the needs or entitlements of other regions. If this procedure was continued with other areas, sooner or later it would become clear that either promises were going to exceed the nation's capabilities or, alternatively, the areas which were considered last might find the cupboard bare when their turn came. This is not to deny that some areas may need more public investment than others, and that Central Scotland and the North-East may have been such areas; but a rational allocation of investment resources can only be made properly after the rival claims of different regions have been considered. One of the principal purposes of regional planning must surely be to arrange the regional spread of the nation's resources in a thought-out rational manner. This, the approach of the White Papers, which highlighted the problems of two such areas while leaving the rest in darkness, was unable to do.

Another example of planning in a region suffering from labour surplus is provided by the Wilson Report on Northern Ireland.[1] This Report which was commissioned from an independent consultant, Professor Thomas Wilson, was adopted by the Northern Ireland Government as its plan for the period 1964–70. Although it was not published until the early months of 1965 it was similar in approach to the two White Papers already referred to. Like them, it sets objectives in terms of the amount of employment to be created and provides detailed targets for public investment, but it eschews any attempt to put forward detailed output targets for individual industries. The Wilson Report is, however, a much more comprehensive document than either of the White Papers. This is, in part, because it is more of a survey inquiring into the obstacles to growth in Northern Ireland, and in this role it has some similarity to the Toothill Report on the Scottish economy.[2]

[1] *Economic Development in Northern Ireland* (including the report of the consultant Professor Thomas Wilson), Cmnd. 479, Belfast 1965.
[2] *Op. cit.*

But it also outlines a detailed programme of action covering the establishment of growth areas, amenity, transport, training and the offer of inducements to industry. These questions are fundamental to a faster rate of economic development, and in setting out to tackle them the Report is trying to provide an economic climate which will be conducive to growth. This Report still forms the basis of Northern Ireland's policy on economic development.

Before the Conservatives left office a further document was published which dealt with the South-East.[1] This was a study prepared by the Ministry of Housing and, unlike the two White Papers referred to above, it did not tackle a small area, but three standard regions.[2] This study is more the child of the physical and urban planning of the 1940s, referred to at the start of this chapter, than an economic plan. The overriding concern is with the physical problems of trying to accommodate within the densely populated confines of the South-East a certain increase in population. The alternatives are not evaluated in economic terms, nor, since the study was purely concerned with the South-East, is the contribution which other regions could have made properly considered. The study is principally concerned with trying to check the growth of the London conurbation which it believes to pose impossible problems for physical planning. These, it may be assumed, could not be solved or could only be solved at intolerable cost. As a solution it advocates the setting up of more new towns and the expansion of some existing towns in the South-East. But although these are not referred to as growth areas, that is what they would be, and as such would be in direct competition, so far as attracting industry is concerned, with the growth areas set up in the depressed regions. Indeed, the result of the policy could well be to accelerate the drift from other regions to the South-East rather than solve London's problems.

The lesson of these first attempts at regional planning was that many of the most important decisions, such as the allocation of public investment, can only be taken at the national level where the priorities of different regions can be seen in perspective and promises equated to what the nation can afford. This requires a process of constant consultation between regional and national

---

[1] *The South-East Study, 1961–81*, Ministry of Housing and Local Government, HMSO 1964.
[2] London and the South-East, the Eastern and Southern Regions. The standard regions were used for census purposes and differed in a number of respects from the 1964 planning regions.

authorities. The former identifying the problems and making proposals for their solution, the latter reconciling the demands of competing regions. Moreover, the problems of one region might easily require a solution to be found in another: just as, with an adverse industrial structure, the development of local firms could not supply all the employment which was required in the North, so it was a mistake in trying to accommodate the expansion which was taking place in the South-East not to look beyond the borders of the region.

we need some National/Regional Planning Machinery.

II. THE PRESENT SYSTEM—REGIONAL COUNCILS AND BOARDS

No doubt, because these problems were increasingly recognized, the Labour Government, on coming to office, set up an entirely new machinery for regional planning. The first step was to fix a regional division of the country. If co-ordination and reconciliation of priorities was to be an objective, there must not be too many regions or the task would be impossible. There was no difficulty about Scotland, Wales and Northern Ireland, each of which had been, for historical reasons, treated as a region. Economically, Wales is something of an oddity as a region, since the South is really part of an economic unit centred on the Bristol Channel and the economic focus of the North is Liverpool. However, in this matter the ties of culture and history are strong and any alternative based on questionable economics would be unacceptable. A regional division of England, on the other hand, is bound to be highly arbitrary and the boundaries cannot help but produce anomalies. The eight planning regions eventually agreed are those shown on Map 6. They differ somewhat from the old standard regions used for Census purposes, as an attempt was made to remove the more anomalous features of the latter. In particular, it was felt desirable that the whole of the Humber estuary should be in one region for planning purposes and the South-East, which hitherto comprised three standard regions, was made into two.[1] As far as possible, each region has an industrial centre round which it gravitates; but some have two, and there are cases of towns such as Poole, which always seems to be awkwardly caught at the boundary in all regional divisions of the South.

Within each region there is a Regional Economic Council and a Regional Economic Planning Board. The Councils vary in size

[1] Now named the South-East and East Anglian planning regions.

228

Map 6
THE PLANNING REGIONS

Scotland

Edinburgh

Newcastle

1

N. Ireland

Belfast

2   3

Manchester   Leeds

Nottingham

Norwich

4   5

Birmingham   8

Wales

Cardiff   6   7

Bristol   London

1 Northern   5 East Midlands
2 North-west   6 South-west
3 Yorkshire and Humberside   7 South-east
4 West Midlands   8 East Anglia

● Offices of Planning Councils and Boards

from eighteen to thirty-seven; their members are appointed by the Government and consist of businessmen, trade unionists, academics and other professional men all prominent in their regions. As an example, the chairmen of the eight councils in England include two Vice-Chancellors, two industrialists, a local politician, a professor, a trade unionist and the chairman of a hospital board. In Scotland the Secretary of State and in Wales the Minister of State are chairmen of the Councils. Thus, the Councils are not in any way electorally responsible, but they are intended, nevertheless, to represent the interests of the region.

The Boards, on the other hand, consist entirely of civil servants from a great variety of Government departments. The chairman is appointed in each case from the Department of Economic Affairs. The essential feature of the Board is that it brings together members of different Government departments, most of whom would be in the region anyway, and gives them, as it were, lateral links at the regional level as well as the existing vertical ones with their own departments. In this way the activities of different departments within the region should be better co-ordinated.

The objectives in setting up this machinery were set out by the First Secretary of State in the House of Commons:

'The purpose of the Regional Councils and Boards . . . is to provide effective machinery for regional economic planning within the framework of the National Plan for economic development. . . .

The economic planning councils will be concerned with broad strategy on regional development and the best use of the region's resources. Their principal function will be to assist in the formulation of regional plans and to advise on their implementation. They will have no executive powers.

The economic planning boards will provide machinery for co-ordinating the work of Government departments concerned with regional planning and development, and their creation will not affect the existing powers and responsibilities of local authorities or existing Ministerial responsibilities.'[1]

Whilst this machinery was being created, studies were already under way in some of the regions. Thus, the reports for the North-West and the West Midlands appeared under the auspices of the Department of Economic Affairs and were essentially sur-

[1] Hansard, December 10, 1964.

vey documents prepared by the Civil Service.[1] Since then the Councils have taken the responsibility and reports have now been published for all the other regions except for East Anglia.[2] The reports for the English regions are similar in character: they provide a mine of information about their regions, they analyse its problems, its economic structure and its future prospects; they also put forward a great number of recommendations for policy. Essentially they try to provide the analysis on which a discussion of the regions' future can be based. There is a tendency for the prosperous regions to be concerned with the physical problems of accommodating their expansion, while giving insufficient weight to economic projections and assessments; the problem regions, such as the North, are much more concerned with the economic problems of stimulating expansion. Such an emphasis is perhaps natural. But the reports are not and are not intended to be regional plans. Detailed forecasts and targets are not given— could not be in the absence of greatly improved statistical data. Neither do the recommendations involve any Government commitments. Indeed, a year after the publication of their Report the Northern Regional Council were still waiting for the Government's reaction to their proposals. The difference between these surveys and regional planning is well put by the South-West Council:

'It has come to be recognized that it is too soon in the experience of regional planning to aim at achieving a set of Government-approved plans for all regions which will neatly dovetail with each other and which, in numbers of population, distribution of manpower, growth and location of industry, scale and disposition of public investment, etc., will in aggregate coincide with the forecasts, intentions and capabilities envisaged by the Government for the economy as a whole. . . . The immediate aim should be for each Council to provide themselves with a "regional strategy" by which recommendations can be made on decisions affecting their regions which cannot wait, and advice be given immediately on the implications for their regions of national and local policies.'[3]

---

[1] *The North-West*, HMSO 1965; *The West Midlands*, HMSO 1965.
[2] *The East Midlands Study*, HMSO 1966; *A Review of Yorkshire and Humberside*, HMSO 1966; *Challenge of the Changing North*, HMSO 1966; *A Region with a Future: a Draft Strategy for the South-West*, HMSO 1967; *A Strategy for the South-East*, HMSO 1967.
[3] *A Region with a Future: A Draft Strategy for the South-West*, HMSO 1967, p. 8.

231

The presence of a Government Minister as chairman of the Council both in Scotland and Wales gives the Councils in those regions a political focus and responsibility which is lacking elsewhere. Moreover, the Scottish Office and the Welsh Office provide a team of civil servants already organized on an interdepartmental basis. The effect of this on the Welsh study was rather inhibiting.[1] Since the Secretary of State was responsible for the Report, it represented a greater degree of Government commitment than the reports for other regions. Proposals could, therefore, not be made with quite the same degree of freedom. Furthermore, by the time the Report was published, the targets of the British National Plan had been abandoned as a result of the 1966 deflationary measures and planning was everywhere in disarray. It was impossible, therefore, to put forward targets in the Welsh study.

The document produced for Scotland, however, stands out in marked contrast to all the other reports.[2] Published early in 1966, it was the first regional report to appear under the Labour Government and it followed in the steps of the National Plan which was at that time still operational. The Scottish Office had been in the forefront of thought on regional development and had had its first shot at planning in the White Paper already referred to. *The Scottish Economy 1965-70* is, therefore, a plan as well as a survey. It purports to carry with it the political commitment of the Government and it attempts to set out targets of output and employment growth to be achieved by 1970. As a survey the document is good. It analyses in an interesting way the problems of the Scottish sub-regions, the Highlands, the North-East, the Borders and the South-West, and the proposals it puts forward to build up centres of growth are well conceived. On Central Scotland, which was covered by the earlier White Paper, it has understandably less to say that is new. As a plan, however, it is poor. Before the 1964 election the Labour Party had virtually committed themselves to producing an economic plan for Scotland, just as they were committed to a National Plan. The techniques of planning, however, take time to build up and the rudimentary state of Scottish statistics only permitted a crude attempt.

As was well known, Scotland suffered from a higher rate of unemployment than the United Kingdom and her income per head was 12 per cent below the British average. At the time in question she was also losing over 40,000 a year in emigration. It

[1] *Wales: The Way Ahead*, Cmnd. 3334, Cardiff, HMSO
[2] *The Scottish Economy 1965-70*, Cmnd. 2864, HMSO Edinburgh, Jan. 1966.

seemed, therefore, that whatever rate of growth Britain was expected to achieve, Scotland should aim a bit higher. Statistics of gross domestic product, however, did not exist and it was necessary to make projections on the basis of the index of industrial production.[1] But this was unsatisfactory since the index only covered about 50 per cent of the economic activity of the region and it was impossible, therefore, to match in any reasonable manner the projected growth of the economy with labour resources.

In the event the target rate chosen for the growth of Scottish industrial output was slightly above the British rate as given in the National Plan, 4.8 per cent compared with 4.5, and this, indeed, seemed to be its main justification. On the face of it, there seemed even less likelihood that this target would be achieved than that Britain would achieve the National Plan's rate.

Actually this was not so implausible as it seemed. Cameron and Reid have argued convincingly that the targets were realistic provided: (a) incoming firms continued to provide employment at the same rate as from 1960 to 1964, approximately 3,000 to 4,000 jobs per annum; (b) industry within the region expanded to provide 4,500 to 5,000 jobs per annum, and (c) job losses in declining manufacturing industry fell from 16,000 per annum, the 1960–64 figure, to 4,000 per annum.[2] A case could be made for all these assumptions, but the Scottish Plan falls down in failing to make it. If planning is at least in part an exercise in persuasion, it is important to demonstrate that the targets adopted are realistic. The Plan is extremely weak in tracing the effects of British expansion, as foreseen in the National Plan, on Scotland. Here a form of input/output model, as demonstrated by Nevin, Roe and Round for Wales, could be useful.[3] This Welsh model was largely experimental, but tested on past data it did give better predictive results than any other system of forecasting. The data, of course, did not exist for Scotland and its preparation would have taken

[1] At the time of writing the only estimates of Scottish Gross Domestic Product are those contained in my *Scotland's Economic Progress 1951–60*, George Allen and Unwin 1965. These do not go beyond 1960 and the Scottish Plan was concerned with the period 1965–70. The Index of Industrial Production is published in the *Digest of Scottish Statistics*, HMSO Edinburgh.
[2] G. C. Cameron and G. L. Reid, 'Scottish Economic Planning and the Attraction of Industry', University of Glasgow Social and Economic Studies, Occasional Paper No. 6, Oliver and Boyd 1966.
[3] E. T. Nevin, A. R. Roe and J. I. Round, 'The Structure of the Welsh Economy', Welsh Economic Studies No. 4, University of Wales Press 1966.

233

time. But one is forced to the conclusion that though many types of survey and plan could be prepared without undue difficulty, the setting of meaningful targets for the various sectors of the economy can only be done if there are at least some rudimentary social accounts for the region.

As a first attempt at a proper regional economic plan, the Scottish Plan is valuable. Its faults serve chiefly to show that regional planning is a highly complex technical exercise. In the first place, the regional plan must rely on the assumptions of the National Plan. If these are unrealistic and the National Plan's targets are abandoned, the regional plan must fail also. Secondly, the preparation of meaningful targets, if it is to be done properly, requires the development of sophisticated forecasting techniques. Over and above this, there ought to be some reconciliation at national level of the claims of competing regions, to ensure that when all their targets and forecasts are put together they are within the capability of the nation.

These Regional Councils and Boards comprise the present system of regional planning in Britain; but, before leaving this description of the institutional framework, mention must be made of one other body which, because of its unique role, is of considerable interest for the future development of regional planning institutions. This is the Highlands and Islands Development Board. The Board was set up with the task of developing the Highlands and Islands of Scotland, an area which has been suffering a fall in population for over a century and exhibits many symptoms of a decaying economy. To convert such an area to economic health is perhaps the hardest regional development task in the country. The unique feature of this Board is that it has executive powers. It is, therefore, charged not simply with formulating policy or drawing up a regional strategy, but with carrying it out. Indeed, this Board is not so much a planning body as a development authority. Nevertheless, if it is to achieve any success, its policy must rest on a development strategy in the same way as for any region. The Board's budget is somewhat meagre, being only about £1 million a year, but it has power to borrow. It may acquire land or business by compulsory purchase and may run its own enterprises. These are remarkably wide powers for a board of officials, for the only electoral control is exercised indirectly through their responsibility to the Secretary of State for Scotland.

The Board has taken up its task in an active manner. Its general strategy and the projects to which it has given assistance are

234

described in its first Annual Report.[1] It is the first body which has been able to take an overall view of the Highland problem; its activities have covered an extremely wide range of projects and it is engaged in the preparation of a variety of studies. Nevertheless, on the political side it has run into difficulties from time to time, principally over the reaction of public opinion to some of its major projects. In particular, this arose over a proposed petrochemical complex which the Board was trying to induce to set up at Invergordon. This would have easily been the Board's largest project and it appeared to offer a number of economic advantages. In the event, however, it unleashed a storm of criticism. In part this was due to the activities of one of the members of the Board, but it also reveals the problems inherent in this type of system. The Board's difficulties were undoubtedly aggravated by its exercise of an executive function without electoral responsibility. In its executive role the Board finds itself fulfilling some of the functions which might be undertaken by a regional government. Yet the public feel they have no direct channel of communication with those who are taking decisions. And precisely because it is a board of officials, alternative policies cannot be discussed and debated in public. This means that the opposition to a particular policy can only be expressed in a rather turbulent manner. For its part, the Board's position is also unsatisfactory because it does not have the strength of democratic authority, but must needs rely on the backing of the Secretary of State for Scotland.

On the economic front, the Board's achievements are encouraging. Despite the small scale of its activities, the Board in its short existence has had a greater impact on the Highlands than any other body ever has. Its financial power has enabled it to deal speedily with applications. And it has not had to worry about targets or whether its proposals dovetailed with those of other regions or whether the Government would endorse its recommendations. The limits of its actions have been quite simply set by its financial powers and the number of projects it could induce to set up in the area.

This bears some similarities to the way in which the Italian Cassa per il Mezzogiorno operates, although of course on an infinitely smaller scale, and to the Fund for Northern Norway. The setting aside in advance of specific financial resources for

[1] First Report of the Highlands and Islands Development Board, Nov. 1965–Dec. 1966, Inverness 1967.

regional development avoids many of the intricate problems of co-ordination which arise from the proposals and targets of advisory regional planning bodies. It means that plans are then prepared in the full knowledge of the resources available to back them. Perhaps this is a principle which might yet have wider application in the United Kingdom.

But in many ways the greatest advantage of this type of system is that the Board is able to work out an approach to the regional problem without being limited to the narrow confines of any one Government department. This is no more than what any regional planning authority should do. It should, however, be possible to carry these advantages much further. The Highland Board has been additional to the other multitude of public authorities already operating in the area. It has thus replaced nothing and its contribution has been in a sense marginal. A regional authority would be able to make a much greater impact if it replaced many of the existing authorities and took over some of the work of Government departments in the area. There would then be a greater chance that public policy could be more closely matched to the needs of the area. But this is something which undoubtedly calls for some form of regional political administration.

It is clear that the various Councils and Boards described in this section represent only the first stage in the development of regional planning in Britain. Though there may be much disagreement about its future, no one imagines that regional planning is yet playing the full role that was intended for it. Obviously it cannot yet be credited with altering the course of the regional problem in any fundamental way. Yet, all the same, it is useful to have a body specifically responsible for posing and analysing a region's problems, for assessing the implications of different aspects of policy, for forecasting the probable development of a region and suggesting ways in which problems, to which that development gives rise, may be overcome. There is absolutely no doubt that the problems of various regions are now much better understood as a result of the Councils' reports. This, then, has been a limited though important function. If a particular Ministry, say Transport or Housing, puts forward a scheme which will affect a region, it is now much more likely that its economic impact on regional development will be properly considered.

But if regional planning is not to remain confined to these rather limited functions, it is necessary to consider how it might be developed. No doubt, it was originally intended that the

236

English Regional Councils would eventually produce regional plans containing output targets by sectors and dovetailing in some way with the National Plan, rather in the way that the Scottish Plan tried to do. The difficulties of this type of system are much clearer than they were as a result of the experience of the last three years, and all forecasts must be in some disarray owing to the abandonment of the National Plan. It is worth considering, therefore, whether it should after all be the aim to give so much attention to detailed industry and sector targets in future plans. A plan which has the more limited task of co-ordinating public investment and setting out the broad strategy of a region's development may still be of value.

On the institutional side, too, there is uncertainty. The English Regional Councils are expected to represent their regions and fight for their interests, yet they have neither money, executive power or electoral responsibility. The absence of the latter especially leaves them in a weak position and has enabled the Government to take as much or as little notice of them as it pleases. There has been considerable dissatisfaction among the Councils about the Government's behaviour towards them. Thus, the chairman of the Northern Council had to threaten to resign to attract the Government's attention to the problems of his region, and the South-East Council were neither consulted nor allowed to influence the matter when the siting of London's third airport at Stansted was decided. It may be considered satisfactory to leave the Councils in their present rather nebulous advisory role; but if it is decided to strengthen them, this may involve making them electorally responsible and perhaps giving them some executive powers. This would put them on the way to being a form of regional Government. Evolution in these directions is at present held up until the Royal Commission on Local Government reports. Both as regards its economic role and its institutional framework, therefore, the future of regional planning is still in the melting pot. It is the purpose of the next section to consider how the system might be developed.

III. THE FUTURE OF REGIONAL PLANNING

As the last two sections of this chapter have shown, Britain now has experience of several different types of regional planning. Yet the fact remains that it does not yet seem to have made the contribution expected of it to a solution of the regional problem.

Clearly there are several ways in which it might be developed, some of which have already been indicated. But the choice of system depends on what it is intended to achieve. It is plain that the present system of planning was started with no very precise idea of what it could or could not achieve. To consider its future development, therefore, it is necessary to start from fundamentals by asking how planning regions should be defined and what the possible functions of regional planning are. It may then be possible to see the merits of different types of planning more clearly.

(a) *The Planning Regions*
The present regional division of the country, by which England is divided into eight planning regions and Scotland, Wales and Northern Ireland comprise one each, dates only from 1964. It is possible that the reform of local government, particularly if this results in a system of regional Government, may cause it to be altered again. Meantime it is worth considering what economic reality the concept of a region has and whether economic planning imposes any particular constraints on a regional division of the country.

There are obviously a great number of factors which may influence the choice of a regional division for a country. It has already been suggested in the Introduction to this book that there are no very sure economic criteria on which this can be based. However, three possible methods may be discussed. The first of these is to try to define homogeneous regions; areas which suffer from a common problem and appear to require a common policy to deal with it. This was the type of approach followed in the Conservative Government's White Papers. The disadvantage is that it may lead to very small fragmented regions and to large areas of the country being left out because they suffer from no particular problem or because they lack homogeneity with a neighbouring problem area. Co-ordination between regions and between the regions and the nation then becomes impossible. Moreover, to press the homogeneity argument too far is to misunderstand the purpose of regional planning. Regional planning is largely a process for settling priorities and for reconciling the needs of different areas. If each tiny area is considered separately, on the grounds that its problems are slightly different from elsewhere, reconciliation may be made more difficult instead of easier. It must be expected, therefore, that a region should embrace areas with different needs and different problems and that one of the tasks of the regional plan is to take these into account.

238

Secondly, regional divisions may be based on some sort of economic unit, such as the area dependent on and served by a large city or industrial complex. This is a useful approach and it has been applied in some measure in the British planning regions. But it presents some impossible problems in practice. Two cities or industrial areas may be very close together, so that their sphere of influence overlaps and in reality the region has two hearts, not one. Moreover, the boundary between two regions in this sense is almost impossible to define, since it is extremely hard to say with any certainty where the sphere of influence of one centre gives place to another. Inevitably there will be some absurdities with towns placed awkwardly at the border.

A third type of region is that which arises from historical or administrative factors. Thus, there is no doubt that a sort of regional consciousness exists in Scotland, Northern Ireland and Wales, though the latter country, at least, is not an economic unit in the sense outlined above. Such regional consciousness may make the task of regional planning and development simpler if only because it is hard to think in regional terms or work up much enthusiasm for its development if the region, as defined, seems an unnatural creation to its inhabitants.

There is, therefore, no simple way to work out the regional division of a country and clearly much sterile argument could be devoted to the merits and demerits of alternative schemes. Where historical factors are important and regional consciousness is strong, this should probably be allowed to determine a regional division where practicable. Otherwise the notion of dividing the country roughly in accordance with the sphere of influence of cities or industrial areas has some application.

Since there are no very clear-cut economic criteria for determining the regional division of a country, and since that division is bound to be arbitrary in some degree, it is important to make it as easy to handle as possible. The procedures of regional planning are complex and the implementation of regional plans depends upon close co-operation at the national and local levels. Plans for a region must be realistic in terms of the resources which the nation can devote to them and the aspirations of different regions must be reconciled. Obviously, this task, and the techniques it requires, become more difficult the greater the number of regions. On economic grounds, therefore, there is a strong case for a small number of fairly large regions. These may often include areas which are very different from each other in character, but it is the task of the regional planning authorities to reconcile their own order of priorities.

The planning regions of Britain accord very closely with these general guidelines. The total number, eleven, is quite small enough to enable the claims of each to be reconciled. Though each contains areas of differing circumstances, the main characteristics and problems of each region can be readily identified. It is now of the first importance that all Government departments work to these new divisions and build up the appropriate statistics for them. For some regions the division is the same as the old standard regions used for the Census, so the task for them should not be too difficult. Adequate statistical data is vital not only to an analysis of the regional economy but to the forecasting which is an essential part of planning.

(b) *The Functions of Regional Planning*

In Chapter I it was stressed that some aspects of the case for a regional policy, while intuitively plausible, could not be properly assessed without a proper cost-benefit analysis. This applied principally to the argument that further expansion in certain large and congested centres was unduly expensive to the community and ought, therefore, to be diverted to other areas. Data on this and on the effects on industrial costs of operating in alternative locations are largely lacking. But it was suggested that this type of analysis ought to be one of the basic elements in regional planning. If policy makers are to make meaningful decisions about the spatial distribution of economic activity they wish to achieve, they must have the means of discovering which distribution will provide the greatest social benefit at the lowest social cost. In other words, the nation should be able to consider what regional pattern of economic activity will give it the greatest amount of development for the smallest input of real resources in the same way as a business has to decide between alternative investment projects. Modifications may be made to this pattern in the light of social or political factors. But this is the problem with which regional planning must be concerned. If regional planning, therefore, is to become a useful instrument, attempts need to be made to gather the information required for such a cost-benefit study.

A second function of regional planning is to forecast a region's probable future course of development, so that problems may come to light in advance and appropriate action be taken in time. It is impossible to do this task adequately with the present state of

240

regional statistics. Since social accounting statistics do not exist for regions, one can hardly be expected to forecast future growth in ignorance of current performance. Professor Nevin's input/output model, though still in the stages of development, was used to show how the Welsh economy is likely to evolve in the next few years and the attempt illustrated particularly clearly the labour surplus problems that are likely to arise.[1] At present this method is probably more accurate than simple interpolation, but it is, as its authors point out, still very rudimentary. It is a complicated technique and it has serious drawbacks. Adequate regional data on input/output relationships are not available and the use of United Kingdom inter-industry co-efficients may well be unsatisfactory. Moreover, the operation of such models with fixed inter-industry co-efficients may be seriously misleading over the period of the projection in a region which is subject to particularly rapid structural change. In any case, all such regional projections depend on National Plan targets; and if these are invalidated by balance of payments constraints, the whole structure falls to the ground. Nevertheless, these techniques have been used with considerable advantage for the Republic of Ireland, and the Irish economy is in many ways as closely tied to that of the United Kingdom as any British region.[2] Thus, if reasonably accurate regional projections could be made, this would be of fundamental importance to regional policy and regional planning.

Forecasts would indicate the probable gap between regional development and regional aspirations. They would, therefore, give time for corrective measures to be implemented and bottlenecks to be removed. This leads to the third and perhaps most important objective of regional planning: the outlining of a regional development strategy. The regional body must attempt to discover the region's growth potential, it must identify the impediments to development so that they can be tackled and it must decide in what places within the region growth can be most satisfactorily promoted. This task is obviously made simpler if the type of economic activity best suited for promotion in different places within the regions can be identified. Obviously, in some areas the

---

[1] E. T. Nevin, et al. Op. cit.
[2] W. J. L. Ryan, 'The Methodology of the Second Programme for Economic Expansion', *Journal of the Statistical and Social Inquiry Society for Ireland* 1966. The Irish projections were seriously upset by the British Import Surcharge, but the Programme is nevertheless of great value as a feasibility study of Irish economic growth.

range of industries which might successfully be started will be very limited while in others there will be few constraints. Knowledge of these factors, together with physical conditions, would assist the regional authority in choosing growth areas and assessing the needs for public investment. The case for growth areas has already been discussed at length in the last chapter; but any attempt to implement such a policy would be largely the responsibility of the regional planning body, whether this simply took the form of attempting to concentrate public investment expenditure or of establishing a full industrial complex.

But even if there is no attempt to plan growth areas or to select and promote a particular type of industrial complex, it will still be the task of the regional body to assess public investment requirements so that ports, transport, housing, new towns, educational facilities, etc., can be provided and their probable economic effect taken into account. All this implies reconciling the competing claims of sub-regions, and assessing the possibilities of expansion.

Since the public sector is under Government control it ought to be possible to plan its activities with some confidence of fulfilment. In fact, this is seldom the case. But the private sector presents even greater problems. It is tempting, therefore, to conclude that regional plans should be largely limited to the public sector. But this is to ignore the inter-related nature of the economy. The provision for housing, education and medical services depends on future trends in population. Power, transport, ports, etc., depend on the scale and nature of industrial growth. The public sector cannot be planned, therefore, without some projections or at least growth assumptions for the private sector. Moreover, the more reliable these are, the more likely it is that the provision of public investment will match requirements. The need to prepare as accurate projections as possible of the development of the regional economy therefore cannot be evaded.

This does not necessarily mean that a regional plan should contain a detailed set of targets industry by industry. Apart from the fact that this is impossible in the current state of regional statistics, it appears to commit Government to a particular pattern of development, which may be invalidated by any one of a long chain of assumptions breaking down. If this happens, the whole exercise is likely to be discredited. Rather the purpose of this type of planning should surely be to foresee what type of regional action would be necessary to cover a series of possible eventualities. Forecasts should, therefore, be built up on a variety of different assumptions and a plan should be as flexible as possible to enable action to be adjusted to circumstances as they unfold.

Any type of regional planning, of course, requires a complicated organizational framework. There is no Western European country where this appears to work satisfactorily so far. And, largely because of this, regional plans seldom become operational or turn out to be much more than a chronicle of regional aspirations. As such they may later be of interest to historians but they cannot be a basis for action. This is because most plans emerge entirely from the region and are dominated by regional rather than national priorities. Not only are the objectives of different regions often incompatible, but action to implement them depends on national Government, and this is usually beyond national capabilities, given the other important claims on Government expenditure. The importance of this is not always realized. Many of the most important decisions of regional planning involve choosing between regions. For instance, is development in the Midlands to be restricted in favour of the North? How is public investment to be shared between projects which are essential to promote growth in Scotland or the North-East and to cater for the accommodation of expansion which is taking place in the South-East? The appointment of regional bodies does nothing to solve this; indeed, it may make it more difficult if these bodies assume the role of pressure groups. It is natural that a regional planning body sees its problems purely in the context of its own region. Yet a solution to the problems of that region could perhaps more easily and more cheaply be found in action taken in other regions. This tends to be ignored if the country is divided up so that each Regional Council is purely interested in its own region. It is then necessary for the Central Government to take an inter-regional view establishing a clear scale of priorities and overruling, when necessary, the demands of some regions in the interest of others.

Co-ordination between central and regional authorities is therefore vital to any fulfilment of regional planning objectives. If a detailed plan with output targets of individual sectors is attempted, this at once imposes a number of important constraints. No targets or commitments can be accepted without a two-way process of discussion and consultation between the regional and national authorities. Thus, the preparation of regional plans might involve the following stages. First, the preparation of forecasts, indicating how the economy as a whole is likely to evolve and the effect on

243

particular industrial sectors, such as coal or iron and steel. Second, an assessment of the consequences of these developments for the region and the preparation of a draft strategy. This would indicate how any problems which these trends pose might be met and how the region's development is to be directed or promoted. Thirdly, an appraisal by the national authorities of the resources which can be devoted to regional development and an attempt to relate these to the regional draft strategies of different regions. This, of course, entails establishing a scale of priorities so that a choice can be made both between the claims of different regions and between various alternative objectives. Only when this is done may the final stage be reached: the preparation of agreed regional plans entailing some measure of Government commitment, and fitting in with the objectives of the National Plan.

It would clearly be somewhat simpler if such regional plans could be worked out after the preparation of the National Plan, so that the objectives of the latter could be taken as given. This, however, is hardly possible owing to the great extent of inter-dependence between national and regional planning. A National Plan will have to make assumptions about regional economic growth and about resources available for development in the regions. Thus, the British National Plan's objectives were dependent on the utilization of labour resources in the problem regions. But the Plan's assumptions here were far too crude. It is not an easy matter to utilize regional labour reserves unless they are suitably trained and available where development is taking place. Proper utilization of such resources is, therefore, dependent on regional measures; and the extent of their possible contribution to national development can best be assessed by regional planning authorities. The objectives of the National Plan therefore depend, at least in part, on regional action and on the contribution which individual regions can make to national growth. There is, therefore, a close interaction between national and regional planning. Neither exercise can be properly done without reference to the other and to a great extent they must be worked out simultaneously.

(c) *Alternatives in Regional Planning Systems*
The nature of regional planning and the type of plan produced obviously depends on the sort of regional body which is charged with producing it. Even in Britain's short experience this much is clear. As has been shown, the Scottish and Welsh documents,

since they both appeared under the signature of a Government Minister, involved a much greater degree of official commitment than the others. Many people regard the English Regional Councils and Boards as a sort of interim machinery either to be developed or replaced. Therefore, if this is so, the nature of regional planning in the future will be very heavily dependent on the character of such bodies. An obvious possibility is that these bodies become democratically elected with executive powers. This would turn them into some sort of regional Government. It is conceivable that some such structure might be among the recommendations of the Royal Commission on Local Government or that the movement towards regional devolution in Scotland or Wales might in time compel its adoption at least for those regions.

To assess the importance of this it may be useful to distinguish three types of approach to regional planning. First, one may have, as at present, advisory bodies lacking executive power whose job is to produce a report on which the Government may, if it chooses, take action. This is similar to the role played by any Royal Commission or advisory committee. While there is the obvious danger that the Government may pay insufficient attention to the report, it has the advantage that the Council, precisely because it lacks executive power, may outline the problems of the region and the possible policies which might be followed with much less inhibition than if the report constituted a commitment to action. Indeed, under such a system the Council's report is of particular importance because its persuasiveness is the only means of inducing the public authorities to take action. If, therefore, it is the purpose of regional planning to produce such reports, largely in the form of surveys or draft strategies, then there is much to be said for an advisory rather than an executive body doing it.

This approach could be carried much further than has been possible in the present series of reports. These, for the most part, concentrate on the strategy of development, but they are weak in some of the other functions described above. Clearly, economic forecasting at the regional level is still extraordinarily crude and needs much development. And the cost aspects of different types or patterns of development have hardly been tackled. Thus, though the South-East Economic Planning Council's report is largely concerned with the need to build up major new centres situated on the fringe of the region to act as countermagnates to London itself, the cost of this type of development compared with any other pattern, or with development in other regions, is not analysed

245

at all. The inclusion of forecasting and cost-benefit studies requires the use of tools of analysis and expertise which are largely lacking at present, but an attempt to tackle them would greatly improve the value of this type of report. However, the weakness of this approach to regional planning, no matter how well it is executed, is that the reports may never receive the attention they deserve. Thus, the public reaction to the present series of reports has been disappointing, and they have had very little effect on Government policy.

An executive regional body, on the other hand, would be likely to put much less emphasis on the publication of a report or draft strategy. Instead, it would be directly concerned with forming a policy, as the Highlands and Islands Development Board has been. If such a body has its own source of revenue, whether earmarked in advance from Central Government or by means of local taxes, it can implement its own programme on its own initiative. This reduces the problems of co-ordination with other regions and with the Central Government so far as the availability of public funds is concerned. Problems of regions outbidding each other and pushing objectives which were incompatible would arise, however, and these would require central co-ordination. This type of planning would seem to require elected regional Councils with their proposals subject to the normal democratic processes. Since this would approximate closely to regional Government, it would have the advantage that legislation could be more suitably geared to regional needs instead of giving rise to the curious anomalies which national legislation sometimes produces in the more remote regions. The main disadvantage is in the provision of finance for regional development. It would clearly be unsatisfactory to oblige regional authorities to rely entirely on regional taxes for their development programmes, since on this basis rich regions would have an advantage over poor. State subventions would obviously be required, but the criteria for determining these between the needs of different regions would give rise to much difficulty.

The third possibility is for regional plans to be prepared which imply a commitment on the part of Central Government to fulfil them. It seems that this was the ultimate objective of the British approach to regional planning. Such regional plans would have to neatly dovetail with each other and be compatible with the National Plan. They would be endorsed by the Central Government which would then implement them, possibly through its regional offices. But there would be no independent regional

Government. Regional Councils could be either Government nominees, as at present, or elected representatives, but they would have no executive power. Such a system implies a full reconciliation of national and regional objectives, and provided this is done it should be possible for the regional plans to be carried out. The problem is that co-ordination to this degree involves extremely complex and difficult procedures. It involves adding a geographical dimension to the National Plan, so that not only must targets be produced indicating *how much* the output of different industries in the economy is to be, but also *where* the increases are to take place. Since Britain's present attempts at planning have so far failed to tackle the quantitative aspect satisfactorily, there is little likelihood that they can deal with the spatial one in the foreseeable future.

Rather than build such a complicated edifice of targets at the national and regional levels, which will almost certainly have to be abandoned until the techniques are much more sophisticated than they are now, there seems much to be said for further improving the present advisory type of planning or of gradually moving towards a regional executive body with some clearly defined spheres in which it can use its own initiative. It is essential that the activities of the different Government departments be properly co-ordinated at the regional level instead of sometimes conflicting with each other. It is essential that the regional economic impact of public investment schemes be properly considered, that the regional growth centres be identified and built up and that the problems of the regional economy are diagnosed before they become critical. These are less ambitious tasks than a blueprint of regional expansion including targets for all the industries, but they are important and, if they can be accomplished, regional planning will have filled a useful role.

CHAPTER XI

BRITISH POLICY AND THE EUROPEAN COMMUNITY*

'The task laid down by the Treaty, i.e. to ensure the
harmonious development of economic life within the
Community and a steady and balanced economic expansion, cannot be accomplished without an active regional
policy.'
EEC Memorandum on the Action Programme for the
Second Stage

Britain has not only had a regional policy in operation longer than
most other European countries, but it is in many respects more
developed. The emphasis of the problem, too, is rather different:
though other countries have depressed industrial areas, notably
Germany and Belgium, the scale of this problem in Britain is
unique. In Europe the predominant problem of regional policy is
the development of underdeveloped rural regions and the avoidance of excessive concentration on the existing centres, notably
Paris and Randstadt—Holland.

Britain has twice attempted to join the Common Market and
full membership remains the official policy of the Government,
provided certain vital British interests can be safeguarded. One of
these was said to be the continuation of an effective regional
policy. Since there is a chance that the French veto on the negotiations may not last indefinitely and the whole question of British
membership may be re-opened sometime in the future, it is worth
considering how British policy might be affected by membership
and to what extent there is a common European policy to which
Britain would have to adhere.

Regional policy measures are, of course, in operation in all the
member states of the Common Market. They are most developed
in Italy, where the problems of the underdeveloped South are par-

* Part of this chapter was included in a paper which the author gave on 'Regional
Policy in the European Community' to a Conference on 'The Mechanics of European Integration' at Reading in December 1967. The proceedings of the conference are published under the editorship of G. R. Denton.

ticularly pressing, and least developed in Germany and Belgium. The Community authorities have for some time recognized the need for measures at the European level and, accordingly, both the Coal and Steel Community and the European Economic Community have provided various types of assistance for regional development.

I. THE REGIONAL PROBLEM IN EUROPE AND THE NEED FOR A POLICY

The nature of the regional problem in Europe differs widely from one country to another. The Italian problem is commonly regarded as the most severe. The southern half of the country, the Mezzogiorno which is densely populated with a population of eighteen million, has an income level per head barely half the Italian average. Here agriculture still employs 55 per cent of the population, productivity is low, underemployment is severe and a high rate of emigration has only been prevented from causing a fall in population by a rate population increase which is about twice the Italian average.

In France there is a serious imbalance between the industrialized North and East, but particularly between the heavy concentration on Paris, and the agricultural underdeveloped South and West. Unlike Italy, however, the French underdeveloped regions are for the most part sparsely populated and income levels are much higher than in the Mezzogiorno. Germany is much less centralized than France and, therefore, has nothing comparable to the concentration on Paris. There are, however, some agricultural problem areas, such as Schleswig-Holstein and areas of declining industry, associated mainly with the coalfields in the Rhur. In addition, special difficulties are associated with the frontier region abutting East Germany. This strip of country has been cut off from its hinterland and offers an unattractive location for new industry.

In Benelux, the Netherlands suffers from over-concentration on the urban area of Randstadt/Holland, comprising the three cities Amsterdam, Rotterdam and the Hague, while the provinces in the East are in need of development. Belgium has enjoyed rapid growth in Brussels and Antwerp, and most of the Flemish provinces, which used to suffer from low incomes and unemployment, have been attracting considerable development. The principal problem now is the stagnation in Walloon Belgium, caused by the sharp run down in the coal industry and the difficulties of the steel industry. This was originally sited on the coalfields to obtain cheap fuel, but now finds itself at a disadvantage when competing with modern integrated plants situated on the coast.

The reasons for establishing a common European regional policy may be briefly stated. First, co-ordination of national policies must be achieved if confusion is to be avoided. Second, there is a danger that the setting up of the Common Market may itself aggravate the regional problem. And third, the avoidance of serious regional disparities either between member states or within them is essential to the political cohesion of Europe.

As regards the co-ordination of national policies, just as regional problems differ considerably in intensity from one country to another, so the policies vary greatly in emphasis and in the generosity of the inducements they offer to attract industry. Without co-ordination this could lead to an attempt on the part of Europe's problem regions to outbid each other in the offer of favourable terms to industry; and attempts to control the growth of, say, Paris or Randstadt/Holland so that new development could be diverted to Brittany or Friesland would be vitiated if it went instead to Brussels or Cologne.

For the most part, all the countries offer some combination of grants or fiscal inducement to attract industry to their problem areas. Industrial estates are also provided, though this policy has not been so highly developed as in Britain. But otherwise there are some important differences in emphasis. Italy, for example, has spent enormous sums on public investment. New motorways have been built to the South, the standard of the public services has been improved and costly irrigation and land reclamation projects have been undertaken. Of particular importance in Italy has been the part played by the public holding companies, IRI and ENI, already referred to in Chapter VIII.[1] These have carried out much of the public investment and have also developed many of the major industrial projects in the South: the steelworks at Taranto, petrochemicals in Sicily and the proposed Alfa-Romeo works in Campania. France and the Netherlands have both undertaken heavy public investment in certain areas to encourage development. Furthermore, France is the only country among the Six to use physical controls to restrict development. Unlike the British IDC, however, this control is not nationwide but is limited to the Paris area. In Belgium, though there has been some heavy public investment in canals and new motorways are proposed,

[1] Istituto Reconstruzione Industriale and Ente Nazionale Idrocarburi. See p. 205.

regional policy is mainly limited to inducements to private industry.

With these wide differences in approach there is thus a serious danger of a chaotic situation arising when complete freedom of movement for capital and labour becomes a reality. Some problem regions may gain at the expense of others, either because the terms offered are more generous or because problem regions by the standards of one country are not problem regions at all by the standards of another. Some parts of Italy outside the Mezzogiorno, for example, which would not be regarded as problem regions by Italian standards, may yet be in a more serious economic condition than some of the scheduled problem areas in Belgium or the Netherlands. It is, therefore, necessary to establish some agreement not only on the measures applied to regional development, but on the definition of problem regions and whether it might be desirable to have different categories of problem area.

The second problem is that the establishment of the Common Market itself may aggravate the regional problem. This may arise in three ways: first, the increased competition and the gains from specialization will cause the industries in some countries to gain at the expense of those elsewhere. This has serious regional implications particularly in agriculture and the fuel industries. The agricultural problems have already led to difficulties in certain areas and the fall in demand for coal has naturally affected most seriously those areas where coal-mining was least productive. The steel industry, in a time of over-capacity, has been suffering from similar problems.

Secondly, the gradual replacement of national markets by a European market may lead firms increasingly to prefer a location at the centre of Europe. Sites which were satisfactory for supplying, say, the French or Italian markets, may be sub-optimal for a European market and sites in South-West France, the Mezzogiorno or Schleswig-Holstein, which were peripheral to the French, Italian or German economies, will be even more peripheral to the European economy. One might, therefore, expect the Common Market to increase the relative advantages of a location within, say, the central zone roughly bounded by Cologne, Amsterdam, Paris and Milan and to aggravate the disadvantages of Northern Germany, South-West France and Southern Italy. The extent of this effect, of course, depends on the importance industries attach to being near the centre of their market area. Obviously this will be more important for some types of industry than others and in the

251

present state of knowledge no clear picture can be obtained. Suffice it to note that, in the past, within the national economies there has been a marked tendency for economic activity to be attracted to the market centres or areas of highest economic potential as defined by Clark.[1]

The third way in which the Common Market may aggravate the regional problem is through a gradual tendency to equalize factor earnings. This follows closely the effects of trade on regional development as analysed in Chapter II. There it was suggested that, whereas trade between countries commonly took place on the basis of comparative advantage, freedom of factor movements and institutional effects such as national collective wage bargaining caused regional factor earnings to approach equality.[2] In consequence, regional trade was limited to absolute advantage. Weaker regions were thus typified by unemployment and outflow of factors of production. The setting up of the Common Market may be expected to have something of this effect in Europe. Labour and capital are already able to move relatively freely from one country to another, though complete freedom of movement is not yet a reality and many legal and institutional barriers still exist. In time, however, it may be expected that factor earnings will tend towards greater equality in Europe; and, if that is so, weaker regions which may previously have survived by paying their factors of production at a lower rate than elsewhere will be forced to increase their efficiency or decline. Thus, capital and labour may tend to flow to the more advanced regions of the European economy, not necessarily limiting their movement within one national state.

This process, of course, tends to be cumulative. The expansion of the advanced regions and the decline of the less prosperous increases the economies of scale and the external economies of economic activity in the former compared with the latter. The tendency is, therefore, for the advantages of the advanced regions to be increased and their power of attracting new economic activity to become stronger, so that the problems of the less prosperous regions become harder to resolve. Yet on economic grounds alone such a process would be highly undesirable. The tendency towards increasing concentration, which has already been discussed in Chapter I, almost certainly involves a disproportionate rise in

[1] Colin Clark, 'Industrial Location and Economic Potential', *Lloyds Bank Review*, Oct. 1966.
[2] See pp. 79–80 above.

social costs, increases the dangers of inflationary pressure and leaves some resources which are not fully employed. It is to correct these tendencies that regional policy is necessary.

If the formation of the Common Market were to aggravate regional disparities in any of the ways described above, it would, of course, be disastrous to the political cohesion of Europe. With different languages and cultures, separatist tendencies must be strong and it would take little to fan the flames of mutual distrust and misunderstanding. The attempt to achieve economic, and later perhaps political, union is therefore a bold experiment. It is a condition of success that each member state must be able to gain from the union. If one state were to become a depressed region while the others prospered, the project would be doomed. Similarly, if important areas of any member state were to suffer serious adverse effects, this would impose such political pressure on the Government of that state that it might have to block further development towards economic union.

An effective regional policy is thus a necessary condition of successful economic, and eventually political, union. This does not mean that measures have to be taken to cushion the effects of increased competition and specialization by bolstering up the industries adversely affected. If regional aids were used for that purpose there would certainly be little point in having a Common Market. The purpose of regional policy is rather to ease the structural readjustment of the problem regions by identifying the possibilities for development, introducing new expanding activities which can be made to flourish in the area, removing where possible the obstacles to development by means of labour training and public investment and creating an environment conducive to growth. If this can be done, regional policy can assist the realization of the Common Market by resolving the very problems which, if left to themselves, might force national Governments to impede its progress.

II. THE ACTION TAKEN BY THE COMMUNITIES

The possibility that European economic integration may aggravate the regional problem has been clearly recognized both by the European Economic Commission and by the High Authority of the Coal and Steel Community.[1] The importance of regional policy

[1] EEC *Memorandum of the Commission on the Action Programme of the Community for the Second Stage*, Brussels 1962.

towards the achievement of European unity is therefore well understood. It has also become clear that the general policies followed by the Communities in fiscal policy, tariffs, etc., and the common policies adopted for particular sectors, notably agriculture, transport, energy and social affairs, are likely to have profound regional repercussions. However, both organizations up to the present time have taken the view that action in this field is mainly the responsibility of national Governments and that the role of the two Communities is primarily to co-ordinate the policies of Governments and to give supplementary assistance in particular cases.

A general aim of the EEC is, of course, to remove subsidies and restrictions of various kinds which distort, or threaten to distort, competition, thus adversely affecting trade between member countries. However, under Article 92 of the Treaty of Rome, exceptions are made for certain specific types of aid, among which are the following:

(a) aids intended to promote the economic development of regions where the standard of living is abnormally low or where there exists serious underemployment;

(b) aids intended to facilitate the development of certain activities or of certain economic regions, provided that such aids do not change trading conditions to such a degree as would be contrary to the common interest.

Moreover, the preamble to the Treaty speaks of the 'harmonious development' of economic activities and 'balanced expansion' which will be attained by 'reducing the differences existing between the various regions and by mitigating the backwardness of the less favoured'.

It is thus clear that from the start regional policy was intended to be a matter of concern for the EEC Commission. The Treaty also gave the Commission certain powers. On the one hand, policies pursued by national Governments might be found to be incompatible with the Treaty; this might apply to regional policy as to other fields of policy, and in such cases the Commission could demand amendments to be made. On the other hand, many common Community policies which came to be adopted might have regional implications and these were to be taken into account in forming the policies. The Treaty also set up two financial institutions, the European Investment Bank and the European

Social Fund, which had powers to provide finance to assist in the removal of regional disequilibria.

The European Coal and Steel Community has, of course, a more limited concern with the regional problem, in that its interest is confined to the coal, iron and steel industries. On the other hand, these industries have given rise to some of the most acute examples of the regional problem in industrial areas; and particularly with the contraction of the coal industry in the late 'fifties, the need for special measures was manifest. Moreover, the Coal and Steel Community has been in existence much longer than the Economic Community and it has, therefore, had more time to evolve a policy.

In 1951, when the Treaty of Paris was signed, there seemed little likelihood of a contraction in demand for coal or steel products and little emphasis was laid on regional or social problems. However, in Article 2 the Treaty outlines its aim to achieve 'the most rational distribution of production at the highest possible level of productivity, *while safeguarding the continuity of employment and avoiding the creation of fundamental and persistent disturbances in the economies of member states*'.[1] Article 56 permitted the compensation of workers who had become unemployed as a result of technological change, but only under rather strict conditions, and Article 46 permits the High Authority to undertake and participate in studies designed to raise the living standards of workers or to re-employ those who are unemployed.

Greater scope was provided by the Convention which set out measures necessary for the five-year transitional period. In this document it was foreseen that the rationalization of Europe's coal and steel industries was likely to lead to unemployment. Section 23 of the Convention, therefore, permitted the High Authority, at the request of member Governments, to assist the retraining and resettlement of workers, to compensate the unemployed until they found new employment, and to assist enterprises with reconversion. In addition, the High Authority could participate in studies to find ways of re-employing the unemployed.

The Convention was only applicable to the transitional period and this came to an end officially in 1958. However, the operation of Section 23 was extended for a further two years until February 1960. In the meantime the coal and steel industries had run into a period of structural readjustment brought on largely by competition from other fuels. It was clear that this was producing

[1] My italics.

255

greater dislocation of the labour force than could be ascribed merely to the transitional period of ECSC and that permanent policies were desirable. Article 56 of the Treaty was too restrictive as it stood; from 1952 to 1959 no assistance had been granted under it, since no application had fulfilled all its conditions.[1] Accordingly, a revision of this article was made which empowered the High Authority to continue to provide the type of readaptation and reconversion assistance which had up till then been given under the Convention. Such assistance could be given where an enterprise had to cease, reduce or change its activities due to changes in market conditions, even if this was not related to the establishment of the Common Market in coal and steel products. This revised article now forms the basis of the High Authority's regional measures.

The Co-ordination of Policies

The Commission saw its first task in the co-ordination of regional policy measures. No measures instituted by individual Governments have so far been disallowed, but efforts have been made to increase inter-Governmental understanding and communication. The Commission's first move, therefore, was to call a conference of experts from the different countries at which a number of papers on Europe's problem regions were presented.[2] Working groups were then set up to prepare reports on three different aspects of the regional problem: (1) the problem of regions in need of development, (2) the conversion of old industrial regions and (3) the effectiveness of different measures pursued by member countries.[3] These reports were summarized and developed to form the Commission's own views on regional policy in a memorandum published in 1965.[4] This document, however, is not really the basis of a common policy so much as a survey of the existing situation with the Commission's own view of the type of measures which are most suitable.

In this document the Commission suggested that member states

[1] F. Finck, *L'action de la Haute Autorité pour le réemploi des travailleurs,* in ECSC *Collection d'Economie et Politique Régionale, I, La Conversion Industrielle en Europe,* Vol. III.
[2] *Documents de la Conférence sur les Economies Régionales,* Vol. I, Brussels 1961.
[3] *Rapport de Groupes d'expert sur la politique régionale dans la CEF,* July 1964.
[4] *Regional Policy in the European Community,* Community Topics document 24 1965. This report also forms the basis of the Chapter on regional policy in the *Preliminary Draft of a First Medium Term Economic Policy Programme, 1966–70,* 788/11/1966/E Brussels 1966.

should make regional plans for as many regions as possible in the Community. The plans should be compatible with general economic policy and steps should be taken to provide forecasts of employment and population by region and to improve regional statistics. In the underdeveloped regions the Commission favoured the creation of 'development poles' or growth areas in which development would be concentrated in the hope that it could become self-sustaining after the initial period of assistance. It pointed out the need for improved agricultural structure and for public investment in infrastructure. In old industrial areas it found a need not only to attract new industry but to train workers in new skills and to undertake urban renewal. It took the view that financial aids should only be given to new development which would ultimately be able to face competition on its own; but it stressed that public services should not be allowed, in setting their charges, to discriminate in favour of the concentration of economic activity.

For itself, the Commission agreed to undertake a number of detailed studies. These were to cover (1) the techniques and methods of regional planning in order to assist with the preparation of regional plans; (2) the progress of certain large regions in the Community since the EEC was founded; (3) the establishment of 'poles of development' in certain areas, and (4) the effect on costs which would arise from an excessive concentration of economic activity. The Commission also undertook to have regard to regional implications in framing agricultural, transport and energy policies.

Some of the studies have now been prepared and others are under way. A study of the development pole to be based on the area comprising Bari, Brindisi and Taranto in the heel of Italy was commissioned from independent consultants and is now published.[1] This is the first full-scale study of the techniques for establishing a development pole; it concentrates attention particularly on the selection of industries and employs a variant of input/output analysis for this purpose. Studies are also in progress of the border areas between France and Belgium and their development as an integrated economic region and on the Eifel-Hunsrück area in Germany. A committee has been set up to examine the employment situation in Sicily and to report on the possibilities of developing the sulphur industry.

[1] EEC: *Studio per la creazione di un polo industriale di sviluppo in Italia Mendionale*, Serie economia e finanza No. 5, Brussels 1966.

257

The European Coal and Steel Community has also devoted a large part of its effort to studies of problem areas. Some of these it carries out itself; others it helps to finance. The studies are now much too numerous to mention, but examples of the former type are those dealing with the Saar, the Ghent-Zelzate district, Lorraine, Liguria and Piombino. Studies where assistance was given include Westphalia, Borinage and Auvergne/Aquitaine. In each case the area covered is dependent on one of the industries for which ECSC has responsibility and in most cases the studies have provided invaluable information for the subsequent introduction of readaptation and reconversion assistance.

Financial Assistance
(a) *European Investment Bank*
The main EEC organs for providing financial assistance with regional problems are the European Investment Bank and the European Social Fund. The former is charged with granting loans and guarantees to assist various different types of project associated with the development of the Common Market, including projects for developing the less developed regions. The Bank's Capital is subscribed by the member states and it may raise loans from the capital markets or borrow direct from member states. Aid is subject to unanimous approval by the Commission and the management committee of EIB and must also be approved by the member state in whose territory the project is to be carried out. Moreover, the Bank participates in the financing of projects only if finance from other sources is also used. Indeed, in 1966 the Bank's average participation in the projects it helped to finance was 22 per cent.[1] Rates of interest are calculated so as to enable the Bank to meet its obligations and build up a reserve of 10 per cent of subscribed capital. The selection of projects to be assisted is based on their expected profitability.

Up to the present time the majority of the Bank's loans have been given to projects in underdeveloped regions, notably the South of Italy. This is clearly shown by the figures for loans approved at December 1966: 58 per cent of ordinary loans had been given for projects in the South of Italy compared with 67 per cent for Italy as a whole. The loans to other countries, although much smaller in total, were also largely devoted to projects in problem areas. The loans for the South of Italy were administered through the Cassa per il Mezzogiorno and cover agricultural

[1] EIB Annual Report 1966, p. 51.

258

development, modernization of road and railway networks, as well as industrial investment. Indeed, the Bank's loans at December 1966 were distributed between sectors in the following manner: industry 40 per cent, of which by far the largest shares went to mining and chemicals; transport 26 per cent, power 18 per cent and agriculture 14 per cent.

The Bank's powers, of course, depend on its ability to raise capital, and member states have been urged to improve its access to national capital markets. The need to operate on a commercial basis also compels it to approach regional development projects with some caution. Nevertheless, it has made an important contribution to regional development.

TABLE I

BREAKDOWN OF EIB LOANS BY COUNTRY 1958–66
AT DECEMBER 31, 1966

	No. of projects	Loans million units of account	Share in total %
I. *Ordinary loans*			
Belgium	1	4.8	1
Germany	1	51.2	7
France	14	84.7	11
Italy	85	458.5	61
Luxembourg	1	4.0	1
	112	603.2	81
Associated Countries	21	75.1	10
II. *Special loans* (Turkey)	13	67.8	9

Source: European Investment Bank Annual Report 1966.
Note: 1 unit of account equals 1 US dollar.

(b) *European Social Fund*

Unlike the Bank, the European Social Fund is not concerned with the setting up of new enterprises: its main contribution to the regional problem comes in the promotion of labour mobility both between occupations and between regions. Under the EEC Treaty the purpose of the Fund is to contribute towards expenses incurred by a member state in (1) occupational retraining of the unemployed, (2) resettlement and (3) the maintenance of wage levels of workers made temporarily or permanently redundant owing to

259

the conversion of the enterprise for which they worked. Its contributions under these headings may be up to 50 per cent of total expense incurred.

The payments made by the Fund are subject to the following conditions. Resettlement assistance may be given if the unemployed have had to change their place of residence within the Community, provided that they have retained their new employment for at least six months. Contributions to the wage level in cases of reconversion are subject to the proviso that the workers concerned had been with the enterprise in question for at least six months and that the Government concerned has submitted a conversion plan drawn up by the enterprise and approved by the Commission.

Up to the present time the largest share of the Fund's expenditure has gone to Italy (see Table II). Its activities have been mainly limited to reimbursing expenditure incurred in different member states rather than initiating any scheme or programme of its own. It has been criticized on this ground in the European

TABLE II

ACTIVITIES OF THE EUROPEAN SOCIAL FUND

	Aid granted in 000 units of account			Persons Benefiting		
	Retraining	Resettlement	Total	Retraining	Resettlement	Total
			January 1 to December 31, 1966			
Germany	1,374	54	1,428	1,840	5,057	6,897
Belgium	596	—	596	1,017	—	1,017
France	1,314	51	1,365	1,966	6,657	8,623
Italy	3,766	33	3,799	34,716	298	35,014
Luxembourg	—	—	—	—	—	—
Netherlands	1,509	—	1,509	2,081	—	2,081
EEC	8,559	138	8,697	41,620	12,012	53,632
			September 20, 1960—December 31, 1966			
Germany	7,696	616	8,312	38,780	64,377	103,157
Belgium	2,490	2	2,492	5,864	9	5,873
France	10,628	415	11,044	20,588	58,836	79,424
Italy	12,653	1,940	14,593	142,830	167,652	310,482
Luxembourg	9	—	9	92	—	92
Netherlands	3,925	15	3,940	8,502	205	8,707
EEC	37,402	2,989	40,390	216,656	291,074	507,735

Source: EEC Tenth General Report on the Activities of the Community.
Note: I unit of account equals 1 US dollar.

Parliament and it seems likely that it will be given greater powers of initiative in the future.

(c) *The High Authority*

Under the revision of the Treaty of Paris, referred to above, the new Article 56 enables the High Authority of the Coal and Steel Community to provide assistance both for readaptation of labour and for industrial reconversion. As with the European Social Fund, under the heading of readaptation aid may be given to assist with the cost of retraining, resettlement, compensation for up to twelve months for a drop in pay sustained by the re-employed and to provide towards the cost of commuting to a job in a new location. Like the Social Fund, the Authority will not normally contribute more than 50 per cent of the total expenditure incurred, the remainder being borne by the Governments concerned.

Table III shows that the greatest beneficiary from readaptation expenditure has been Germany. Indeed, during the seven years since the revised Article 56 came into operation, 45 per cent of the total expenditure has gone to Germany and this has covered an even higher proportion of total employees. Belgium, too, has received assistance throughout the period and so has France. Italy and the Netherlands, on the other hand, received no assistance from 1960 till 1965 and Luxembourg until 1966. The total expenditure has fluctuated remarkably, falling to a low figure in 1964 but rising to an all-time high of 16.5 million units of account in 1966. As might be expected, by far the largest group of workers to receive assistance were coal-miners, these forming 88 per cent of the total assisted in 1966. No doubt, this also explains, to a large extent, the national distribution of total expenditure, since Germany and Belgium are the two countries in which coal-mining plays the largest part in the economy.

Assistance with industrial reconversion did not get under-way until the late 1950s when it became increasingly apparent that readaptation of the labour force fell far short of a complete solution to the problem. The High Authority is empowered to give assistance for the reorganization of existing coal, steel and iron ore industries, as it did in the case of the Sulcis mines in Sardinia or the Belgian mines. In such instances, assistance may provide towards the costs of new investment or temporarily subsidize the loss made on output while reorganization is being carried out. Alternatively, it may give aid for the attraction of new enterprises

261

TABLE III
HIGH AUTHORITY AID

I. Expenditure on Readaptation of Labour

	Feb. 1, 1966—Jan. 31, 1967			Mar. 29, 1960—Dec. 31, 1966		Under Section 23 of the Convention Mar. 18, 1954—Feb. 9, 1960	
	000 units of account	*Forecast Employees Affected*	*%*	*000 units of account*	*Forecast Employees Affected*	*000 units of account*	*Employees Affected*
West Germany	7,619	34,369	59	19,436	100,999	17,346	55,100
Belgium	3,022	10,090	17	7,952	30,225	10,560	28,900
France	1,027	2,659	5	5,969	12,251	2,512	11,905
Italy	1,302	1,624	3	5,119	6,130	12,100	19,180
Luxembourg	100	150	—	100	150	—	—
Netherlands	3,480	9,500	16	4,171	12,200	—	—
	16,550	58,392	100	42,748	161,955	42,518	115,085
of which:							
Coal	13,902	51,132					
Iron ore	674	2,121					
Steel	1,974	5,139					

II. Expenditure on Industrial Reconversion
February 1, 1966—January 31, 1967

	Loans, 000 units of account	*Forecast Employment*
West Germany	2,800	1,026— 1,036
Belgium	15,000	—
France	15,250	22,000—34,000
Italy	10,350	1,580— 2,580
Netherlands	11,360	6,200— 6,300
	54,760	

Source: EEC 15th General Report.

and the provision of public services and infrastructure which are necessary for this; the only condition is that such development must utilize unemployed workers from the coal, steel or iron ore industries. An example of this type of scheme, in which the High Authority participated, is provided by the programme prepared by the Société Provinciale d'Industrialization for Liège. This aimed to create 4,000 jobs and included the clearing of colliery sites, the provision of industrial estates and the building of factories.

Such assistance may take the form of either loans or guarantees. The interest rates charged have not normally exceeded 5 per cent and the Authority will raise the money from the international capital market. Until 1965, the terms of each reconversion loan were negotiated individually and depended on the terms on which the High Authority itself could raise the money. In 1965, however, in order to give a greater boost to reconversion, standard terms were introduced and the Authority used money from its special reserve to keep interest rates well below market levels. These terms are as follows:[1]

(1) Loans are normally granted for 30 per cent of the capital cost of a project but may be increased in special cases.
(2) The normal duration of a loan is ten to thirteen years.
(3) Redemption will be by equal annual instalments beginning from the end of the third year.
(4) Interest is at 4.5 per cent for the first five years and 6.5 per cent thereafter.

The Authority expected that these terms would attract a larger flow of applicants and that they would, therefore, stimulate a wide range of projects.

Table III shows that expenditure on reconversion in 1966 was more than three times the total spent on readaptation. Belgium and France were the main beneficiaries with Germany getting the smallest share. The effect of the 1965 measures is certainly evident in the figures, since the expenditure authorized in 1966 at 54.8 million units of account exceeds the combined total of thirty million units for all the years 1960 to 1965.[2]

(d) *The European Agricultural Guidance and Guarantee Fund*
The fourth organ which may provide assistance for regional development is specifically concerned with agriculture. Under the

[1] ECSC 14th General Report.
[2] ECSC 15th General Report.

common agricultural policy a guidance and guarantee fund was established with two explicit functions.[1] The first was support buying of agricultural produce when the market price fell below the intervention price; this is not relevant to the present discussion. But the second was to help finance the structural improvement of European agriculture. Up to the present, the Fund has been financed partly by contributions from national exchequers and partly from the import levies on imported agricultural produce, but eventually it is intended that import levies will finance the guarantee section almost entirely. The guidance section will continue to be financed according to a fixed scale. By far the greater part of the expenditure has gone in support buying. This can be extremely expensive if the produce bought has then to be exported at the much lower prices prevailing on international markets.

It is not yet clear how the structural reform will be organized, in particular whether the Commission will simply contribute to national schemes or take an initiative of its own. This is, however, regarded as an important part of its activities, since the promotion of greater efficiency in European agriculture is the only method of reducing the industry's very high level of protection without acute social and economic distress for the farming community. At present, owing mainly to historical and social factors, the EEC countries suffer from a very poor agricultural structure, much worse than the British or Scandinavian. Farms are not only much too small but fragmented into several pieces. The average farm in Germany, for instance, is fragmented into eleven separate parts and the total size is only twenty acres.[2] The industry is consequently heavily overmanned and output per head in Germany, France and Italy is only about half what it is in Britain or Denmark.[3] Expenditure on structural reform, whether in the form of amalgamation of holdings or the draining and reclaiming of land, can improve this situation. It will tend to raise agricultural incomes and so greatly help the economies of many underdeveloped agricultural regions. But by raising labour productivity it is also likely to make a considerable part of the labour force redundant. Here there is an important interconnection with the creation of new activities in such regions. The availability of alternative employ-

---

[1] *Fond Européen d'Orientation et de Guarantie Agricole*, usually known by its initials FEOGA.
[2] *Statistique Agricole*, 1961, No. 1. Office Statistique des Communantés Européenes.
[3] G. Sharp and C. W. Capstick, 'The Place of Agriculture in the National Economy', *Journal of Agricultural Economics*, May 1966.

ment would encourage the surplus labour to leave agriculture and so raise productivity, while the raising of agricultural productivity is one of the surest means of making an increased labour supply available for other activities. The attraction of new industry and agricultural improvement, therefore, need to be considered together as complementary parts of a regional policy;[1] this the present machinery, operating through the Agricultural Fund, is not yet able to do.

France has so far enjoyed the lion's share of total payments from FEOGA. Although she contributes only about 30 per cent of the Fund's receipts, she received in 1966 80 per cent of the payments. This, however, is mainly from the guarantee section of the Fund. The guidance section is much smaller financially, amounting to £17 million units of account in 1966. Of this the largest share went to Italy, 5.9 million units for forty projects, followed by Germany 5.0 million and France 3.7 million. Many more projects were submitted than could be financed and the grants made amounted on average to 25 per cent of the total investment cost. It is expected that annual expenditure under the guidance section will rise to 250–300 million units of account by 1970. The distribution of payments from the guidance section is always likely to give France and Italy a large share since both these countries have large agricultural land areas; agriculture accounts for a large share of their gross national product, and, particularly in Italy, agricultural improvement is essential for the elimination of rural poverty.

TABLE IV

FEOGA EXPENDITURE UNDER THE GUIDANCE SECTION 1966

	000 units of account	%
West Germany	4,969	29
Belgium	755	4
France	3,692	21
Italy	5,866	34
Luxembourg	275	2
Netherlands	1,577	9
	17,134	100

Source: Tenth General Report EEC 1967.

It may thus be seen that each of the foregoing organs, in providing finance, tends to favour a particular part of the EEC,

[1] Report by Professors Priebe and Möller, *La politique régionale condition du succès de la politique agricole*, EEC Série agriculture 4, Brussels 1961.

265

depending on the purpose for which it is applied. The largest share of the funds from the European Investment Bank and the European Social Fund go to Italy; Italy has also been the largest beneficiary from the guidance section of the Agricultural Fund so far. But Germany and Belgium get the preponderant part of the assistance from the High Authority. Such a division is natural, given the particular problems of individual countries. But though each organ may apportion its own funds according to appropriate criteria, there is little evidence that the total combined expenditure is apportioned between reconversion, readaptation of labour and agricultural improvement according to any thought-out scale of priorities. Yet such a scale ought to be a fundamental part of a European regional policy.

III. BRITISH MEMBERSHIP AND THE DEVELOPMENT OF EUROPEAN POLICY

The measures so far taken by the European Economic Community and by the Coal and Steel Community are of considerable value in helping to tackle the regional problem; but they cannot be described as a common European regional policy. At the very least, a common policy would require agreed criteria for scheduling problem regions and an agreed scale of incentives and inducements. If physical controls on development were used, these would also require co-ordinated procedures. Ideally the role and techniques of regional planning also need some supranational co-ordination so that a European view can be taken of the spatial distribution of economic activity and population. At present none of this exists and the action so far taken at a European level is limited to co-ordination by means of inter-Governmental consultation, the sponsoring of regional studies and the provision of various types of financial assistance, all of which supplement national regional policy measures. Under such an arrangement it is still possible for regional policy to vary widely from one country to another, both as regards the meaning of a problem region, the determination with which regional policy is implemented and the generosity and effectiveness of individual measures.

As far as Britain is concerned, her entry to the Common Market in present circumstances would clearly raise many fewer problems of adjustment than if a common European regional policy existed to which she was obliged to conform. Britain's regional policy is, perhaps, more far-reaching and accorded higher priority than in

266

any of the Six save Italy, but the policy itself is similar in kind to Continental policies. All rely on a broadly similar range of incentives and inducements; and the provision of industrial estates, following its early success in Britain, is now an important part of policy in most EEC countries. The roles of public investment and growth points are being discussed and tried out in several countries. Regional planning is in vogue in France, Italy and Benelux, though it is doubtful if it has yet achieved any more in these countries than it has in Britain. With all these similarities there is no reason to suppose that Britain would be compelled to follow a different *kind* of policy if she joined EEC. The terms of Article 92 are sufficiently broad to permit the type of incentives and inducements which are currently offered.[1] Insofar as any differences existed between the scale and generosity of British measures and those used in EEC countries, this would pose no problem at present, since Continental practice varies so widely. Similarly, differences between the British definition of Development Areas and Continental practice is no greater than between EEC members themselves.

There are, however, two specific problems which could raise serious difficulty. British policy has always relied heavily on the use of controls over new development. The Industrial Development Certificates go back to the 1947 Town and Country Planning Act and have always been regarded as one of the most important weapons of regional policy. In recent years the exemption limit has been lowered and offices have been brought under control by the Office Development Permits. It may be that these negative measures are less important than they used to be since the inducements have been stepped up. But they are still an essential feature of British regional policy. There is, of course, nothing in the Treaty of Rome which would compel such controls to be dropped; but there is a serious danger that their effectiveness would be diminished. Capital movements are already less restricted between members of the Six than they are between Britain and the Six. In time it must be expected that there will be complete capital and labour mobility and that the present administrative and legal restrictions impeding mergers between companies in different member states will be eliminated. In such conditions the application of controls to new development in one member state, while having others unrestricted, may seriously backfire. An attempt to control new development in the South and Midlands of England

[1] See p. 254 above.

for the purpose of diverting it to Scotland, Wales or Ireland, could just as easily result in it going to Rotterdam or Antwerp and yet serve the same market. Of present EEC members only France, as pointed out earlier, attempts to use such controls and these are limited to Paris and, therefore, much more restricted than the British system. Given that controls are an essential part of British policy, there seems no solution to this problem in the event of British membership save their adoption by all EEC members. This is a step they may be reluctant to take, but it would do much to give European regional policy more meaning.

The second problem arises over the Regional Employment Premium. This is one of the most far-reaching measures of tax discrimination in favour of regional development to be found in Europe. No similar incentive is applied by any of the Six and it might easily provoke complaints of unfair competition. Nevertheless, it does appear to come within the terms of Article 92 and therefore would be perfectly legal. What is much less certain, however, is the position of Selective Employment Tax. Nothing similar to this tax exists in EEC and the discrimination in favour of manufacturing industry and exports which it implies would almost certainly be regarded as incompatible with the Treaty. The Common Market is, in any case, evolving its own system of company taxation based on the Value Added Tax. Britain would have to adopt this in place of much of her present system. The question is whether the abolition of SET would also entail the removal of REP. REP is, of course, an offshoot of the SET system, from which it was developed. There seems no obvious reason why REP should not survive even if SET were to be abolished, but the maintenance of the administrative machinery for one without the other would be clumsy and expensive. An alternative, already suggested in Chapter VIII, is to see whether a form of regional discrimination could be built into the Value Added Tax. A regional VAT, if practicable, could have much the same effect as the present REP and it would, perhaps, be more readily adopted for regional policy by other European countries. Britain, having at last evolved a major weapon of regional tax discrimination which appears to offer substantial advantages, should not lightly abandon it. Moreover, a REP or regional VAT system, or some variant of the same idea, offers tremendous possibilities as one of the foundation stones for an effective European policy.

The effect of membership on British policy, however, would also bring some advantages. The activities of the European Investment

Bank in this country would probably be limited, as they are in Germany, though possibly Ireland could obtain substantial aid from this source. Little can be expected either from the social Fund or the guidance section of the Agricultural Fund. Britain's agricultural structure is far from perfect, but it is superior to that of any of the Six. The High Authority, on the other hand, could be expected to give Britain a generous share of its loans. Britain has easily the largest coal industry of any nation in Western Europe and the output is very little less than the coal output of all six member states of EEC combined. Like every other country, however, Britain will suffer a continuing decline in her coal industry and this could easily be the dominant problem of British regional policy for the next decade or more. Much redeployment has already taken place, but large sums are going to be needed in the years ahead for retraining, resettlement and the setting up of new industries where possible. Britain would have a right to expect substantial aid from the High Authority for this.

The effect of membership on the regional problem, as distinct from policy, would be much the same in Britain as in other countries. For the various reasons outlined in the first part of this chapter, there is a danger that the regional problem would be aggravated by economic union. British agriculture, generally, especially since devaluation, would do well from the EEC system. But the main beneficiaries would be the grain growers and, to a smaller extent, the beef producers. The present production grants, of which about £50 million a year is given in fertilizer subsidies, would probably have to go and this would have a particularly serious effect on farmers on marginal land and hill land. Producers of pigs, eggs and milk would suffer from a sharp rise in the cost of grain feedingstuffs. To some extent these types of farms are concentrated in certain parts of the country, Wales, Northern Ireland and parts of Scotland, and in this respect there might be regional difficulties. Another problem is that the peripheral regions of Britain are even more peripheral to the European market than they are to the British. If the centre of the British market is somewhere between Manchester and London, the centre of the European market would be somewhere between London, Paris and Cologne. Efforts to develop East Coast parts such as Humberside, the Tees, the Tyne and the Forth could do something to remedy this. While it would be a grave mistake to overemphasize the importance of a central location, yet the fact remains that Northern England, Scotland and especially Northern Ireland are not

269

ideally placed geographically for a European market.

Whether or not Britain joins EEC eventually, it is clear that the need for a common European regional policy is urgent. If Britain were a member, with her long experience of regional measures, she would be well placed to play a key role in the development of such a policy. It would be in her interest to do so since the chaos which could result from overconcentration, attempts by regions to outbid each other, and widening regional disparities, would have as serious an effect on the British economy as on the economies of any of the present members. Moreover, Britain has experience of the IDC system and the REP, modifications of which could form the basis of a European policy.

The problems of evolving such a common policy, however, must not be underestimated. Whatever the economist may like to think, regional policy springs in part from political pressure and the policy-makers must tread warily. Not only are the views of Governments so different that policies are hard to co-ordinate, but the regional issue can easily arouse strong and disruptive passions, especially where historical boundaries and linguistic or cultural differences are concerned. Various political separatist groups or regional enthusiasts may try to use the EEC's interest as a means of embarrassing their own Governments. And there could be no clearer prescription for disaster than for the Commission to appear to be championing such groups against Brussels, Paris, Rome or Bonn. In a British context this might appear as backing the Scots or the Welsh against London. Yet, the paradox remains: in the long run separatism feeds on economic grievance. An effective regional policy is, therefore, essential to Europe's political and economic cohesion and to the success of the European Community.

CONCLUSION

As a result of the changes made in the last six years, Britain now has a more developed and far-reaching regional policy than ever before. Probably no other Western European country employs such a comprehensive range of measures, and few give regional development the priority which Governments of both major political parties in Britain have done in the 1960s. From its humble and ineffectual beginnings in the 1930s, regional policy has grown to embrace controls on development, capital incentives, the regional employment premium, industrial estates, public investment and regional planning. As this book has shown, this development of policy was not continuous, nor was policy pursued with equal determination throughout the thirty-five years or so since it was started. Only in two short periods, 1945–48 and in the 1960s, was regional policy given really high priority. These were the times when the biggest changes were made in the legislation, when the measures were applied with greatest emphasis and significant results obtained.

The gross expenditure on regional policy measures is now at a rate in excess of £200 million per annum, certainly a large increase when compared with the paltry sums, less than £10 million a year, which were spent in the 1950s. Clearly the incentives offered to stimulate regional development are now much more generous than ever before. But sums of this magnitude seem not unreasonable when compared with other items of Government expenditure. And in any case it must be remembered that a high proportion of the amount spent returns to the Government in company taxation, so that the net benefit to the Development Areas is much less than the gross figure would suggest. As a result of these measures the Government can certainly claim to have made an impact on the regional problem. Though the Development Areas contain only about 20 per cent of the nation's population, they have received in recent years nearly half the new employment created by projects for which Industrial Development Certificates were granted, or one-third of the new factory building in terms of floor space. The only other time when results on this scale were

271

achieved was in the immediate post-war years. These results by themselves do not mean that regional disparities in income levels and employment are being reduced, since the problem regions still have an excessive share of declining industry. But the analysis of regional performance in this book did show that the problem regions had done much better in the 1960s than they did in the second half of the 1950s. Whereas in those years regional disparities tended to widen, they have been held and in some cases narrowed in the 1960s. Thus, the problem regions did not suffer such high levels of unemployment in the 1967 squeeze as they did during the 1962–63 recession, although for the country as a whole 1967 was certainly a worse year. Regional growth rates have kept up and in some cases exceeded the United Kingdom rate in the 1960s; and there is some evidence that the gap in labour earnings and in incomes has narrowed slightly. Regional emigration remains a serious problem especially from Scotland, but while the booming parts of the South-West and the Midlands still attract population, it is most significant that the inflow to the South-East has been virtually halted.

For those who seek a rapid cure, these results may seem disappointing. But in reality they are most important. A solution to the regional problem requires a drastic change in regional economic structure. This is not something which can be rapidly accomplished. The coal industry will be subject to a continuing decline for many years yet and the areas in which it is located will remain in need of measures to revamp their economies. Moreover, industries which are booming today may become the declining industries of twenty years hence. Though the regional problem may change both in intensity and in aspect, it is always likely to be present in some form. It is not so very long since Governments learnt to manage the aggregate level of economic activity in the economy as a whole; the achievement of regional balance is a much newer sphere of Government intervention and the measures are still in the early stages of their development. Yet, despite all these qualifications, the measures have had an impact on the problem. Provided they are maintained with the same determination, one may expect the regional problem in its present form to be gradually overcome. Though many countries now apply regional policies, there are few where such a claim could be made with confidence.

But if policy is achieving some results, it has still a long way to go and it is important to consider what improvements might be made. It has to be admitted that regional economics is still a rather unsatisfactory branch of economic science. Too often, policy tends to be based on assertion rather than analysis, and the forces which give rise to the regional problem are still insufficiently understood. In part the shape of policy is determined by the strength of the social and political pressures to which the regional problem gives rise; but the economic analysis on which it might be based is often too weak to exert much influence over it. In particular, this is due to the comparative neglect of this subject in economic theory and to the gross inadequacy of the statistical data which is necessary not only for an analysis of regional economic conditions, but to provide a basis for choosing between different policy alternatives and to assess the effects of policy on growth, income levels and the economic structure of regions.

In many ways the key to a more satisfactory policy lies in being able to fill the gaps in a cost-benefit analysis of alternative patterns of regional development. At present, too little is known both about congestion costs and the effect on business efficiency of requiring firms to operate in locations other than those of their first choice. It is expected that an increase of twenty million in Britain's population may have to be accommodated by the end of the century. There are various ways in which this might be done. To take some simple and extreme examples, should the increase be absorbed in the existing cities of the prosperous regions, spread fairly evenly across the country or concentrated in new cities or growth centres? Up to the present time such questions have been almost exclusively the province of physical planners. Yet, though the economic data is still largely lacking, the choice between these alternatives is an important economic question. The wastage of economic resources which an unsatisfactory spatial distribution of economic activity may involve, either through congestion or business inefficiency, could be enormous. If these matters could be subjected to quantitative analysis, it would not only settle once and for all some of the rather sterile arguments about the case for a regional policy; but more important, without this, the economic basis of regional policy and regional planning will remain unsatisfactory.

The 1960s did, however, witness an increasing awareness of the economic issues in regional policy. In particular, the replacement of Development Districts, based simply on unemployment blackspots, by the new Development Areas was a change of major importance. A larger proportion of the country is now scheduled than ever before and development can be attracted to the natural growth points within the regions where it has the greatest chance of success. But some ambiguities in policy remain. While economic objectives favour a growth area policy, political and social pressures demand emphasis to be given to black-spots. Thus, while some moves have been made in the direction of a growth area policy, the siting of certain advance factories, the refusal to include Plymouth in the South-West Development Area although it was the natural growth point, and the scheduling of the new Special Development Areas on distressed coalfields, all indicate the continuance of a black-spots approach. In cases where black-spots are capable of development as growth areas, of course, no conflict need arise in policy objectives. But in other instances an attempt to face both ways produces a dispersal of effort which may prejudice success.

Despite the much wider coverage of the Development Areas, and indeed partly because of the greater incentives now offered, the condition of some of the excluded areas is now causing concern. In particular, towns near the borders of Development Areas which suffer from similar problems, though in less marked degree, may be robbed of their potential development by the incentives which the Areas offer. The Hunt Committee on Intermediate Areas is due to report on this question shortly. It would seem that some graduated form of assistance will be required, but the Committee will no doubt have to review the whole procedure for scheduling Development Areas and the importance to be attached to the degree of distress suffered by an area or to its development potential.

The purpose of incentives must be to stimulate development in the problem regions while imposing the minimum additional strain on the rest of the country. It is the task of policy to provide the means of obtaining a finer balance of macroeconomic aggregates than has been possible hitherto with national monetary and fiscal policies. This requires the use of measures with greater regional flexibility. Much progress has been made in this respect in recent years. Capital incentives can trigger off substantial private investment in relation to the expenditure of public money. The regional employment premium may have a less direct effect on investment but it corrects the capital-intensive bias of investment grants and should help to improve the competitive position of regional economic activity. Other ways in which fiscal policy may be made regionally flexible should, however, be considered. This could secure greater growth, fuller utilization of labour and a better control of inflationary pressure. It offers what is perhaps the most fruitful approach for the development of regional policy.

One of the changes made in the 1960s was to replace tax incentives with investment grants. In part this followed from the introduction of corporation tax, which reduced the value of tax allowances. But it was also argued that the new system had the benefit of greater simplicity, so that its attractions could be more readily grasped by a potential investor, and that it helped the newly-established firm which was not yet in a position to earn much profit. It seems that both of these advantages can be easily exaggerated. As regards simplicity, while the apparent value of the new grants is high, their real value after allowing for tax effects is much less and this can only be calculated by using the same discounted cash flow analysis as was necessary in estimating the benefit of tax remissions. As regards liquidity for the firm which has newly set up, it must be remembered that when introduced the grants were subject to an eighteen-month delay in payment, and although this is to be reduced, it is still in excess of a year at the time of writing.

Against this it seems unnecessarily cumbersome to hand out apparently large sums for the development of the problem regions only to claim a high proportion of it back in taxation revenue. It is psychologically bad for the problem regions to make them appear to rely on large grants, without which it may readily be assumed they would not be viable, when in reality a large part of this expenditure goes eventually neither to the firm nor to the region but back to the Inland Revenue. From the firm's point of view, too, the grant system has disadvantages. Tax remissions, such as investment allowances or accelerated depreciation, rather than giving a free handout, enable a firm to retain profits it itself has earned. The more profitable the firm, and the more efficiently it is run, therefore, the greater the benefit it obtains. This is an increased incentive. The grant system gives the same handout to any firm no matter how well conceived or faulty its investment project; if the project does prove profitable, almost half the profit goes in taxation. Such a system weakens incentives.

Controls, such as the Industrial Development Certificate or the Office Development Permit, are a unique feature of British regional policy. In the past they have been regarded as one of the most effective weapons in British policy, but their use could more easily distort the pattern of economic activity and result in inefficiency

275

than is likely with incentives. Moreover, their use imposes a heavy burden on the Civil Service. Board of Trade officials have the responsibility for deciding which developments should be permitted and which refused, a task calling for considerable expertise. Perhaps one of the gravest dangers with this system is that it might block desirable investment which could raise output per man in the areas of labour shortage. For this reason it may seem desirable to shift the emphasis of policy from controls to inducements; some would advocate the abolition of controls altogether. A shift of emphasis has, of course, occurred in the 1960s as inducements have been increased, but policy is not yet sufficiently effective, nor are the results achieved so substantial, that much relaxation in the use of controls can be contemplated.

One of the most widely discussed developments during the 1960s was the birth of regional economic planning. The present machinery is probably little more than an interim arrangement until the Royal Commission on Local Government reports and the question of regional devolution can be properly worked out. Regional planning cannot be said to have had much impact on the regional problem so far and in many respects it has still to find its role. Much depends on whether the regional bodies are to remain advisory or are to be given some executive power. But valuable as these bodies may be, it is important to understand their limitations particularly in tackling the type of problem with which this book has been mainly concerned. The regional problem as traditionally understood involves inter-regional imbalance and policies to tackle it are primarily concerned with the allocation of resources *between* regions. This may be a task for inter-regional planning at the national level, involving the type of cost/benefit analysis already discussed, but it is not a job for the present type of Regional Planning Councils. They are concerned with problems *within* each of their regions. In developing regional strategies they are not concerned with the requirements or priorities of other regions; there is, therefore, little likelihood that the aspirations or proposals of individual regions will be compatible with each other or within the nation's capability when taken in the aggregate. It is, therefore, not surprising that the Government finds it is unable to accept some of the regional proposals, and the regional strategies seem to be prepared only to be ignored. This is unsatisfactory and it has led to some disillusion among the Councils. To solve this by producing plans which neatly dovetail with each other and with the National Plan must remain a planner's dream for the time being. But regional planning can still play a useful role in forecasting and charting the future course of the regional economy, in identifying the growth possibilities and building up growth areas and in co-ordinating and planning public investment expenditure. The locational advantages or disadvantages of particular regions, perhaps through an oversimplification in economic theory, are too often thought of as natural and unalterable. In fact, they depend as much on factors within man's control as those imposed by nature. Communications, harbours, housing, siting of new towns, the planning of the industrial structure so as to provide external economies and economies of scale, appropriate training for the labour force, all these may contribute to a region being in a good or bad industrial location. These questions are the province of regional planning.

Much remains to be accomplished, therefore, and there is much scope for further improvements in regional policy. But the regional problem, involving as it does immense changes in economic structure, is one of the most intractable problems which Governments have to face. Yet failure to tackle it may result in serious political and social consequences as well as the wastage of economic resources. The application of economics to spatial questions may have only just begun, but the experience of British policy gives some encouragement to those who believe these problems can be effectively tackled.

INDEX